W9-DBS-982

German Moral and Political Philosophy, 1785-1908

German Moral and Political Philosophy, 1785-1908:
A concise introduction

by Sabrina P. Ramet
and Torbjørn L. Knutsen

with an afterword by Jonathon W. Moses

NEW ACADEMIA PUBLISHING

Washington, DC

Copyright © 2022 by Sabrina P. Ramet
New Academia Publishing, 2023

All rights reserved. No part of this book may be reproduced or transmitted in any form or by any means, electronic or mechanical, including photocopying, recording, or by any information storage and retrieval system.

Printed in the United States of America

Library of Congress Control Number: 2023903228
ISBN 979-8-9852214-6-6 paperback (alk. paper)

New Academia Publishing, 4401-A Connecticut Ave. NW, #236,
Washington, DC 20008
info@newacademia.com - www.newacademia.com

For Steven Kennedy

Contents

About the Authors

Sabrina P. Ramet is a Professor Emerita of Political Science at the Norwegian University of Science & Technology (NTNU) in Trondheim, Norway. Her most recent books are: *Alternatives to Democracy in Twentieth-Century Europe: Collectivist visions of modernity* (Central European University Press, 2019) and *Nonconformity, Dissent, Opposition, and Resistance in Germany, 1933-1990: The Freedom to Conform* (Palgrave Macmillan, 2020).

Torbjørn L. Knutsen is a Professor of Political Science at the Norwegian University of Science & Technology (NTNU) in Trondheim, Norway. His most recent books are: *A History of International Relations Theory*, 3rd ed. (Manchester University Press, 2016) and *Ways of Knowing: Competing methodologies in social and political research*, 3rd ed., co-authored with Jonathon W. Moses (Palgrave Macmillan, 2019).

Jonathon W. Moses is a Professor of Political Science at the Norwegian University of Science & Technology (NTNU) in Trondheim, Norway. His most recent books are: *Ways of Knowing: Competing methodologies in social and political research*, 3rd ed., co-authored with Torbjørn L. Knutsen (Palgrave Macmillan, 2019) and *Workaway: The Human Costs of Europe's Common Labour Market* (Bristol University Press, 2021).

Preface

The years from 1785, with the publication of Immanuel Kant's *Groundwork for a Metaphysic of Morals,* to 1908, with the posthumous publication of Friedrich Nietzsche's *Ecce Homo,* may be counted as the Golden Age of German philosophy. In between these two books, other authors – Hegel, Fichte, Schleiermacher, Bauer, Strauss, and others – produced volumes that had a lasting impact on moral and political philosophy.

They wrote during or in the wake of the French Revolution. They elaborated on the meaning of "citizens" and "rights" and "duties", supplanting the pre-revolutionary notion that, aside from the ruling class, there were only subjects (some of them serfs). But, if people had rights and duties as citizens, what kind of rights and duties were they? And where did they come from? Were they ordained by God and anchored in Divine or Natural Law? Or were they politically defined, expressed in secular law and enforced by the power of the state? Closely associated with this were the questions whether people had the right to rebel against an oppressive government, as the English philosopher John Locke had argued, or rather owed their obedience to whatever government was in control. Kant, for example, addressed this question by asserting that people – citizens – owed allegiance to the established government but only until such time as it might be overthrown and replaced by a new (and revolutionary) government. At that point, Kant argued, citizens should transfer their allegiance to the new government. But the French Revolutionaries did not proclaim the rights of citizens, but the rights of man, establishing thereby that some rights could not be abolished by any government and raised the banner of equality for women – a banner which Schleiermacher, for example, embraced.

The French Revolution attacked Christianity, at one point replacing God with Reason-incarnate. All of the philosophers discussed in this volume confronted this challenge, with Kant judging that belief in God was "useful", while Feuerbach, writing several decades later, concluded that belief in a supreme deity had proven damaging. Nietzsche simply asserted that God was dead – a bold declaration which has been given diverse interpretations. David Friedrich Strauss advanced the argument that Jesus of Nazareth was a mere mortal and that most of the stories about him recorded in the Gospels were myths or legends, in some cases taken over from other religions. And Marx and Engels looked to a future when national attachments and religion, states and Churches, would all wither away.

Nor did the reimagining stop there. Both Schleiermacher and Nietzsche insisted that it made no sense to affirm a universal and uniform moral code which everyone should respect; although coming to this contention from different vantage points, both of them believed that what was morally right or wrong for each person hinged on that person's character. In Schleiermacher's case, this notion came as a reaction to Kant's categorical imperative – a rule applicable equally to everyone – which Schleiermacher rejected. Hegel, Schleiermacher's colleague at the University of Berlin, rejected both Kant's abstract formula and Schleiermacher's personalist approach and sought to make rights and duties concrete, by lodging them variously in the family, the community, and the state. Stirner, Marx, and Nietzsche all responded to the moral courses charted by Kant and Hegel, with Stirner rejecting all morality, Marx contending that in any society the dominant moral code was always the moral code of the ruling class, and Nietzsche urging that some people were simply superior to others and their creative talents were cramped and constrained by the human herd and by conventional moral law.

And finally, the French Revolution threw open the question of political legitimacy. When the French revolutionaries beheaded King Louis XVI – whom the revolutionaries called Citizen Louis Capet – they claimed a right of popular sovereignty, and when Napoleon crowned himself Emperor in 1804 he argued that one could establish a royal title *ex nihilo:* both were radical ideas. The German philosophers responded in different ways, with Hegel endorsing constitutional monarchy, Bauer applauding the absolutist monarchy of Russia, Young Hegelian Arnold Ruge subscribing to classical liberal values, and Marx calling for the overthrow of bourgeois states and the subsequent withering away of worker-led states.

We hope that the chapters that comprise this book will offer the reader a reliable, uncontroversial introduction to the Golden Age of German philosophy and help the reader to understand how the thinkers of that century were grappling with pressing political and moral issues of their day.

Finally, we wish to thank the editors of *Eastern Review* for permission to republish here the chapters on Kant and Hegel, originally published in that journal.

Sabrina P. Ramet
Torbjørn L. Knutsen

1

Introduction

Torbjørn L. Knutsen

At the end of the 18th century German philosophy experienced a remarkable burst of energy. Launched in the 1780s, it sped like a rocket across the sky of European thought, spreading a fiery trail of metaphysical systems in its wake – each trying to master the human experience in its totality. It was an impressive flight – a philosophical fireworks "whose status and influence has been frequently compared to nothing less than the golden age of Athens."[1]

Its brightest displays were brief. The climax of this philosophical revolution occurred roughly between 1790 and 1815. After 1815 its lights dimmed. However, its blaze did not burn out. Its ideas and visions ignited fiery debates. These gave rise to organized arguments and ideological systems which mobilized popular masses. During the second half of the 19th century, there emerged political movements which altered the political landscape of Europe and the world.

Then it disintegrated and fell to earth. As the 20th century progressed, German philosophy gained a reputation of being speculative and impenetrable. Much of it disappeared from view in the Anglo-American world during the 1930s, largely based on the suspicion that German philosophy and Nazism had something to do with each other. However, it revived during the late 1960s – when West-Germany was a wealthy, stable, and successful democracy. After the Cold War, when Germany was reunified, German philosophy gained a new relevance. One reason was that the West grappled with late 20th-century challenges and conditions which have sometimes been referred to as a "crisis in modernity".[2]

At a most basic level these challenges involve economic and political change. This may stem from the introduction of new technologies that require social adjustments in the form of new forms of production and exchange. Or it may stem from new bodies of knowledge, new insights and new forms of social understanding. Regardless of cause, such novelties often break up stable, inherited ways of life and dislocate familiar views and values. Many people resent changes to established ways of life. Some do not readily adapt to them. Some oppose the changes or refuse to recognize them. Some even reject new, scientific knowledge and cling rigidly to conceptions of the old order.

Germany is a graphic illustration of this. Enlightenment impulses from north-Atlantic states challenged the old (often religiously-based) cultural norms and values. The industrial revolution in Britain and the political revolution in France shook the traditional institutions of a largely fictional Holy Roman Empire. The German nation struggled to adapt.

Late-18th-century Germany is significantly two-dimensional with regard to those challenges. On the one hand, Germany serves as an example of structural crisis and the need to establish new institutions of social organization. On the other, it is a vital resource for our own, 21st-century challenge to understand how a society might come to terms with a "crisis of modernity". The metaphysical systems of 19th-century German philosophy provide us with useful terms and valuable perspectives on the challenges to our old, familiar order of national capitalism and liberal democracy.

This book discusses some of the most important contributors to this dynamic epoch of German philosophy. It examines the arguments of Kant, Herder, Fichte, Hegel, Marx, Nietzsche, and others. It investigates their key ideas and places them in their proper historical context: a period in which "everything established melts into air, everything holy is desecrated."[3]

This introduction is organized in three main parts. The first part places Germany's remarkable philosophical efflorescence in a quick historical context. The second compares some well-known German thinkers with those of Britain and France. This is done to illustrate some of the key differences between the German, the British, and the French intellectual traditions and thus define some of the unique features of German thought. The third part zooms in on some of the central, characteristic themes in German thought itself. It is a quick review of the central thinkers whose ideas are discussed in the chapters of this book.

The European Context

It is necessary to note first, that the thinkers who suddenly lifted German philosophy into European prominence toward the end of the 18th century, did not live in a state but in a fictional empire (the Holy Roman Empire of the German People) held together by a common language. Consequently, the political philosophy of the Germans differs from that of thinkers who lived in Great Britain and France. Late 18th-century French thinkers tended to advocate the virtues of a strong state; British thinkers, by contrast, tended to prefer a limited state. German thinkers had no national state. They tended to conceive of law, order, and politics in other, more abstract terms.

It is also necessary to note that the end of the 18th century was a time of upheaval – not just of political revolution, but of economic and mental turmoil as well. Impulses from the industrial revolution in Great Britain and the political revolution in France impinged upon the German nation. Dutch, English, and French thinkers formulated modern, rational, and secular arguments that challenged the doctrines and theological certainties of the old order.

The personal context: Immanuel Kant and his world

This book begins with Immanuel Kant, because Germany's philosophical revolution begins with him. He was the first and, perhaps, the greatest of the great German philosophers. His three "critiques", written during the final quarter of the 18th century, had enormous impact. They were read and admired not only in Germany, but throughout Europe. Kant contributed significantly to elevate Germany's scholarly reputation.

Kant addressed the epistemological challenges from the West in particular. In his earliest writings, Kant was interested above all in the philosophy of knowledge, and rarely addressed political questions head on. One reason for this was that "Germany" did not really exist as a political entity at the time. German thinkers were scattered across some 300 social formations. The vast majority of them were land-locked, agriculturally self-sufficient, and culturally self-contained. Some of them were integrated in Europe's over-land trade routes. But most of them were untouched by the maritime discoveries and the systems of communication and trade that evolved along the north-Atlantic rim. They were uninvolved in the processes of national integration and state-building that took place in the West. They existed among the fragments remnants of an empire that had been destroyed by war a century previously.

German philosophers were long shielded from Enlightenment impulses of the Western states. They lived in different regions of a fragmented empire. They were separated from each other. Kant spent his whole life in Königsberg – a city that had been established just a short time before he was born. However, there was one thing that united them: a common, written language – the standardization of which was largely the result of the Protestant Reformation. Toward the end of the 18th century, that unifying medium was strengthened by a veritable media revolution. German society saw, like other Western societies, a growth in the number of newspapers, magazines, and books – which included translations of French and English writers, philosophers as well as novelists.

Germany was, in other words, exposed to a communications revolution. First came new ideas about reason, rights and liberty from revolutionary France, washing across the German nation. Then came Napoleon's soldiers. They conquered the fragmented empire and reorganized it. They introduced a more rational administration and a greater unity upon its nation by reducing its more than 300 social formations to about 30. Napoleon's reforms made Germany's intellectual life more united and centralized. During the Napoleonic Wars, King Frederick Wilhelm III of Prussia built a new, large university in the capital, Berlin. Prussia became a political and a cultural hub and the center of 19th-century German philosophy.

The academic context: the professorial domination

One reason for this dominance of Berlin was a peculiar feature of German philosophy: its major contributors were university professors. In Britain and France, famous thinkers were often independent writers – independently wealthy aristocrats or publicists who lived by their pen.

British and French publicists earned their income from the number of texts they could sell. In short, they wrote for the market. And they wrote texts that would attract attention. Some of them were scandalous, such as the texts of Denis Diderot. Others were philosophically or politically radical – like those of Voltaire and David Hume. Some would write both – like Jean-Jacques Rousseau and William Godwin.

German writers were rarely publicists; they were mostly university professors. They tended to be both more elaborate in their style and more careful in their claims. German philosophy professors had risen slowly through a competitive system that tended to remove rebellious views and sharp edges, and their careers might be put in danger by careless radicalism. In 1799, the University of Jena fired Fichte for his radical views – interestingly enough, not so much for his defense of the totalitarian turn of the French revolution as for his criticism of religion.

Two notable free thinkers appeared on Germany's philosophical scene toward the end of the 19th century: Karl Marx and Friedrich Nietzsche. They were polar opposites when it came to political and moral philosophy – Marx was a radical socialist, whereas Nietzsche despised socialism. But their social situations had some striking similarities. First, they lived and wrote in exile. Second, they still wrote in German. Third, they travelled abroad and absorbed impulses from French and British thinkers.

Marx was never a professor; he fled Germany and ended up in England as a political refugee and an independent publicist. Nietzsche had briefly held a university chair but he resigned early for reasons of ill health and eked out a meagre existence in the mountains of Switzerland and Italy. Both were outsiders looking into Germany from abroad, writing zinging critiques of what they saw as an insulated, limited, self-absorbed, and stifling German culture. They both found German debates parochial and theological. Marx noted that the Germans thought of themselves as wolves, but that their arguments amounted to a mere bleating of sheep.[4] He argued that German philosophy was obsessed with far-fetched ideas and abstract concepts, and that it was necessary to counter this German idealism with a more "materialist conception" of society and history. Nietzsche was even more damning. He found German politicians poor in spirit, vulgar, puerile and boisterous. German thinkers were in his view inward-looking and obsessed by Christian theology.

The European Context: Germany and its neighbors

France was the leading land-power in 18th-century Europe and culturally dominant. Great Britain was an emerging sea-power – evolving rapidly along the north-Atlantic rim, controlling The Netherlands and exerting a growing economic dominance by virtue of an expanding, global empire.

Britain and France were geopolitical rivals. Both had contributed greatly to the Enlightenment -- Britain with arguments based on a pragmatic and empiricist orientation, which expressed itself in the political contract theories of Hobbes and Locke and, later, in the political-economy doctrines of David Hume and Adam Smith. France had contributed to Enlightenment philosophy with logical and systematic approaches to knowledge, the towering monument of which was Diderot's and d'Alembert's *Encyclopédie* (1751-77). German philosophers were slow to embrace the new scientific and secular outlooks of the West. They lingered long around old theological quarrels.

Kantian ambiguities

The arrival of the Enlightenment in Germany is associated with Immanuel Kant. "'Have courage to use your own reason!' – that is the motto of enlightenment", wrote Kant in the introduction to his essay "What Is Enlightenment?" (1784). This is a fine manifesto for the whole movement. However, it should also be recalled that Kant also wrote texts that criticized and challenged the tenets of the Enlightenment. This is apparent in his three famous critiques on Pure Reason, Practical Reason, and Judgment. Here he turned his critical eye on some of the major concepts of Enlightenment thought.

In other words, Kant's relationship to the European Enlightenment was ambiguous. He expressed doubts about its emphasis on observation and reason; he criticized both British empiricism and French rationalism. He boosted the reputation of German philosophy, but he also placed its development on a different trajectory from that of Britain and France. This philosophical *Sonderweg* was pursued by Kant's successors. Among them were Herder, Hegel, Fichte, and Schelling – all of them great system builders who demonstrated the strength and uniqueness of German philosophy.

They did not follow the lead of British thought, which remained practical and empirical. Nor did they pursue the themes of the French tradition, which sought to uncover the regularities and laws in the physical world. No, German thinkers were searching for abstract principles that governed the mental and spiritual universe.

The Germans and the British

British thinkers built on a tradition of pragmatic rationality along lines established by Thomas Hobbes and John Locke. They were materialistic, individualistic, and eminently practical. They saw society as the sum of human relations, and they viewed relations in terms of social contracts negotiated by rational human beings. These assumptions informed the British approach to politics, economic and law. German philosophy developed differently. Influenced by Kant's theory about the set categories of the human mind, German thinkers tended to distrust the human faculties of sense perception.

Kant's successors – Hamann, Herder, Fichte, Hegel, Schelling and many others – followed Kant's lead. Each contributed to the Kantian legacy in his own way. All contributed to a German tradition of social thought that was different from that of Britain. Where the British ended up with a tradition of moral philosophy built around a vision of society as innumerable rational individuals entering into contractual relations, the Germans – working from the assumptions of Kant – ended up with a tradition that distrusted contractarian reasoning, market theory and commercial practices. Hamann and Fichte were particularly critical of the free-market doctrines and the international free-marked practice of the British.

The Germans and the French

Kant and his students followed the American Revolution with only lukewarm interest. The absence of philosophical discussions in Germany of the 1780s about the American experiment in republicanism and its federative innovations is striking. Also, the disregard for the American Revolution contrasts starkly with the close attention that German thinkers paid to the Revolution in France during the 1790s.

Kant followed the French Revolution with great interest. Hamann, Herder, and Fichte were initially enthusiastic supporters of the revolutionary upheaval in France. However, when the Revolution produced a repressive regime of terror and when the forces of the Revolutionary Republic invaded German lands, they protested and turned against it. Hand in hand with this protest went a growing rejection of Enlightenment values. Herder and Fichte, who criticized the pragmatic commercialism of the British, also condemned the universalism and the militarism of the French. German thinkers rejected both the British explanation of social cohesion and political order as an outcome of rational interaction and social-contract theory. They also rejected the French explanation of universal reason and rights. Instead, German thinkers invoked historical evolution and culture to explain social cohesion and political order. They viewed social cohesion in organic terms and saw it as the outcome of sustained interaction within a culture that was carried by a common language and evolved into a closed, self-aware community through historical time. The first inklings of this view were expressed during the French Revolution by some of Kant's students.

Johann Gottlieb Fichte, played a particularly important role here. During the French Revolution, he attacked the British free-market argument, and argued for a strong state and a planned and closed economy.[5] During the Napoleonic Wars, he railed against the French occupation of Prussia, and instilled in the German nation a romantic defiance against French militarism.

The German Sonderweg

Following the lead of Kant, Hamann, Herder and Fichte paved the way for a distinct German tradition in social theory – one which differed from that of Britain and France. It is worth recalling that Great Britain and France had political philosophers who had long been preoccupied with the origins and the workings of the state. German thinkers were latecomers to this kind of thinking. They paid less attention than British and French thinkers to the workings of the state and the relationship between the state and the individual citizen; instead, they tended to emphasize the ordering effects of a common spiritual authority. Some of them referred to the unifying effect of a common "spirit" and conceived of this spirit as an organic, rational entity that evolved and developed a steadily more mature self-consciousness during the course of historical time. Some stressed the importance of language and the culture carried by it.

The main concerns of 18th-century German thinkers were not political in the narrow, concrete and pragmatic sense of the term. Their topics were lofty, abstract and ideational. They probed the workings of a human society that was unified by a common language and a collective human Reason. They evolved huge, abstract systems that revealed the laws of Reason and the impact of a communal "spirit". They explained the progress of History, solved the riddle of the social world, and delineated the meaning of human existence.

Paving the Sonderweg

Not all German thinkers did this. Many of them observed the development of Enlightenment thought in neighboring nations. Immanuel Kant was among them. From the Baltic port city of Königsberg, he followed the events in France and Britain. Deeply disturbed by the skeptical empiricism of David Hume and dissatisfied by the rationalism in the tradition of Descartes, Kant drew on both to create a synthesis of the two traditions. The result was three major *critiques* – of Pure Reason, of Practical Reason, and of Judgment – three volumes that released a remarkable burst of philosophical energy among Kant's students and younger contemporaries. Kant's *critiques* were in turn criticized. And this released what we might call the "German philosophical revolution".

Kant's critics

Some of Kant's critics were impressed with the West. They argued that Kant was too independent and too critical of British and French Enlightenment thought. They feared that he and his disciples were pulling German philosophy away from the European mainstream and that Kantianism was placing every fundamental concept of the Enlightenment project in jeopardy. Another group of critics disagreed, and argued that Kant was too close to British and French thought. The first group included several luminaries who were famous in their day. But their fame faded quickly. They are rarely read today and will not be further discussed in this book.[6] It is the second group of Kant's critics that will receive pride of place in this volume.

This book offer chapters on Hamann (1730-1788), Herder (1744-1803), and Fichte (1762-1814); on Friedrich Schleiermacher (1768-1834), on George Wilhelm Friedrich Hegel (1770-1831), and on the left Hegelians. These thinkers were not only skeptics of British and, especially, French philosophy; they were also critics of Enlightenment thought as such. They tended to be dissatisfied with the way in which Kant and his disciples embraced Enlightenment concepts of Reason, Man, God and Nature.

Kant, in other words, had a polarizing effect on German philosophy. But only one of the poles was to formulate the characteristic features of German moral and political philosophy: viz., Kant's anti-Enlightenment critics. This group included some of Kant's own students, who, impatient with their master's doctrines of perception and reason, struck out on their own. Hamann, Herder and Fichte rejected the intellectualism of Kant and argued that there are other sources of knowledge besides observation and reason.

Laying the Philosophical Foundation: Ontology, Epistemology, and Methodology

Hamann quarreled with Kant's proposition that universal categories of the human mind organized sense perceptions and affected human knowledge. He stuck to old, theological ideas and argued instead that knowledge was anchored in divine revelation. But he added that knowledge was also maintained by language – which he reduced to a divine creation. Herder, too, disagreed with Kant's theory of perception. He distanced himself from Hamann's theological claim, but embraced Hamann's emphasis on language. However, for Herder, language was not created by God; it evolved through History. All languages consist of concepts and terms by means of which their users grasp the world. And since there exist many different languages in the world, there are many different ways of grasping reality. Besides, Herder continued, languages store and transfer human knowledge from one generation of users to the next. In fact, a distinct language carries an entire distinct culture and shapes the perceptions of its users in very particular ways.

It was a powerful theory. And it involved an ontology that was at odds with the Enlightenment notion of universal values and reason-based absolutes. On the strength of it, Herder and his followers rejected the idea of universal values and eternal moral principles. They argued instead that values were rooted in culture, which in turn were shaped by geographical conditions and historical events and carried by language. The world was composed of many languages, each carrying a culture that was produced by unique circumstances, each forming a unique *Volk*, and each deserving respect and tolerance. As a result, Herder defended diversity of values, plurality of principles, and a deep respect for the cultural diversity of humankind.

Schleiermacher was as weary of Kant's theory of perception as were Hamann and Herder. He rejected the idea that human reason was limited by universal categories of the mind, and argued (like Hamann) that reason was not the only source of knowledge and understanding available to Man; humans could also obtain knowledge and understanding through direct insight – through faith, instinct, or *Ahnung*. This epistemology stands in clear contrast to the reason-based arguments of British and French philosophers. And in close association with it, German thinkers evolved methodological arguments that contrasted sharply with those of the Atlantic world.

Romantic Politics

Kant's critiques were published during the years of the French Revolution. They triggered an ontological shift.[7] The shift was quick, but many-faceted. In its most simple form it was a reaction to the sudden intrusion of the modern world. First, to late-18th-century pressures from the Dutch, British and French Enlightenment and to its pursuit of knowledge through reason and objective, sense-based evidence. Then, to the military shock of Napoleon's invasion and the French occupation of German lands.

The Germans lacked the central institutions of the modern, centralized, Western state. And they rejected the institutions that Napoleon's soldiers imposed upon them. They resisted the laws, and the universal norms and values that these institutions brought with them. Instead, they constructed an identity around their own, local values – around language, the traditional Christian culture carried by that language, and around notions of socio-cultural evolution.

The result was the rise of a peculiar German variant of Western moral and political philosophy. The ontological consequences of this German variant were momentous. Not only for Germany, but for social and political philosophy all over the world.

Paving the Way

To capture this ontological shift, it is convenient to return to Immanuel Kant for a moment. He was the first major German thinker who explicitly perceived a challenge from the Enlightenment impulses of the West, and who self-consciously decided to formulate a response to challenges posed by British empiricism and French rationalism.[8]

During the late 1790s – as the French revolutionary government slid into dictatorial practices and French generals were replaced by the revolutionary regime -- Kant reached the peak of his fame. His critical philosophy was introduced to every important German university. He was consulted as an oracle on all kinds of questions. Young men flocked to Königsberg as to a shrine. But at one point some of Kant's students began to criticize their master. They berated him for accepting the Enlightenment emphasis on the rational individual and the idea of social development as a reason-driven process of linear improvement.

Kant's critics did not reject reason, but they argued that human beings could not be reduced to reason alone. They did not reject individualism, but they insisted that humans exist in and are shaped by their social context. Humans cannot be reduced to individual thinking-machines. All individuals enter into relations with others; they create webs of meaning and social order, which they maintain and refine through language and continued interaction.

Within each individual are energies and attributes which affect their actions and provide insight and understanding that reason alone cannot deliver. These are individual qualities. They are subjective, hard to account for, and impossible to describe in objective terms. Yet, they are recognizable, because they are common to all humans. Indeed, some of them – such as anger, attraction, love, and a protective instinct – are common to all living things. They are universal and attributes of nature itself. Some thinkers found in these ideas a way to preserve the old, theological approaches.

Schleiermacher, for example, noted that individual qualities are divinely inspired. This dovetailed nicely with traditional dogmas – that all things are created by God, and that He had invested in His creations a spark of His divine Self. It was on this old, theological basis that Schleiermacher added revelation and a divinely inspired *Ahnung* as sources of insight and understanding.

Writers such as Schelling, Schleiermacher, Schlegel, Tieck, and Novalis, developed similar arguments. Many of them turned to the pre-Enlightenment past to find well-ordered, simple societies. They looked back to the Middle Ages with nostalgia, where they found an authentic and integrated culture unified by Christian faith. Their reactions sowed the seeds of a culture-based romanticism that made a deep mark on German moral and political thought. Napoleon's invasions made them grow.

The German Scene – Disciples and Critics

Napoleon's occupation of German lands created a deep resentment of and opposition to the universal ideals of the French Revolution. This was expressed early by Herder, whose works paved the way for an anti-modern admiration for ancient societies, early civilizations, and authentic cultures. But it was Fichte who developed Germany's idealistic romanticism into its fully fledged form and gave it a nationalistic thrust.

Both Herder and Fichte invoked ancient collective ideas. They found them in Medieval myths and in Greek tragedies, and they used them to critique Kant's conception of individual freedom. They considered Greek tragedy a unique, historical phenomenon as well as a timeless literary genre – an idea which was later embellished by authors such as Schiller, Schelling, and Hegel.[9] Fichte criticized the reason-based, cause-and-effect logic of the Enlightenment and of modern science. Instead, he reverted to classical philosophy and to the dialectical method developed by the ancient Greeks.

Kant had criticized this ancient method. He had presented its core logic as a three-step procedure: It began with a proposition (or thesis), continued with a reaction or a negation (an antithesis) that resulted in a tension or a contradiction, and it ended in a deeper insight or a resolution (or a synthesis). Kant had rejected this procedure. He found it vague and unsatisfactory. Fichte, by contrast, lauded it. He recommended it as a method of investigation. Schelling and other German thinkers heeded Fichte's recommendation. They embraced the dialectical method and employed its terminology to discussions of nature and history. Some German thinkers even invested ontological features in it, regarding dialectics as a fundamental aspect of reality. Fichte's dialectics implied a *process*. It involved development. And on the basis of it, Fichte constructed a vast system of historical evolution, which he then applied to events of his own times, with great effect.

International Events and German Resistance

To capture the essence of Fichte's system, it is necessary to appreciate that Fichte was, like many of Kant's students, an enthusiastic supporter of the French Revolution. Indeed, he was more enthusiastic than most: when the Revolutionary government in France became a repressive regime of terror, Fichte continued to defend it. Even when Napoleon seized power and led the French army against Prussia, Fichte stuck to his revolutionary convictions.

But later Fichte condemned Napoleon as a traitor to the revolutionary ideals, and turned his analytical energies against France and Napoleon. In a series of public speeches he rejected Napoleon's occupation, his legal reforms, and his claims to universal reason. Instead, he defended the specific culture of the German nation. He extolled those cultures that were authentic, strong and pure; while he derided those that he considered artificial, effete, and corrupt. The French culture was corrupt, Fichte argued, whereas the German culture was authentic and pure. In fact, German culture was superior to all other cultures, and the German people deserved a place at the very top of the world's hierarchy of peoples.

Napoleon invaded German territories. He dissolved the ancient *imperium*, integrated the old 300+ social formations of the Holy Roman Empire into a secular confederation, and imposed *Code Napoléon* on it. He contaminated and corrupted the German nation, Fichte argued. Napoleon had removed the German *Volk* from its original "Innocence" and plunged it into a state of "Sin". The German nation must oppose Napoleon. Through an effort of collective will, it must chase the French occupants out and regain its authenticity in a stage of "Sanctification". It goes without saying that Fichte's argument was radical nationalism, justified by Christian theology.[10]

The French occupation convinced Fichte that, if the German people were to preserve their distinct culture and enjoy freedom and dignity, they must possess a strong and independent state. Fichte died in 1814, just before Napoleon's defeat and before the Congress of Vienna founded the German Federation – a loose league of 39 states. But Fichte's call for a German state took hold, especially in Prussia, the largest of the German states. Here Hegel expressed similar views. For him the state was the precondition for freedom and dignity, and the institutional embodiment of Reason. The State "is the march of God through history", as he put it.[11]

Like Fichte, Hegel saw the state as the product of a long evolution, an unfolding development driven by an inner, dialectical logic. This evolutionary view differed from the static and mechanical philosophy of the Atlantic West, with its fixed concepts and its universal categories of right and wrong. Also, it differed from the victors of the Napoleonic Wars. They sought to contain Prussia's rising influence. At the Congress of Vienna the Great Powers of Europe appointed Austrian emperor Franz I as permanent president of the German confederation. The emperor perceived the German protests as revolutionary and dangerous and tried to repress them. The Germans reacted with resentment and resistance. They responded with protests and demands for national unity and freedom.

Realpolitik: Towards Unity and Empire

Friedrich Wilhelm III, King of Prussia, welcomed the protests. The monarch was encouraged by economic progress – in 1818 he created the *Zollverein* a tariff union which stimulated production, trade, and economic and political unity. Economic progress and political support sustained both his expanding ambitions, his military capabilities, and his claims that he reflected the will of the whole German *Volk*.

The Rhetoric of Prussia

The Prussian King echoed the idea of an historical evolution, propelled by spiritual forces towards German unity. These ideas also guided the moral and political philosophy of Hegel. He understood, just like Fichte, that the progress of Reason, German unity, and national freedom depended on the establishment of a strong, independent state. He described this establishment as the outcome of a spiritual evolution of the German people, which Fichte described as a dialectical process through History, and divided into distinct historical stages.

There are differences between Fichte and Hegel. Hegel does not describe the evolution of the German *Volk* in clear, Biblical terms, and he avoids the hyper-patriotic language that portrays the German *Volk* as superior to others.[12] However, the two philosophers shared the same holistic ontology, the dialectical methodology, the evolutionist epistemology. They shared the idea that human society is an unceasing process of citizen interaction – an idea they both illustrated with examples from ancient Greece and discussions of the *polis*. They both held that individuals are born into an extant community and are shaped by it.

Hegel died in 1831, at a time when a wave of protests washed across France and the German federation. The protests were partly the result of climatic vagaries – a period of drought resulted in bad harvests, hunger and hardship. But they were also reactions against industrial change and social dislocation that made the hardship worse. Popular dissatisfaction created a tense political environment. Popular masses expressed their dissatisfaction in mass demonstrations with demands of bread, unity and freedom. The Habsburg emperor and his powerful chancellor Metternich, responded by arresting demonstrators, restricting civil liberties and tightening censorship. Tensions in German society intensified. German patriots repeated the view that the nation would unify as History evolved. The German people would build a steadily stronger state, which would attain increasing consciousness of itself. And as the state grew stronger and more self-conscious, its citizens would progress towards greater unity and greater freedom.

Hegel's legacy was complex, abstract, sweeping, and controversial. A succession of new interpretations peeled off the philosophical system that he had left behind. Its many interpretations tended to be sorted into two camps – the Right and the Left. Both camps expressed their arguments in a dialectical vision of History and a progressive evolution of Reason and freedom. Yet, they differed greatly in political orientation.

The "Right Hegelians" (or "old Hegelians") were conservative, patriotic and theologically informed. They held knowledge to be a spiritual component in the divinely created universe. They believed that the advanced societies of Europe were products of a historical dialectic that was nearing its end, and that Reason and freedom were reaching their culmination in the Prussian state. Any effort to reform or change Prussia, was seen by them as dangerous and destructive.

The "Left Hegelians" (or "Young Hegelians") were radical, internationalist, and secular. They abandoned theological arguments and rejected the idea that the dialectical advancement of Reason and freedom was nearing its end. They observed that the world around them was marked by the presence of great irrationality, especially in the form of blind, religious faith. They spurned the idea that the Prussian state was the summit of social evolution. Germany was neither united nor sovereign. Freedom had not expanded. In fact, foreign rulers constrained the nation and repressed its citizens.

Left Hegelians worked to remedy the sorry situation. They followed the strategy that had been drawn by Fichte: the German people must first be spiritually unified through education, and then collected under a single constitution. They put pressures on several local rulers to call for an all-German constitutional assembly. But to little avail.

They fought an uphill battle. However, a great glimmer of hope appeared in May 1848, when representatives from all states met in Frankfurt, to draw up a German Constitution. They declared themselves a National Assembly and invited the King of Prussia – Germany's leading state – to be emperor of a united Germany. It was a revolutionary act and King Friedrich Wilhelm IV of Prussia declined. The Frankfurt assembly was dissolved and the local uprising repressed, and the German Confederation was quickly re-established.

Then followed a period of political reaction. German Universities did not hire Left Hegelians: Strauss taught briefly at the University of Tübingen and Stirner taught briefly at a school for young girls in Berlin, while Bauer was hired to teach at the University of Bonn in 1839; Feuerbach and Marx never taught; in general, German universities hired uncontroversial or conservative teachers. Dissent was vigorously suppressed. Many German intellectuals and political leaders went into exile. Public offices were filled with men who advocated the old virtues of clericalism and divine monarchy. It was a boom time for philosophers of the spiritual, Right-Hegelian persuasion. It was a time of reckoning for the Left-Hegelians. They distanced themselves from Hegel's abstract idealism. They interpreted Hegel's social philosophy within a materialist framework. They found Hegel standing on his head, and turned him right side up again, as Karl Marx put it.[13]

Materialist Reactions

This development was part of a materialist reaction against the idealist system builders. It had gathered force for some time, encouraged by developments in the natural and the new social sciences, and was reflected in a circle of Left Hegelian publicists. One of its members was Ludwig Feuerbach, who delivered a stinging criticism of Christianity, arguing e.g. that God had not created man; rather, man had created God. Another was Karl Marx, who wrote his doctoral dissertation on two Greek materialists.[14]

Feuerbach, Marx, and others tended to echo the methodology of Fichte and Hegel – they approached social questions from a romantic view of human history as driven by a dialectical process of conflict and struggle; its overall direction is progressive, describing a teleology that moves towards greater Reason, tighter social unity/ solidarity, and more freedom. However, most of the Left Hegelians encased their arguments in a materialist ontology. Some of them were well acquainted with French and British arguments. This was the case of Marx, who fled Prussia, lived in Paris and Brussels during the 1840s, and then settled in London. His materialist views were influenced by French rationalism and British empiricism – especially by theories of development from British classical political economy and by Darwin's theories of evolution.

Marx lived in London when Prussia's King Friedrich Wilhelm IV died in 1857. He was briefly encouraged when the old king was succeeded by his more active and ambitious brother Wilhelm. The new king quickly introduced economic, military and political reforms. Then he appointed Otto von Bismarck as his Minister President. Bismarck was entirely in tune with the materialist attitude of the age. He observed that wars had disrupted the old European order and concluded that continued international disarray would serve Prussia's national interests. He exploited the patriotic rhetoric of German nationalism to serve his foreign-policy goals.

The big political questions of the age "will not be resolved by speeches," Bismarck averred, "but by iron and blood." He launched a series of cleverly conducted wars to conquer neighboring territories. First, he allied with Austria, waged a victorious war against Denmark, and subjected Schleswig and Holstein to Prussian laws (1864). Next, he attacked Austria, his old ally, and won a victory which excluded Austrian influence from German politics. This enabled him to create the North-German Confederation, an imperial construction in which Schleswig, Holstein, and 20 other German states became satellites to Prussia's metropolis. It was a complex and loose construct. To convert it into a single state, Bismarck needed a single, outside enemy to declare war on the German Confederation. In 1870, he craftily created a *casus belli* that ensnared France and caused her to act aggressively. The result was a defensive war for which Prussia had long prepared. The Prussian army advanced quickly, occupied Paris, and brought the war to a spectacular victory. In August 1871 Bismarck travelled to Versailles. From the splendid French Palace he proclaimed the founding of the German Empire.

Bismarck had achieved German unity. At last. But not in the way German philosophers had imagined, and without the results they had hoped for. Unity had been purchased at the expense of freedom. Marx followed the events from London, and portrayed the German Empire as "military despotism cloaked in parliamentary forms, with a feudal ingredient, influenced by the bourgeoisie, festooned with bureaucrats and guarded by the police."[15] Nietzsche was in Bern when he read about Bismarck's proclamation. He did not know whether to laugh or cry. He saw the spectacle as German pretentiousness at its most vulgar, and considered the new Empire an artificial, inauthentic, entirely hollow construct. *"Deutschland, Deutschland über alles* – I fear that was the end of German philosophy", was his ascorbic comment.[16] During the subsequent years, Nietzsche would subject German philosophy to an increasingly ruthless criticism. He ended in total condemnation, arguing that German philosophy was superstitious, vulgar, decadent, and self-serving. It was based on ancient Hebrew myths and Christian fiction. It all had to go.

Yet, even in his periods of most savage criticism, Nietzsche retained elements of the tradition that he so thoroughly condemned. He kept the idea of historical evolution. He made linguistic analysis an important tool in his philosophical queries. And he drew on tropes and themes from ancient Greece.

Conclusion

Kant marks the beginning of Germany's philosophical revolution. Nietzsche marks a convenient end. The distance between them is vast. Nietzsche argues that Kant began a development that must be suppressed. In *Twilight of the Idols*, Nietzsche argues that the slate must be swept clean so that German philosophy can be rebuilt from scratch. The arc of German philosophy is vast. Yet, it is marked by a few lasting features. One of them is the acknowledgement that the world we experience may not be the way the world is in itself. This epistemological position would intersect with other features which informed discussions on prominent German themes about Reason, Spirit, History, and Language.

German thinkers from Kant to Nietzsche had a tendency to slide into a subjectivist epistemology. Its groundwork was laid by Kant, who criticized both empiricism and rationalism and worked to create a unique synthesis of them both. His critiques have greater force than his synthesis, and caused many of his successors to reject both empiricism and rationalism and to search for their own alternatives. One of the alternatives was the dialectical approach, developed by Fichte and Hegel.[17] This methodology, together with a skepticism towards the empiricist ontology, drove many German thinkers to speculate about a reality that might lie outside of the purview of human perception. This opened up a new space for God: if human beings were not equipped to perceive Him, His existence could neither be proven nor disproven. This meant that God's existence was based on individual faith. But it also meant that He was immune to attacks by empirical or rationalist arguments. It was an ontology that preserved traditional Christian arguments, which continued to play guiding roles in German social and political thought. Finally, this ontology gave rise to abstract speculations about Spirit and its relationship to the Christian God, to Reason, to nations and the German people, to History, to historical change… Fichte and Hegel are, again, important contributors. They expressed Historical change in abstract, ideational terms. Arguments about events being phenomena, driven by Spirit that obtains increasing knowledge of itself, gave rise to a literature that was voluminous and abstract and gained a reputation for being impenetrable and abstruse.[18]

These discussions about Reason, Spirit, History, and Language were shaped by German reactions to intrusions and threats from the Atlantic Powers.[19] In turn they changed the political and moral philosophy of 19th-century Europe. But the Atlantic Powers intruded upon other regions as well. Upon Russia, for example, not to mention extra-European regions in Asia and Africa, where the Atlantic sea-powers had consolidated colonial presence since the "long 16th century." These regions were primed for critical philosophies from Germany. They embraced German arguments that rejected the universalist pretentions of the West and criticized British commercialism and French militarism.

A line can be drawn from the legacy of Fichte, Hegel, and Marx to Lenin and the Russian Revolution. Lines of influence can also be drawn from Marx and Lenin to Mao, to wars of national liberation, to revolutionary movements in the Third World. Leaders of the 20th-century decolonization movement have regularly justified their actions in terms formulated by 19th-century German social philosophers. Non-Western nations have often criticized the Atlantic powers with arguments that have relied on Marx' understanding of repression and exploitation, Fichte's demand for an independent state, and Hegel's dialectical understanding of the political process.[20]

Then, towards the end of the 20th century, rapid changes in communication technology, knowledge, economic reform and social adjustments began to shake the familiar institutions in the West itself.[21] Large segments of Western populations felt threatened by increased competition in the labour market, immigration, multiculturalism, and the retreat of familiar institutions and outlook on life.

Among the popular masses, there were groups which stubbornly protested the changes. Some of them rejected science and clung to traditional beliefs. Among the intellectuals, analytical or positivist approaches were challenged by a growing number of new theories and approaches. Boosted by decolonization and globalism, these approaches have interrogated received ideas – they have for example argued convincingly that traditional judgements of society and culture rest on ethnocentric assumptions. Such criticisms are often associated with French post-modernists – with names like Michel Foucault, Jacques Derrida, François Lyotard, and others. However, the deeper roots of their arguments lie with 18th-century German thinkers, notably with thinkers like Kant, Herder, Fichte, Hegel, and Nietzsche. This book may discuss dead, white males and terms and ideas that emerged from Germany's remarkable 19th-century transformation. But we still rely on those terms and ideas to discuss the present "crisis of modernity."

Notes

1 Karl Ameriks (ed.), *The Cambridge Companion to German Idealism* (Cambridge: Cambridge University Press, 2000), p.1.

2 Daniel Weinstock, Jacob T. Levy, and Jocelyn Maclure (eds.), *Interpreting Modernity: Essays on the Work of Charles Taylor* (Montreal: MacGill University Press, 2020).

3 Karl Marx and Frederick Engels, *The Manifesto of the Communist Party* (Moscow: Progress Publishers, 1977 [1848]), p. 39.

4 Karl Marx and Friedrich Engels, *The German Ideology* (New York: Prometheus Books, 1998), pp. 27-658.

5 Johann Gottlieb Fichte, *The Closed Commercial State* (New York: SUNY Press, 2013 [1800]).

6 Among these critics were thinkers such as Johann Augustus Eberhard (1739-1809), Johann G. H. Feder (1740-1821), Christian Garve (1742-1798), and Ernest Platner (1744-1818). They were famous luminaries who were influenced by French and particularly British ideas – Eberhard adopted the epistemology of John Locke and the British empiricists; Garve admired the Scottish Enlightenment and translated Adam

Smith into German. They criticized Kant because they feared that he and his disciples were pulling German philosophy away from the European mainstream and that Kantianism was placing every fundamental concept of the Enlightenment project in jeopardy. Although famous in their day, their popularity quickly waned.

7 Kant's *Critique of Pure Reason* was published in 1781. His *Critique of Practical Reason* came in 1788. *The Critique of Judgement* was issued in 1790.

8 Kant's *Critique of Pure Reason* (1781) addressed the shortcomings of Rationalism. The *Critique of Practical Reason* (1788) tackled the challenges of Empiricism. On the one hand, Kant rejected the rationalist idea that the human mind can arrive, by pure reason, at knowledge about the world. On the other, he rejected the radical empiricist idea that all knowledge comes from sense perception alone. Such perception is important, of course, but it is not reliable, Kant argued. Then he added the argument that fueled an ontological change in Western philosophy: that sense perception is shaped by mental conditions which cannot be reduced to sensory experience. These conditions are not the result of pure and abstract reason; it is a form of practical reason – it is conditioned and limited by categories that belong to the mind itself. Kant's two Critiques, plus his *Critique of Judgement* (1790) offered nothing less than a new metaphysic. It inaugurated a new era in the development of philosophical thought. Kant approached a wide gamut of philosophical and moral questions from his new, metaphysical vantage point. His comprehensive and systematic work greatly influenced all subsequent philosophy, especially in Germany.

9 This admiration of the Greek tragedy was later embellished by authors like Schiller, Schelling, Hegel, and others. See Joshua Billings, *Genealogy of the Tragic: Greek Tragedy and German Philosophy* (Princeton, N.J.: Princeton University Press, 2014).

10 Fichte's five stages of spiritual development corresponds perfectly to the Christian division of Biblical History into "Paradise", "Fall", generations of suffering and sinful struggles, and the appearance of Christ with His promise of salvation, and the regaining of Paradise.

11 Georg Wilhelm Friedrich Hegel, *Philosophy of Right,* trans. by T. M. Knox (London and Oxford: Oxford University Press, 1967), section 258.

12 See Hegel's criticism of Fichte's simple triangulation of "thesis, antithesis, and synthesis" in his Preface to *The Phenomenology of Spirit,* trans. by Terry Pinkard and Michael Baur (Cambridge: Cambridge University Press, 2019).

13 It might, however, be more accurate to say that in the case of Marx, he stood Fichte on his head, as Marx's dialectical method is closer to Fichte's Kant-derived triplicity of thesis-antithesis-synthesis than to Hegel.

14 See Peter Fenves, "Marx's Doctoral Thesis on Two Greek Atomists and the Post-Kantian Interpretations", in *Journal of the History of Ideas*, Vol. 47, No. 3 (1986), pp. 433-452.

15 Marx, quoted in Hans Ulrich Wehler, *The German Empire, 1871-1918* (Leamington: Berg, 1975), p. 30.
16 Friedrich Nietzsche, *Twilight of the Idols*, trans. from German by Walter Kaufmann, in Kaufmann (compiler), *The Portable Nietzsche* (London: Penguin 1986), p. 506.
17 Another alternative would be elaborated later and emerge as the phenomenological approach.
18 Hegel explains it all in his *Phenomenology of Spirit*. For many critics of German philosophy – such as Bertrand Russell, this book is the epitome of German obtuseness and it illustrates an important thing: "that the worse your logic, the more interesting the consequences to which it gives rise." See Russell, Bertrand, *A History of Western Philosophy* (London: Routledge, 2004), p. 674.
19 Émile Durkheim, «*Allemande au-dessus de tout* ». *La mentalité allemande et la guerre.* (Paris: Librairie Armand Colin, 1915).
20 Theodor Von Laue, *The World Revolution of Westernization* (Oxford: Oxford University Press, 1989).
21 Marshall Berman, *All That is Solid Melts into Air* (New York: Simon & Schuster, 1982).

2

Kant on Ethics and Politics[1]

Sabrina Ramet

Summary: Best known for his ethical works, Immanuel Kant was part of the liberal Enlightenment and addressed most of the principal political issues of his day. Several of his major works were written in the wake of the storming of the Bastille in Paris, while Europe was engaged in the French Revolutionary Wars. His rejection of revolution but endorsement of the principles for which the French revolutionaries were fighting, as well as his plea for a federation of European states that would settle disputes peacefully, reflected his engagement with the controversies raised by the Revolution. But, although he could not countenance revolution, he declared that, once a revolutionary government has succeeded in establishing itself, citizens should obey the new government, rather than try to restore the ousted authorities. Kant's ethical philosophy was focused on the individual, but he distinguished between the rights and duties of a person qua individual and the rights and duties of a person as a citizen.

Immanuel Kant lived in revolutionary times. Some of his earlier works were devoted to issues related to morality and religion; he spelled out what he called the 'categorical imperative', which called for people to act only in a such a way that, if everyone did likewise, the world would be a better place. Later, as the French Revolutionary Wars got underway and Europe was shaken by revolutionary currents, Kant advised that people should be loyal to whichever government was in place, seeking neither to overthrow an existing regime nor to restore a fallen one. In his *Perpetual Peace*, he sketched a vision of a more peaceful world and argued that, as the rule of law and republican rule spread across Europe, the continent would see fewer wars.

Early Career

Kant was born on 22 April 1724 in Königsberg (now Kaliningrad) in East Prussia. Except for occasional journeys into the immediate vicinity just outside the city limits, Kant never left Königsberg during the 80 years of his life. Königsberg in the eighteenth century – unlike Kaliningrad today – was a lively, cosmopolitan city with flourishing trade and participating in the broader European cultural and intellectual trends. Kant himself was no recluse; on the contrary, he enjoyed a lively social life and had a wide social circle. In his later years, Kant was extremely regular and meticulous in his habits, unfailingly punctual; locals joked that they would set their watches by the schedule of Kant's daily walk. His parents were Pietists, advocating complete reliance on God and the renunciation of personal moral autonomy. Kant turned his back on his parents' Pietism and, in opposition to their views, came to champion moral autonomy, personal responsibility, and reliance on one's own reason in making moral decisions.[2]

Kant's intellectual gifts were evident already at an early age, and he was admitted to the University of Königsberg, where he excelled. In 1755 (at age 31), he was granted the right to lecture at the university as a *Privatdozent*, meaning that his salary consisted of fees for lectures. Kant proved to be a popular lecturer, offering lectures on many subjects: logic, metaphysics, ethics, jurisprudence, geography, anthropology and other subjects. In 1764, he was offered a full professorship in poetry at the University of Berlin; he declined the offer. Five years later, the University of Erlangen approached him with an offer that he assume the first chair of theoretical philosophy; he turned down this offer as well, hoping to remain in his native Königsberg. He achieved this objective the following year, when he assumed the post of professor of moral philosophy at the University of Königsberg.[3] He continued to present lectures across a range of subjects; thus, in addition to moral philosophy and rational theology, he also presented lectures on anthropology, logic, and mineralogy during 1770-71 and on theoretical physics and physical geography in summer 1776.

At the time of his appointment, the 46-year-old philosopher had not yet written any of the works for which we remember him today. His chief concerns at that time were epistemology and the moral law. Indeed, by 1763, Kant had reached the conclusion that it was necessary to spell out the highest principle of morality and he was convinced that this had to be a rational principle.[4] He set to work on what became his *Critique of Pure Reason*, published in 1781.

Even before 1763, various works of the Scottish ethicist Francis Hutcheson (1694-1746) appeared in German translation[5] and, in 1781, a German translation of David Hume's *Dialogues Concerning Natural Religion* was published. Hutcheson and Hume (1711-1776) agreed that morality was founded on a "moral sense" – a feeling. Kant rejected this view, and interpreted moral understanding in terms of reason.[6] He also rejected Hutcheson's belief that God tendered "kind affections" toward humanity and that He wished to promote the happiness of humankind and all His other creatures.[7] Privately, Kant disclosed that he did not believe in an afterlife or in a personal God, and, in the company of his friends, would mock religious practices.[8] He also had no use for the doctrine of original sin, and wrote that the "doctrine of the Trinity, taken literally, has *no practical relevance at all.*"[9]

His religious scepticism was already revealed in the *Critique of Pure Reason* (1781), where we find him declaring that

[t]he concept of a Supreme Being is, in many respects, a very useful idea, but being an idea only, it is quite incapable of increasing, by itself, our knowledge with regard to what exists. It cannot even do so much as to inform us any further as to its possibility.[10]

In conceding that the concept of a God was, in his view, "a very useful idea," Kant betrayed a functionalist approach to religion which would reemerge in his later writings. But already in the *Critique*, he dismissed the cosmological, empirical, and ontological arguments for the existence of God, only to declare that "the Supreme Being remains, no doubt, an ideal only."[11]

Hume had expressed a similar scepticism in *Dialogues;* indeed, Kant and Hume concurred that one simply could not know anything about a putative Supreme Being. But, reflecting on Hume's supposition that scepticism was the end-point of our reflections on this matter, Kant countered that one could, all the same, *think* about God.[12] But, agreeing with Aquinas on this point, Kant upheld the idea that the moral law did not depend on commands from a Supreme Being; on the contrary, in his *Critique of Practical Reason* (1788), he would argue that "common human reason" was sufficient to identify which actions were good and which bad.[13] In Kant's view, thus, people understood the moral law quite readily, but they demanded a firmer, or perhaps more authoritative, foundation than mere reason – in effect, a divine command.

Groundwork of the Metaphysic of Morals (1785)

In the years preceding the French Revolution, Kant's attention was firmly fixed on identifying the fundamental principle of morality. He conceived of his *Groundwork* as a preliminary investigation of the moral law, and proposed to derive its fundamental principle from a priori concepts alone. As such, his concern in *Groundwork* was above all with defining and clarifying the nature of duty. Kant emphasized that right and duty are interconnected, so that one cannot have one without the other.

For Kant, it followed that, if one relativized one's morality, reducing everything to situational variables (that is to say to "situational ethics", which relies on empirical considerations), then one could, by the same virtue, claim only very relativized and situationally determined rights, again as conditioned by empirical considerations. Or again, if one chose to construe one's duties as purely subjective, then, to be completely consistent, one should construe one's rights as dependent on the purely subjective opinions others may hold concerning their own duties. Yet again, if one were to believe that the only duties one has are those specified by positive law (the position of Thrasymachus in Plato's *Republic*), then it would follow that one might claim only such rights as are granted by the statutes of the government under whose jurisdiction one happens to live. And finally, if and only if one accepts the rock-hard ethics based on Natural Law (whether in Kant's form or in some other), can one presume to postulate inalienable and unabridgeable natural rights. Hence, by endeavoring to set forth an air-tight system of natural duties, Kant laid the groundwork, at the same time, for a metaphysics (a system of a priori knowledge from concepts alone) of *rights*.

Duties, rights, and respect for the rights of others became *absolute* in Kant's system, which means that they are ends in themselves, and should never be regarded as mere means to realize some other end. For Kant, "Duty is the necessity to act out of reverence for the law."[14] It followed, for Kant, that "An action done from duty has its moral worth, not in the purpose to be attained by it, but in the maxim according with which it is decided upon; it depends therefore, not on the realisation of the object of the action, but solely on the principle of volition in accordance with which...the action has been performed."[15] In other words, the morality of an action does not depend upon the success of one's endeavor, but upon one's motivation. Thus, the only motivation which qualifies as morally worthy, is the desire to be in conformity with the moral law ("because it's the right thing to do"). This, for Kant, must be for its own sake: if one obeys the moral law in expectation of "eternal salvation", then one is acting in the expectation of payment and one's action has no moral content. Again, if one obeys the moral law to please somebody (mother, teacher, pastor, God), then again, one's action, even if helpful to others, has no moral content.[16]

In *Groundwork*, Kant offered three formal statements of his *categorical imperative*:

■   1st statement: "I ought never to act except in such a way that I can also will that my maxim [meaning the maxim from which my action would appear to be derived] should become a universal law."[17]

■   2nd statement: "Act only on that maxim through which you can at the same time will that it should become a universal law."[18]

■   3rd statement: "Act on the maxim which can at the same time be made a universal law."[19]

This may be reasonably paraphrased as follows: "Act in such a way that, if everyone were to act as you are acting, the world would be a better place."

In chapter 2 of *Groundwork*, Kant set forth his opposition to projects of attempting to derive the moral law from examples: no contingent example is capable of serving either as a first principle or as a springboard to a first principle. If then, the moral law cannot be derived from empirical cases, it can only be grounded on "pure reason" (recall that Cicero, Aquinas, and others had equated Natural Law with Right Reason). Now, if, furthermore, all human beings are to be considered subject to the moral law, it necessarily follows that all human beings (with certain exceptions) have the capacity to judge right from wrong.

But Kant was worried lest the appeal to universality could make the moral law contingent upon *general* comprehensibility, which is to say on the *lowest* common denominator among humankind. He therefore wanted principles of morality to be derived not from "the special nature of human reason,"[20] (which might even qualify as an empirical consideration), but more abstractly from notions of rationality as such. (What would a rational person do?).

In chapter 2, Kant also spelled out a "practical imperative": "Act in such a way that you always treat humanity, whether in your own person or in the person of any other, never simply as a means, but always at the same time as an end."[21] This "practical imperative" is, in fact, derived from the categorical imperative, because if everyone treated everyone else only as a means to one's own pleasure or profit (the position of pure "realism"), then there could be no true friendships, no bonds of trust, and no moral behavior.

Toward the end of chapter 2, Kant attacked empirical principles for the second time, and this time singled out the appeal to happiness for especial criticism. He wrote as follows:

> *Empirical principles* are always unfitted to serve as a ground for moral laws...The principle of *personal happiness* is, however, the most objectionable, not merely because it is false and because its pretence that well-being always adjusts itself to well-doing is contradicted by experience; nor merely because it contributes nothing whatever towards establishing morality, since making a man happy is quite different from making him good and making him prudent or astute in seeking his advantage [is] quite different from making him virtuous; but because it bases morality on sensuous motives which rather undermine it and totally destroy its sublimity, inasmuch as the motives of virtue are put in the same class as those of vice and we are instructed only to become better at calculation, the specific difference between virtue and vice being completely wiped out.[22]

The foregoing amounted, among other things, to a repudiation of the "realist" position spelled out by Machiavelli and Hobbes. Further, lest anyone still object that morality should best be derived from God's will, Kant criticized this as a *heteronomous* (non-autonomous) principle.

Kant now took his argument to its logical conclusion, not merely freeing the moral law from any connection with God's Will, but also insisting that his appeal to rationality as the ground of the moral law "...is better than the theological concept which derives morality from a divine and supremely perfect will..."[23] In this way, Kant established a firm secular basis for the moral law. He added that only the postulate of the individual *autonomously* discerning and willing the moral law could succeed in laying the foundation for authentic moral action. In chapter 3 (the final chapter in *Groundwork*) Kant returned to the theme of autonomy and freedom, and developed it further.

There was yet another alternative to Kant's effort to link morality to *a priori* principles, viz., claims registered on behalf of empirical knowledge (in particular the notion that one could build up an ethical system on the foundation of mere empirical observations). What Kant wanted to do, in the realm of ethics, was to develop a purely deductive system of ethics, which could be derived from logically defensible a priori principles.

Justus Möser was among the best known advocates of deducing moral principles from empirical observations. A prominent conservative, he thought that it was mistaken to try to theorize from a priori principles. Kant replied to Möser in *Groundwork for a Metaphysic of Morals*, writing:

> Everything that is empirical is, as a contribution to the principle of morality, not only wholly unsuitable for the purpose, but...even highly injurious to the purity of morals...Against the slack, or indeed ignoble, attitude which seeks for the moral principle among empirical motives and laws we cannot give a warning too strongly or too often; for human reason in its weariness is fain to rest upon this pillow and in a dream of sweet illusions (which lead it to embrace a cloud in mistake for Juno) to foist into the place of morality some misbegotten mongrel patched up from limbs of very varied ancestry and looking like anything you please, only not like virtue, to him who has once beheld her in her true shape.[24]

Clearly, Kant had a talent for sharp polemic, even though he rarely put that talent to use.

Wrestling with the French Revolution

Groundwork and the *Critique of Practical Reason* were Kant's last major writings before the outbreak of the French Revolution in 1789. But even before the outbreak of the Revolution, Kant, who was profoundly influenced by Rousseau's writings,[25] was writing about the subject of revolution. In his 1783 essay, "What is Enlightenment?", he had warned that one could not expect a revolution to engender "true reform" in people's thinking and, thus, one could not expect results as positive as what could come from gradual reform.[26] The French Revolution, which led to the outbreak of continent-wide war in 1792, was the major event in Kant's life and gave him occasion to write extensively on political subjects. During the period of the constitutional monarchy (1789-1792), Kant's comments about the French Revolution were largely positive; indeed, the French constitutions of 1791 and 1793 included principles consonant with Kant's philosophy, most notably in calling for progress in public enlightenment, i.e., education[27]; but he became highly critical of the revolutionaries during the Reign of Terror (1793-1794) and, in 1798, assessed that "the activity of the Committee of Public Safety in the phase of the revolutionary dictatorship under [Maximilien] Robespierre [w]as unjust."[28] By contrast, Kant had a positive view of the bourgeois republic of 1795-1799, with its limited suffrage.

Although he recoiled at the violent excesses of the French Revolution and was outraged by the execution of King Louis XVI, which he considered completely unnecessary and an offense to law, even putting social cohesion at risk, Kant remained sympathetic to the ideals of the Revolution. This sympathy caused him to revise his assessment of Great Britain, once the British went to war against Revolutionary France. Before 1789, he had held a high opinion of the British constitution and even thought it could offer a model for the development of a republican system within the framework of a limited government. But he now reversed his view of Old Albion and concluded that Britain's Glorious Revolution of 1688 had failed to achieve the goals for which Locke, Sidney, and others had been fighting. He also detected traces of both absolutism and corruption in the British system, and faulted it for nontransparency.[29] In his *Conflict of the Faculties*, although addressing primarily religious matters, Kant boldly declared his sympathy for the principles of the revolution and confessed that his emotional response to the events unfolding in France "border[ed] closely on enthusiasm."[30] Kant's last public utterance concerning developments connected with the French Revolution was a commentary on the Egyptian campaign of Napoleon Bonaparte in 1798-1799, which confirmed his (continued) partiality for France. He made no comment about Napoleon's assumption of power in November 1799; by then his mental and physical strength was in decline.[31]

In *Religion within the Boundaries of Mere Reason* (1793; 2nd edition, 1794), he revived his functionalist approach to religion, advancing the proposition that religion could contribute to human progress and, more controversially, calling for an "ethical commonwealth" in which Christian religions would overcome their differences and draw steadily closer to a moral understanding founded on reason.[32] As he expressed himself here, Christianity had placed people "under a slavish yoke of faith" from which people were just beginning to escape; "freedom of thought" was his clarion call.[33] In this work, Kant rejected both the idea of state control of religion (the Hobb'sian solution) and religious toleration (Bodin's solution); he felt that bare toleration would allow outright superstitions and corrupt religious and moral perspectives to flourish. His alternative – the ethical commonwealth – would have no enforcement capacity but would promote shared ethical principles. He intended the commonwealth to overcome the "ethical state of nature" in which he believed people were living, with no recognized ecclesiastical authority to adjudicate and resolve moral and religious disputes.[34] This unique solution may be viewed as the ethical counterpart to the political federation of states he would shortly outline in *Perpetual Peace*.

Religion within the Boundaries of Mere Reason, with its reference to the "slavish yoke of [Christian] faith", enraged the King of Prussia, Friedrich Wilhelm II (1744-97; reigned 1786-97). (His uncle and predecessor, Friedrich II, had been an advocate of religious toleration, but Friedrich Wilhelm II did not believe in toleration and apparently did not subscribe to Kant's notion of an ethical commonwealth either.) The King ordered his minister of education and religious affairs, Johann Cristoph Woellner, to write to Kant to extract a promise that he would not write again on religion: this was tantamount to a Royal command. Kant reluctantly agreed, writing in reply that he would never again write on religious matters "as Your Majesty's most loyal subject". When the King passed away in 1797, Kant resumed writing on religion, explaining that the phrase "as Your Majesty's most loyal subject" had served to limit the promise to the lifetime of King Friedrich Wilhelm II.[35]

Kant was of a mixed mind about his decision to comply with the King's orders; but consistent with the principles he defended in his writings, he considered himself duty-bound to obey the King's orders, and noted that, although one was morally bound to tell the truth, it did not follow that one had to tell the whole truth in the public sphere. In the meantime, Kant's influential essay, "Perpetual Peace" was published in 1795, and in 1797-98, Kant published his final and definitive statement on ethics, his *Metaphysics of Morals*. Then, in 1798, Kant brought together three shorter pieces of his, publishing them under the title, *The Conflict of the Faculties*. The main focus of the work was the differing perspectives and methodologies of the faculties of philosophy and theology. In the course of this work, as if to spite the deceased monarch, Kant suggested that the

Bible contained "mistakes",[36] expressed skepticism concerning the allegedly divine inspiration of the Bible,[37] and referred to Christianity merely as "the most adequate religion."[38] Yet, insofar as this "most adequate" religion could help to induce people to behave morally, Kant urged the government to promote the Bible as a "great means for establishing and administering civil order and peace."[39] But, by this point, Kant was declining physically and he retired from the university. In 1803 he fell seriously ill for the first time, and on 12 February 1804 he passed away, a few months before his 80th birthday and just over two months before Napoleon Bonaparte would crown himself Emperor of the French.

Kant greeted both the American Revolution and the French Revolution, believing that both of them held the promise of bringing forth systems founded on the rule of law and committed to the common good. But in spite of his sympathy for the French Revolution, bordering on "enthusiasm", Kant was deeply conflicted about it. He considered revolution illegal, by definition. Already in his essay, "On the Proverb, That May be True in Theory, But [it] Is of No Practical Use" (published in 1793, after the French Revolutionary Wars had broken out), Kant declared that

> ...all resistance to the supreme legislative power, all incitement of subjects actively to express discontent, all revolt that breaks forth into rebellion, is the highest and most punishable crime in a commonwealth, for it destroys its foundation. And this prohibition is *absolute*, so that even if that power or its agent, the nation's leader, may have broken the original contract, thereby forfeiting in the subject's eyes the right to be legislator, since he has authorized the government to proceed in a thoroughly brutal (tyrannical) fashion, the citizen is nonetheless not to resist him in any way whatsoever. This is because under an already existing civil constitution the people no longer have the right to judge and to determine how the constitution should be administered.[40]

Put differently, Kant believed that the doctrine of popular sovereignty popularized by John Locke among others involved self-contradiction, since sovereignty – in his view – could not be located both in the government and in the people, and, in any event, there was no such thing as a "people" except insofar as they were united under a sovereign government.[41] But there was another problem with revolution in general, viz., that revolutions typically led, in the short run, to situations of interregnum, which returned citizens to the state of nature. Furthermore, he feared that, in the absence of the changes in people's attitudes which he believed revolutions were ill equipped to promote, they were likely to end with governments which would be worse than what people had before.[42]

Perpetual Peace was published in 1795, the same year in which the Peace of Basel brought an end to the first phase of the wars unleashed by the Revolution. Written during the worst fighting across Europe since the Thirty Years War of 1618-48, the tract may therefore be understood as Kant's response to the French Revolutionary War. In that treatise, Kant laid down the principle of non-interference in the government or constitution of any state, except in cases of civil war, together with a corollary prohibiting partition.[43] Given that this came in the wake of the first (1772) and second (1793) partitions of Poland, with Poland about to be wiped off the map by the third partition (of 1795), Kant's reference to the impermissibility of partition would have had a concrete reference for his contemporary readers. He also declared his opposition, in the same work, to "piracy, enslavement, colonial oppression, and subversion of a foreign people."[44] But it was the war engulfing all of Europe which was most on Kant's mind. He hoped, to be sure, that war would prove to be

> ...the means by which nature drives nations to make initially imperfect attempts, but finally, after many devastations, upheavals and even complete inner exhaustion of their powers, to take the step which reason could have suggested to them even without so many sad experiences – that of abandoning a lawless state of savagery and entering a federation of peoples in which every state, even the smallest, could expect to derive its security and rights not from its own power or its own legal judgement, but solely from this great federation...and the law-governed decisions of a united will.[45]

In his "Idea for a Universal History with a Cosmopolitan Purpose" (1784), he had nurtured a dual concern – to identify what might be called a "perfect civil constitution" and to urge that states enter into a federation which could assure the security of all – a dual concern which likewise animated Kant's *Perpetual Peace*. In this latter work, he explicitly endorsed *republican* government as the only form of government compatible with the moral law.[46] Kant's notion of *republican* government is easily confused with representative government. What Kant had in mind by the term was that the will of the people should be sovereign but, he insisted, not only a representative government but also a monarchy could be republican, provided that the monarch allowed a public sphere to function in which the public could express its opinions and voice its concerns and provided that the system was characterized by the rule of law. Kant laid especial stress on the duty of rulers to respect the rights of their subjects and to promote their welfare. In the second edition of the work (released in 1796), Kant added a chapter stressing that it was in the state's own interest to assure freedom of speech and press to philosophers.[47] The reason for this is that Kant believed that it was precisely the philosophers who were reflecting the most seriously about the problems of the age as well as about prospective solutions.

Hobbes' *Leviathan* had recently been published in German translation, and interest in the English philosopher's views, in the German-speaking world, was high. Kant had read Hobbes and considered the Englishman's arguments dangerous. Among other things, Hobbes thought that a sovereign was above the law and thought the international political order to be of secondary importance for the maintenance of order within any given state. Kant, by contrast, insisted that a republican political order was likely to be less conducive to belligerence and placed great stress on achieving peace in the international political order.[48]

The first step, then, was to construct a well-ordered state in which the laws and institutions of state moderate, neutralize, or even eliminate most of the destructive potential of people's selfish orientation.[49] Kant did not expect people to agree to a republican constitution out of good will; on the contrary, he warned that people had a natural propensity to evil.[50] But the need to counter the self-seeking of other selfish individuals and groups would be – he thought – quite enough to motivate people to agree to a set of laws which would assure some measure of fairness toward all. What is practical, thus, is what is fair and, even from self-seeking motives, it is possible to realize that all are best served by a state having "an internal constitution organised in accordance with pure principles of right."[51] Once such a state would be set up, it would actually serve, Kant suggested, to raise the level of morality among the people living under its jurisdiction.[52] This, Kant pointed out elsewhere, should be embraced as a conscious task, so that the level of morality and sociability could be steadily raised from one generation to the next.[53] Thus, morality should serve as the yardstick by which to measure the health of a state. On this point, Kant urged explicitly that "the well-being of a state" cannot be reduced to the welfare and happiness of the citizens. On the contrary, Kant noted, "By the well-being of a state is understood, instead, that condition in which its constitution conforms most fully to principles of Right."[54] Kant also argued that the inclusion of the citizens in deliberations about public policy would provide an assurance that war would be a rare event since – he was convinced – people would be loath to willingly agree to endure the hardships of war.[55]

The next step, for Kant, was for states "to arrive at a lawful settlement of their differences by forming something analogous to a universal state."[56] But, he cautioned in another work, a unified world state under a single ruler might prove to be inimical to human freedom and, thus, it would be safer and preferable for nations to agree to a "state of nations" (Völkerstaat), in which the distinct cultures, along with the constituent states themselves, would be preserved.[57] Kant specifically cautioned against trying to erect a world state, believing that the project, if successful, would risk creating "the most terrible despotism."[58] At the same time, he also warned that too loose a grouping, such as in what he called a Völkerbund (a league of nations), being oriented only to collaboration and mutual consultation, would not serve the purpose of assuring peace as effectively as a Völkerstaat.

The Völkerstaat which Kant envisioned would, he hoped, establish certain provisional laws and rights – which he linked to his principles of cosmopolitan right, summarized in laws of hospitality. These "laws" should include the right of individuals to visit all parts of the world, the right of travellers not to be treated with hostility by citizens of other countries, the right to engage in public reason, the right to engage in commerce, and the right to be treated fairly in contracts.[59] Insofar as these are rights, they impose certain duties on others, duties which are, in fact, reciprocal and constitute, thus, the foundation for a notion of cosmopolitan or universal rights. It comes as no surprise, then, that one scholar has suggested that Kant's concept of cosmopolitan right and the laws of hospitality can be seen as foreshadowing the human rights embodied in the Universal Declaration of Human Rights issued by the United Nations in 1948.[60]

Kant was, in fact, a cautious optimist. In spite of his concern about "self-seeking energies" and about human selfishness generally, he believed that humanity was improving not only culturally and in terms of scientific knowledge but also in relation to moral principles.[61] Indeed, in his view, the goal of history should be understood in terms of the improvement in humankind's capacity for good – in a word, in terms of humankind's moral improvement; at the same time, progress in morality entailed progress in the understanding of right (Recht), and here he was convinced that the French Revolution marked a watershed in the realization of human freedom and in the evolution of systems based on the concept of right.[62] Accordingly, even while recognizing the imperialistic or irredentist ambitions which drive states, leaving no nation entirely secure,[63] he was convinced that humanity's growing wisdom would serve it well at such point as practical considerations dictated the creation of a federation of independent states. Cautious to the end, he readily admitted that *"perpetual peace,* the ultimate goal of the whole Right of Nations, is indeed an unachievable Idea." But, in the same breath, he insisted nonetheless that "the political principles directed toward perpetual peace, of entering into such an alliance of states, which serve for continual *approximation* to it, are not unachievable."[64]

The Metaphysics of Morals (1797)

Kant was still wrestling with the themes of revolution, political legitimacy, war, and freedom as he sat down to write what has been called his "most important political work."[65] Like many of his philosophical forebears, Kant saw that political theory has a natural and organic connection with moral theory and that, to offer any normative propositions concerning politics, one had to develop them on the foundation of a comprehensive moral theory. This is precisely what he set out to do in *The Metaphysics of Morals.* As he noted there, he believed that people had a duty to strive to improve themselves, even to aspire to "natural perfection"; insofar as this required that people be able to set rational ends for their actions, this entailed at the same time that people had an "innate right to freedom".[66] Accordingly, the purpose of the state was to maximize people's freedom, but people's happiness, as such, insofar as it is to some extent subjective, could not be a legitimate object of government. At the same time, however, he identified freedom with the moral law; to be free is to be free to live morally; there is no such thing as freedom to be immoral.[67]

He also expanded his scope to subsume the political. He argued, for example, that the laws of the state (positive laws) may not infringe upon people's natural rights, including the right of first possession of land. But he further underlined the connection between positive laws and Natural Law, by arguing that the validity of the former depends upon its conformity with the latter. One of the most controversial passages of *The Metaphysics of Morals* occurs in the chapter devoted to "Public Right". Here, he argued that:

> The head of a state has only rights against his subjects and no duties *(that he can be coerced to fulfil)*. Moreover, even if the organ of the head of a state, the *ruler*, proceeds contrary to law, for example, if he goes against the law of equality in assigning the burdens of the state in matters of taxation, recruiting and so forth, subjects may indeed oppose this injustice by *complaints (gravamina)* but not by resistance.[68]

The key qualifier in the foregoing passage is "that he can be coerced to fulfil". After all, Kant had already stressed that positive law *cannot* infringe upon natural rights. The reason that there is no right of resistance, for Kant, is that he did not recognize any notion of popular sovereignty. Rousseau had assumed a basic human innocence (albeit corrupted by conditions of inequality) in his defence of popular sovereignty. But Kant was not prepared to assume human innocence. On the contrary, like most other liberals, he took human shortcomings as a given, warning, at one point, "… of men's maxim of violence and of their malevolent tendency to attack one another before external legislation endowed with power appears."[69]

The difficulty, for Kant, was that, insofar as he viewed sovereignty in *functional* terms, i.e., as being in charge, he could not allow that anyone might judge the state except the state itself, since if there were some higher judge, then – in his view – that higher judge would be the sovereign state, rather than the state itself. Accordingly, rebellion would result in "abolishing the entire legal constitution"[70] which has value in assuring the "negative freedom" of the citizens of the state.[71] But, inevitably, the subjects will draw conclusions about what the sovereign is doing and will conclude – and rightly so – that they have some duties to respond in some way to unjust commands. Therefore, following Richard Hooker on this point, Kant made a provision for passive resistance, in what he called a "limited constitution", but he insisted that "no active resistance…

is permitted,"[72] which is to say, no rebellion and no revolution. But Kant was writing this text even as the French Revolution was unfurling the banner of "Liberté, Egalité, Fraternité", and he did *not* want to end up advocating monarchical restoration. Kant therefore immediately provided the following qualification:

> ...once a revolution has succeeded and a new constitution has been established, the lack of legitimacy with which it began and has been implemented cannot release the subjects from the obligation to comply with the new order of things as good citizens, and they cannot refuse honest obedience to the authority that now has the power.[73]

As for the legitimate jurisdiction of the state, Kant emphasized that the state existed for the good of the entire society, from which he concluded: first, that the government had every right to tax the rich (whether via tax on property or a tax on commerce) in order to use the funds to support vital social services, including providing for the sustenance of the indigent[74]; and second, that the government does *not* have the right to prescribe specific religious beliefs or religious rituals to the society or to favor one religion (in practice, one Christian denomination) over others.

Kant was, as already noted, highly conflicted about revolution as a means to advance human civilization. The best route to expanding the political participation of citizens, building a representative government on republican foundations, was – he thought – for an absolute monarch to launch a gradual transition, reforming the system step by step. In the short run, he favored intellectual freedom and the expansion of public education, combined with a measure of civil unfreedom. In this way, enlightened absolutism could provide a secure environment in which a people could grow and mature intellectually and culturally.[75]

Once again, he employed the categorical imperative,[76] and delineated the duties respectively of citizens and rulers. Citizens, aside from their duty to obey the law and restrict themselves at the most to passive disobedience, also had a further duty, viz., to the extent that they perceived injustice or corruption in the country, they were obliged, said Kant, to bring their information to the attention of the authorities in a public forum and to share their perspectives.[77]

The ruler's duties included the protection of the lives and property of the country's inhabitants, respect for the law, and protection of the lawful (and moral) freedom of the people. In addition, Kant argued that the government was "...authorized to constrain the wealthy to provide the means of sustenance to those who are unable to provide for even their most necessary natural needs. The wealthy have acquired an obligation to the commonwealth, since they owe their existence to...its protection and care."[78] Finally, insofar as a government in which executive and legislative functions are not separate may only be characterized as despotic, an enlightened monarch had a duty to maintain the separation of these functions, thus the independence of the judiciary. At the same time, viewing the state as the guarantee of people's security and freedom, Kant was careful to defend its prerogatives and therefore was prepared to legitimate the government's interference in meetings of private associations and in other domains sometimes thought to belong strictly to the private sphere.[79]

Kant's Importance

With his defense of individual rights, the rule of law, personal freedom, and the separation of powers, Kant is unmistakably part of the liberal tradition and a key figure in the liberal Enlightenment.[80] He advocated the spread of democratic republics throughout the world, and predicted that republican democracy (i.e., respecting the principles of rule of law, individual rights, toleration, and some measure of equality) would eventually be the only legitimate political system. He asserted the importance of individual duty and individual rights. He stressed the centrality of freedom. He sympathized with both the American and the French revolutionaries, despite his philosophical misgivings about revolution as such.

Kant rejected Hobbes' authoritarian view of sovereignty and Hobbes' endeavor to trace the civil compact to nothing more than the fear of violent death. Kant also differed from Rousseau in his interpretation of notions of communal, or "general", will. Among Kant's legacies was his contribution to shaping the doctrine of the *Rechtsstaat* (nomocracy), a state governed by law, and his achievement in revivifying the Natural Law tradition, albeit in a transformed variant.

In sum, Kant's importance may be summarized in four points. First, Kant laid out an ethical system derived from a priori principles and summarized by a single overarching imperative – the categorical imperative. Second he argued that liberal policies must be built on the foundation of a strict ethical system, and that there could be no freedom to be immoral. Third, he argued that it was possible for people to improve (morally) and that the state could play a constructive role in this improvement, among other things by fostering conditions conducive to the promotion of "sociability under laws".[81] And fourth, he made a strong argument that it was possible to build up a network of international organizations and international law, and that this, in combination with the promotion of liberal politics could move the planet *in the direction of* perpetual peace, with steadily less violence and warfare.

Notes

1   This chapter was originally published in *Eastern Review,* Vol. 8 (2019), pp. 183-199.

2   Manfred Kuehn, *Kant: A Biography* (Cambridge: Cambridge University Press, 2001), pp. 53—54. See also Karl Jaspers, *Kant: Leben, Werk, Wirkung* (Munich: R. Piper, 1975). For Kant's comments on Pietism, see Immanuel Kant, *The Conflict of the Faculties*, trans. from German by Mary J. Gregor (Lincoln and London: University of Nebraska Press, 1979; paperback, 1992), pp. 97-107.

3   Kuehn, *Kant*, pp. 158-159, 162-163, 188-189.

4   Ludwig Siep, "What is the Purpose of a Metaphysics of Morals? Some Observations on the Preface to the *Groundwork of the Metaphysics of Morals"*, in Karl Ameriks and Otfried Höffe (eds.), *Kant's Moral and Legal Philosophy*, trans. from German by Nicholas Walker (Cambridge: Cambridge University Press, 2009), p. 78.

5   Dieter Henrich, "Hutcheson and Kant", in Ameriks and Höffe (eds.), *Kant's Moral and Legal Philosophy*, p. 30, notes 1-4.

6   Kuehn, *Kant*, p. 202.

7   Henrich, "Hutcheson and Kant", p. 37.

8   Kuehn, *Kant*, p. 3.

9   Kant, *Conflict of the Faculties*, p. 65.

10   Immanuel Kant, *Critique of Pure Reason*, trans. from German by Max Müller, in *Kant Selections*, ed. by Theodore M. Greene (New York: Charles Scribner's Sons, 1929), p. 251.

11 *Ibid.,* p. 267. For further discussion of Kant's ideas on this subject, see Peter Byrne, *Kant on God* (Aldershot: Ashgate, 2007), *passim.*

12 Beryl Logan, "Hume and Kant on Knowing the Deity", in *International Journal for Philosophy of Religion,* Vol. 43, no. 3 (June 1998), p. 138.

13 Immanuel Kant, *Critique of Practical Reason,* trans. from German by T. K. Abbott under the title, *Theory of Ethics,* in *Kant Selections,* p. 283.

14 Immanuel Kant, *Groundwork of the Metaphysic of Morals,* trans. from German by H. J. Paton (London and New York: Routledge, 1948), p. 66.

15 *Ibid.,* p. 65.

16 Pippin writes, however, that Kant did not, in fact, mean to suggest that acts not motivated purely by a sense of duty have no moral worth. See Robert B. Pippin, "Kant's Theory of Value: On Allen Wood's *Kant's Ethical Thought",* in *Inquiry,* Vol. 43, no. 2 (2000), p. 241.

17 Kant, *Groundwork of the Metaphysic of Morals,* p. 67.

18 *Ibid.,* p. 84.

19 *Ibid.,* p. 98.

20 *Ibid.,* p. 76.

21 *Ibid.,* p. 91.

22 *Ibid.,* p. 103.

23 *Ibid.,* p. 104.

24 *Ibid.,* pp. 88-89.

25 There was only one picture on the wall in Kant's house – a portrait of Rousseau.

26 Howard Williams, *Kant's critique of Hobbes: Sovereignty and cosmopolitanism* (Cardiff: University of Wales Press, 2003), p. 22.

27 Peter Burg, *Kant und die Französische Revolution* (Berlin: Duncker & Humblot, 1974), pp. 56-57.

28 *Ibid.,* p. 20.

29 Dieter Henrich, "On the Meaning of Rational Action in the State", trans. from German by Richard L. Velkley, in Ronald Beiner and William James Booth (eds.), *Kant & Political Philosophy: The Contemporary Legacy* (New Haven, Conn.: Yale University Press, 1993), p. 108; and Ellis, *Kant's Political Legacy,* pp. 24-25, 36, 122-123.

30 Immanuel Kant, *Religion within the Boundaries of Mere Reason,* in I. Kant, *Religion within the Boundaries of Mere Reason And Other Writings,* trans. & ed. by Allen Wood and George di Giovanni (Cambridge: Cambridge University Press, 1998; 11th printing 2011), p. 153. See also p. 159.

31 Burg, *Kant und die Französische Revolution,* p. 20.

32 *Kant, Religion within the Boundaries,* pp. 108-112.

33 *Ibid.,* pp. 180-181.

34 Mark Lilla, "Kant's Theological-Political Revolution", in *Review of Metaphysics*, Vol. 52, no. 2 (December 1998), pp. 423, 425, 427. Regarding the "ethical state of nature", see also Kant *Religion within the Boundaries of Mere Reason*, pp. 106-109.
35 Kant, *Conflict of the Faculties*, preface, pp. 9-19 and 19n.
36 *Ibid.*, p. 121.
37 *Ibid.*, p. 77.
38 *Ibid.*, p. 61.
39 *Ibid.*, p. 119.
40 Immanuel Kant, "On the Proverb: That May be True in Theory, But [it] Is of No Practical Use" [hereafter, *Theory and Practice*] (1793), trans. from German by Ted Humphrey, in I. Kant, *Perpetual Peace and Other Essays* (Indianapolis: Hackett Publishing Co., 1983), p. 79 (299/300).
41 Katrin Flikschuh, "Reason, Right, and Revolution: Kant and Locke", in *Philosophy & Public Affairs*, Vol. 36, no. 4 (2008), pp. 376-377, 382.
42 Lewis W. Beck, "Kant and the Right of Revolution", in *Journal of the History of Ideas*, Vol. 32, no. 3 (July—September 1971), p. 418.
43 Elisabeth Ellis, *Kant's Politics: Provisional Theory for an Uncertain World* (New Haven, Conn.: Yale University Press, 2005), p. 75.
44 *Ibid.*, p. 95.
45 *Ibid.*, p. 47.
46 Immanuel Kant, "Perpetual Peace: A Philosophical Sketch", in Kant, *Political Writings*, p. 101.
47 Ellis, *Kant's Politics*, pp. 108, 110.
48 Williams, *Kant's critique of Hobbes, passim*.
49 Kant, "Perpetual Peace", p. 112.
50 Kant, *Religion within the Boundaries*, pp. 52-53.
51 Kant, "Perpetual Peace", p. 123.
52 *Ibid.*, p. 113.
53 G. Felicitas Munzel, "Kant on Moral Education, or 'Enlightenment' and the Liberal Arts", in *The Review of Metaphysics*, Vol. 57, No. 1 (September 2003), pp. 43-44, citing Kant's essay, *On Pedagogy*.
54 Immanuel Kant, *The Metaphysics of Morals*, trans. from German by Mary Gregor (Cambridge: Cambridge University Press, 1991; reprinted 1993), p. 129.
55 Wolfgang Kersting, "The Civil Constitution in Every State Shall Be a Republican One", in Ameriks and Höffe (eds.), *Kant's Moral and Legal Philosophy*, p. 255.
56 Kant, "Perpetual Peace", p. 123.
57 B. Sharon Byrd and Joachim Hruschka, *Kant's Doctrine of Right: A Commentary* (Cambridge: Cambridge University Press, 2010), pp. 198-199, summarizing Kant's *Theory and Practice*.

58 Quoted in *Ibid.*, p. 197.

59 Brown, "Kantian Cosmopolitan Law", pp. 667-670.

60 Sharon Anderson-Gold, *Cosmopolitanism and Human Rights* (Cardiff, 2001), as cited in Brown, "Kantian Cosmopolitan Law", p. 665.

61 Kant, *Perpetual Peace*, p. 112. See also Kant, *Conflict of the Faculties*, pp. 157, 159, 165, 167.

62 Burg, *Kant und die Französische Revolution*, pp. 37, 62, 65, 67.

63 Kant, *Theory and Practice*, pp. 91-92.

64 Kant, *The Metaphysics of Morals*, p. 156, Kant's emphases.

65 Ellis, *Kant's Politics*, p. 6.

66 Allen W. Wood, *Kant's Ethical Thought* (Cambridge: Cambridge University Press, 1999), pp. 140, 323. See also Kant, *Religion within the Boundaries*, p. 80.

67 Kant, *The Metaphysics of Morals*, p. 52.

68 *Ibid.*, p. 130, first emphasis mine, others Kant's.

69 *Ibid.*, p. 123.

70 *Ibid.*, p. 131.

71 Patrick Riley, "On Kant as the Most Adequate of the Social Contract Theorists", in *Political Theory*, Vol. 1, No. 4 (November 1973), p. 453.

72 Kant, *The Metaphysics of Morals*, p. 133.

73 *Ibid.*, p. 133.

74 *Ibid.*, p. 136.

75 Robert S. Taylor, "Democratic Transitions and the Progress of Absolutism in Kant's Political Thought", in *Journal of Politics*, Vol. 68, no. 3 (August 2006), pp. 557, 559-560.

76 Kant, *The Metaphysics of Morals*, p. 51.

77 Ellis, *Kant's Politics*, p. 145.

78 Kant, *The Metaphysics of Morals*, p. 136.

79 Ellis, *Kant's Politics*, p. 17.

80 As noted by various writers, including: Allen D. Rosen, *Kant's Theory of Justice* (Ithaca: Cornell University Press, 1993), p. 116; and Katrin Flikschuh, *Kant and modern political philosophy* (Cambridge: Cambridge University Press, 2000), p. 2.

81 Munzel, "Kant on Moral Education", p. 67.

3

Hamann, Herder, Fichte, and the Anti-Enlightenment Tradition

Torbjørn L. Knutsen

Summary: Johann Gottfried Herder and Johann Gottlieb Fichte were two of the most consequential thinkers of the early phase of the period covered in this volume. Together with Johann Georg Hamann, they responded to Kant's ideas in various ways. Hamann rejected Kant's claim that one could talk sensibly of "pure reason"; for Hamann, there was no such thing. Herder was influenced by Hamann, but, where the pivotal question of language was concerned, he repudiated the ideas of both Kant and Hamann. For Herder, language is the mirror of a national group's culture and contributes to defining its identity. Herder broke with the key assumptions of mainstream Enlightenment thinking and had a huge influence in his time. Fichte took Kant's philosophy as his starting point but was affected by Herder. While political philosophy was not central to the thinking of either Hamann or Herder, it was central to Fichte. Responding to Thomas Jefferson's claim that human rights are God-given and universal, Fichte rejected the claim that rights have a divine origin; although deeply religious in other questions, he argued that that rights are human constructs that evolved over the course of history. Since rights emerge within human societies, with distinct cultures, it followed that they cannot be considered either universal or inalienable.

Germany experienced a remarkable philosophical revolution during the final quarter of the 18th century. It interacted with and was affected by two other revolutions that shook the Western world at that time: The economic revolution in Britain and the political revolution in France. The effect of the economic revolution of Britain was subtle, slow, and long term. It was the political French Revolution that exerted the most immediate influence on German thinkers, because the radical upheavals in Paris was quickly followed by Napoleon's seizure of power and military expansion. Both had huge consequences.

Many German thinkers were at first enthusiastic supporters of the French Revolution. They embraced its optimistic rhetoric and its republican ideals of progress and popular sovereignty. But when the armies of Napoleon Bonaparte began to march across large swaths of Europe – including German lands – their enthusiasm cooled. War, conquest, bloodshed, and repression turned the Germans against Napoleon and his French empire. At the same time, many German thinkers retained the basic ideals of the revolution. The ideals of popular sovereignty, rights of man, self-determination and mass-participation spread throughout the industrializing regions of Europe and the Americas during the final quarter of the 18th century. But they fractured. The ideals quickly gave rise to two strands of political thought. One was elaborated on the tradition of Enlightenment thought – it carried ideas formulated by writers like Thomas Paine in England, Thomas Jefferson and James Madison in the Americas, and Condorcet in France. The other strand emerged in Germany as a reaction to the core claims of the Enlightenment. It is this second strand that shall concern us here.

Three men stood out as particularly important in the German maelstrom of events: The first was Immanuel Kant. He disseminated the humanist message of the European Enlightenment in Germany; he contributed greatly to the German *Aufklärung*, and exerted a deep influence on a whole generation of German thinkers. The second was Napoléon Bonaparte. He was a catalyst, whose wars helped unify Germany as a political unit and a nation. He also spread the universal values of the Enlightenment across the entire European Continent. The third man was the relatively obscure Johann George Hamann. He criticized Kant and castigated England and condemned Napoleon. His writings were amateurish, but his charisma was substantial: He influenced Herder, Fichte and a generation of thinkers who paved the way for Germany's anti-Enlightenment reaction.

This chapter will not discuss Kant – the previous chapter has done that. It will instead begin with a brief account of Johann George Hamann (1730-1788), before it moves on to the ideas of Johann Gottfried Herder (1744-1803), and Johann Gottlieb Fichte (1762-1814). All three were students of Kant. The latter two were among the most original and consequential thinkers of the late eighteenth and the early nineteenth century. Together with Johann

Georg Hamann, they reacted to Kant's ideas in various ways. They were not the only critics of the Enlightenment; they interacted with a host of other thinkers – with Goethe, Schelling, Schleiermacher (the last of these are discussed more closely in chapter five) and many others. Reasons of space prevent this chapter from presenting the whole, complicated cloth of this formative period of German philosophy; it will limit its attention to the key arguments of Herder and Fichte.

Opposing Britain and France

Germany's philosophical revolution gathered speed during the 1780s – at the same time as Great Britain was shaken by an Industrial Revolution and France was shattered by a Political Revolution. To appreciate the development of political philosophy in Germany, it is useful to recall that the events of Britain and France took place in established territorial states. Germany, by contrast, had no state – during the 17th century the Holy Roman Empire had fragmented, leaving some 1,800 impoverished and independent principalities in its wake.

German thinkers tended to be absorbed by their own history while fearing the expansion of neighboring states – especially Britain and France, whose economic influence and military power threatened to overwhelm the fragmented German lands. Many German thinkers directed their attention towards the heritage of the past and the values they considered to be under threat. They resented the forces that drove the changes of the age and rejected the values that marked them. Most particularly, they rejected the arguments of the Enlightenment *philosophes* and their portrayal of the uni-linear evolution of Reason, knowledge, and human capabilities. They regarded industrialism, travel, trade and increasing commerce with skepticism.

These resentments were notable in Königsberg, the old capital of East Prussia. The city has a reputable university – the Albertina University (founded in 1544) – which contributed to the development of Königsberg into an important German intellectual and cultural center, being the residence of Kant, Hamann and Herder. It was also a considerable Baltic port, tightly tied in with the Atlantic powers through shipping and trade. The British presence was strong. Indeed, Königsberg was the hub of the Baltic trade in timber and grain. Trade was in turn associated with the transfer of impulses and ideas – in this case the ideas of the English, the French, and the Scottish Enlightenment.

From Kant to Hamann

Johann Georg Hamann attended classes at the university of Königsberg – including classes from Immanuel Kant. He took no final exams. But he became one of Kant's acquaintances and developed high opinions of himself. He considered himself an intellectual, although he earned his living as a jack-of-all-trades in the port cities of Königsberg and Riga.

In 1758 Hamann was sent to London on a mission for a Königsberg businessman: he was given money to pay some bills on the behalf of a German company and was told to negotiate new deals with a London firm. He was neither a disciplined businessman nor a tough negotiator. He was led into temptation in London. He partied hard, wasted his money, ended up on skid row and suffered a nervous breakdown. In this moment of darkest remorse, Hamann experienced a religious conversion. Jesus appeared in a revelation and gave him a reason to believe that knowledge could be inspired by divine intervention. In his mind, this revelation supported the skeptical writings of David Hume, which Hamann had discovered in London. It gave him a reason to doubt his senses and reject inductive reason as a basis for solid knowledge.

Hamann returned broke to his native Königsberg. He had lost all his money – and all faith in the British ideals of liberty, wealth, and material progress. But he had found Hume and Jesus. This would have important implications; not only for Hamann but also for his many friends and acquaintances. For Hamann was a charismatic debater, and his new perspectives influenced several members of his intellectual circles – most particularly Johann Gottfried Herder and, more indirectly, Johann Gottlieb Fichte. Both of them had studied with Immanuel Kant in Königsberg. Hamann gave them cause to doubt Kant's philosophical arguments.

There is an odd incongruence between Hamann and Kant. They were acquaintances, even friends. Hamann was an obscure figure. He was hardly a "philosopher" – he was a prophet rather than an analyst; an oracular pronouncer and a mystic. Kant was an analyst; a man of cool reason and an architect of logical arguments. And he was about to emerge as the most famous philosopher of the German Enlightenment. Kant was an inspiration for members of the German *Aufklärung*. Hamann was an inspiration for thinkers who reacted against the theories and the claims of the Enlightenment tradition. Herder and Fichte were taught by Kant but ended up under Hamann's influence. They contributed to a critique of Kant and to the development of new ideas and concepts – among them the concepts of "nation" and *Volk*, two of the most formative political concepts of the 19th century.

Hamann and Herder

In 1762, as Kant was turning 40 and was not yet truly famous, he found in his classes a gifted, introspective youth of 18, Johann Gottfried Herder (1744-1803). Kant observed the talents of the young man with some surprise, for Herder had no academic past. He had grown up in a poor household in Mohrungen in the east of Prussia. He had risen out of his class by sheer ability, learning to read from his father's Bible and songbook.

But Herder had also been lucky. First, a Russian army surgeon, who was on his way back from the Seven Years' War, took a liking to the serious young boy, took him to Königsberg and enrolled him as a student at the university's school of medicine. Second, once in Königsberg, young Herder quickly discovered that he had an inconvenient tendency to faint during dissections. Medicine was not for him. He switched to theology. And as a consequence, he was brought into the classroom of Immanuel Kant.

Herder followed Kant's lectures which introduced him to the great thinkers of the age – among them two of the most influential philosophers on Kant's own life, David Hume and Jean-Jacques Rousseau. In 1764 Herder travelled to the Baltic city of Riga to complete his education. Here he began to write and publish his first reviews and articles. Also, he met Johann Georg Hamann, who would play an important part in his intellectual development.

Hamann had a quick mind, but he was hardly a disciplined scholar. He was a prolific writer, but he was unsystematic and scattered – he did not address any one issue in depth but wrote sketches and essays on a wide range of topics. His comments tended to be cast as opinions rather than reasoned arguments. His statements were often oracular – and earned Hamann the sobriquet "The Wizard of the North". He was imaginative, insightful, and charismatic. He rallied against the fashionable faith in human reason and the general abstractions of the Enlightenment *philosophes*. He criticized them for pulling reason out of its larger, human context and cultivating it as a thing in itself, removed from any social and historical context. Hamann was a holist. For him, the world was an infinitely complex unity. He argued that in order to understand it, it was necessary to capture human relations in their earthy and rich totality. The Enlightenment quest for general laws was a naïve simplification, he argued. He held them to be contextless, hollow and meaningless abstractions.

Hamann had a wide social circle, but he was a demanding friend. In the 1780s, when Kant began to write his celebrated critiques,[1] Hamann launched one crushing criticism at him after the other. There is no such thing as "pure reason" – i.e., reason devoid of experience – argued Hamann. First, reason is not a thing, it is a process. Second, it is impossible to distinguish reason from experience; the two are inseparably joined. Third, both depend on language. Sense experience must be converted into language to be fully perceived. Language, continued Hamann, is not developed by human reason, as Kant seemed to think; it was intertwined with reason.

Three aspects of Hamann's philosophy of language are worth noting. First, that it had theological foundations. Hamann considered language to be God's gift to Man. *The Bible* was perfectly clear on this point, in Hamann's view: "In the beginning was the Word, and the Word was with God, and the Word was God".[2] Second, it followed from this that language was part and parcel of God's creation. It was not *caused* by anything in particular. It just *was*. It flowed from a divine source and was coeval with Man. Finally, language was not just a transparent medium of communication; it was not just a method that Reason used to communicate messages and ideas. No, it was a tool by means of which human beings grasped the world. And since there existed many different languages in the world, different nations or *Volk* would grasp and understand the world in many different ways.[3]

This idea, that language was a tool through which humans grasped and understood the world, broke with the doctrines of Kant and most Enlightenment philosophers. It opened a new and different way of understanding human interaction, history and society. It introduced the idea that language was an active agent in the formation of human societies and a carrier of culture. And since there existed many languages in the world, there also existed many cultures. Hamann merely adumbrated this idea of cultural pluralism. But his basic ideas, which offered a stinging critique of the reason-based, universalist arguments of Enlightenment thinkers, were quickly elaborated by German linguists (like the Grimm brothers) and social thinkers (like Herder and Fichte). Their elaborations have a profound impact on German thought and, eventually, on social and political theories of the Western and extra-Western world.[4]

Herder: Language, das Volk, and Its Glorious Past

Hamann was the charismatic member of a social circle of intellectuals. His comments on Kant and his ideas significantly influenced the others; among them young Herder, who studied theology with Kant. By the time he was ordained in 1767, Herder had distanced himself from Kant and had come to share many of Hamann's philosophical and political concerns, among them a skeptical attitude towards king Friedrich II ("the Great"), who was set on transforming Prussia from a European backwater to a modern, politically reformed state – with the aid of French advisors and British investors.[5] Herder shared Hamann's worry that the world "increasingly came to resemble … a vast machine in which men were like cogs, and whose lives were governed by the inexorable operations of mechanical bureaucracies".[6]

Herder accepted Hamann's skepticism of the rationalistic abstractions of the Enlightenment. He agreed that Reason was tied in with language and that it had to be guided by experience and religious faith. However, where Hamann emphasized the importance of faith, Herder put stock in observation and experience.

This is apparent in Herder's essay *On the Origin of Language,* which won a prize from the Berlin Academy in 1771. The essay began by juxtaposing the views of Kant and Hamann and then rejecting both. Neither view could explain the origin of language; both based their arguments on pure speculation, argued Herder – one anchored his argument in *à priori* axioms about the nature of man; the other in a faith in the nature of God. The only way to settle the question of the origin of language, continued Herder, was by careful, empirical investigations of ancient human history.

This essay on language foreshadowed Herder's subsequent work, which stressed the importance of History, language, and human relations. He wrote much and on a wide variety of topics. Always the holist, like Hamann, he protested the tendency towards scholarly specialization. He opposed the artificial distinction between human faculties and the increasing tendency to study them separately in distinct fields (such as Psychology, Physiology, Logic…). Instead, he insisted on the unity of knowledge and defended his views with arguments that emphasized the indivisible wholeness of human nature.

Herder's addressed the same basic questions as the other thinkers of the age – like them, he sought to capture the basic principles of human history; like them he presented that history as successive phases or stages; also like them, he sought to identify the cohesive force, or glue, of society. But Herder's answers were different. The Scottish philosophers like David Hume and Adam Smith found their answer in "moral sentiments". Immanuel Kant found the answer in human reason. Herder, however, found it in *language*.

At the center of Herder's writings lies a constant preoccupation with the nature and history of language – like a magnet that exerted a steady pull on his vast and varied production. What are the basic forces that keep modern society together? In *Another Philosophy of History* (1774) Herder spelled out his linguistic answer in great historical detail. Language, he argued, is not a transparent medium through which human beings formulate rational claims. Language is part of reason. Indeed, he continued, it is a key element in the very makeup of humanity. When children are born, they are born into a language. As they learn to speak, that language introduces them into a distinct reality, and they become members of a particular social group. Language is the carrier of that group's lifeworld as it is expressed in its culture which in turn constitutes its identity as a *Volk*.

The argument was indebted to Hamann. It was holistic and historical and flew in the face of the cosmopolitan ideas of Kant, Lessing, Schiller, and other members of the German Enlightenment. Where Kant and other proponents of the *Aufklärung* emphasized the role of Reason, Herder stressed the significance of language. Where they were concerned with the steady improvement of the human condition and looked forward to a better future, Herder looked towards a Golden Past. Where they stressed individual Rights and freedoms, Herder placed Rights and freedoms in a cultural and historical context that stressed belongingness, collective identity, and mutual recognition. Whereas the Enlightenment thinkers looked to the development of the natural sciences and its mechanical models, Herder emphasized the importance of organic growth and historical evolution. Here, then, emerged a difference in methodological orientation: Whereas the Enlightenment thinkers pursued the methods of formal logic and mathematics, Herder made History the queen of the sciences.

Herder pioneered "historicism", a mode of analysis that seeks to explain a phenomenon in evolutionary terms and that places great importance on a specific context – such as historical period, geographical place, and local culture.[7] He brought in development and evolution as central concepts to all understanding. To explain any social phenomenon fully, it would be necessary to trace its historical evolution. To explain an event, it would be required to first understand the society and "the people" that brought it forth. "Thanks to Johann Herder, history became the basis of all culture", writes Watson.[8] With Herder, development and evolution became central to the understanding of all social phenomena.[9]

Herder's arguments were learned, original and suited the tenor of the times. Swayed by the progressive arguments that attended the American and the French Revolutions, Herder entertained the idea that the popular masses constituted the mainstay of society. But he gave the idea a new cast that introduced new ways of thinking about the popular masses. Where British thinkers talked about "the People" and French thinkers referred to "*le peuple*", Herder conceived of the masses as *das Volk*. By that term he meant a people that is united by historical experiences expressed in a language that carried norms and values that belonged uniquely to it. Each individual member of *das Volk* has been born into a distinct language and they are united, through it, in a distinct "collective consciousness" or culture. The language was, in other words, embedded in a distinct culture into which human beings were born and formed into a distinct *Volk*.

Herder elaborated his views in an ambitious work that was published in four thick volumes during the second half of the 1780s, *Ideas for the Philosophy of History of Humanity* (1784–91). Here Herder presents a human history that is very different from that of the Enlightenment authors. He presents humans as an organic part of the natural world. He adds that the human race is endowed with unique characteristics, but he does not single out reason as the key distinguishing feature, he singles out language. He explains that language predisposes human beings for reason and freedom.[10]

Herder, in other words, broke with the key assumptions of mainstream Enlightenment views. His influence was big and immediate, not only because his views were controversial and much discussed, but also because he wrote on many subjects. He had an enormous production – of varying quality.[11] He was not particularly interested in politics – and he was scarcely a political philosopher. The nearest he came to a political philosophy was a deep skepticism towards the state. He saw it as a machine which regulates, centralizes, controls, and coerces. It robs humans of their freedom and turns its own citizens into animals of obedience. It is, in short, a cold monster, bent on the acquisition of power. Herder distrusted the state. He believed in the people – *das Volk*.

Kant, Fichte, and the French Revolution

Herder was 40 years old when he issued the first volume of his *Ideas for the Philosophy of History of Humanity*. Immanuel Kant was in his 60s and followed the career of his former student with interest. The great philosopher read the first two volumes of Herder's *Ideas for the Philosophy of History of Humanity*, disagreed with the basic argument, and gave the books ambiguous reviews.[12]

Herder paid back in kind when he wrote his third volume. Here he criticized Kant's cosmopolitan approach to History.[13] Kant built his cosmopolitan approach around a notion of historical progress towards steadily more rational systems of government and increasing human freedom. Herder begged to differ. He proposed instead that a decrease in freedom had occurred over time, that the past was a Golden Age when human beings were genuine and free, and that the evolution of history had brought more alienation and corruption.

At the time of this widening disagreement, Kant was approached by another poor and ambitious youth from the provinces: the twenty-four-year-old Johann Gottlieb Fichte (1762-1814). Like Herder, the poor youth was gifted and showed early talents. And, like Herder, his talents were buoyed by good fortune. First, Fichte was given an unexpected chance at an education by attracting the attention of a local nobleman.[14] To pursue this education, Fichte showed up in Kant's office at the university of Königsberg one day in 1790.

Kant was not particularly impressed on their first meeting. Desperate to make a better impression, Fichte closed himself up for a week and wrote a long essay which sought to justify faith by using Kant's theory of practical reason. Kant was fascinated by the result. He even contacted a publisher on Fichte's behalf and got the essay printed. The resulting booklet, issued in 1792 as *Attempt at a Critique of All Revelation*, was published without the author's name. It was generally believed that it was written by Kant himself. When the mistake was cleared up, the booklet was already widely read and admired. And Fichte was catapulted into fame. He was offered a chair in Philosophy at the University of Jena; a meteoric rise from total obscurity to one of Germany's up-and-coming universities.

At Jena Fichte continued to develop Kant's system of ethics. This resulted in a book on the philosophy of science, *Science of Knowledge* (1794), which presented human knowledge as a vast system of thought with interlocking parts. Fichte also laid the basis for a philosophy of law with his *Foundations of Natural Right* (1796) and a *System of Ethics* (1798). These three books intertwine and support a vast philosophical system.

On Science: Fichte's dialectics

Fichte's *Science of Knowledge* develops a dialectical approach that has often received less attention that it deserves. It springs from Fichte's discussion of Kant's critique of the philosophical method of the ancient Greeks. Kant was, in Fichte's mind, too rash in rejecting ancient dialectics as a "logic of illusion" and favored an experience-based philosophy of knowledge instead. Building on Kant's presentation of dialectics, Fichte sketched a formal process of knowledge acquisition in three steps: A proposition (or thesis) gives rise to a reaction or negation (an antithesis); this creates a tension (or contradiction) which in turn can be resolved (creating a synthesis) and produce deeper insight. Schelling and other German thinkers quickly took up Fichte's terminology, applied it to discussions of nature and history, and made it popular. In essence, Fichte's 1794 book, essentially "discovered the method of speculative thinking which ten years later received the name 'dialectical method'".[15]

This method, which implied a process of growth and development, suited the German predilection for historical arguments as it dovetailed nicely with the notion of historical evolution.

On Rights and Ethics: Fichte's Political Philosophy

Haman and Herder were philosophers who contributed importantly to an anti-Enlightenment tradition. Reasonable doubts can be raised, however, as to whether they were *political* philosophers in the traditional sense of the term. About Fichte, however, there is no such doubt: the three books he wrote during the 1790s were all written under the impact of the French Revolution and were self-consciously political – none more so than Fichte's *Foundations of Natural Right*. It introduced a wholly new perspective to one of the most important ideas of the Enlightenment Age: the idea of Right.

Foundations is an important book. In order to suggest both its importance and its basic argument, it is useful to contrast it with one of the clearest and most authoritative documents on Rights in the Enlightenment Age: viz. the succinct formulation that Thomas Jefferson penned in the American Declaration of Independence. "We hold these truths to be self-evident," Jefferson began: "that all men are created equal, that they are endowed by their Creator with certain unalienable Rights, that among these are Life, Liberty and the pursuit of Happiness."

Fichte would agree with several of these claims – he would for example agree that all men are born equal; although he would demand to clarify that he meant of equal moral standing, not equal in body and mind (as Hobbes had submitted). However, Fichte would protest some of Jefferson's other formulations. He would disagree with the notion that Rights are self-evident.[16] He would reject the proposition that Rights are given to all men by their Creator. Also, he would reject the notion that Rights are universal and inalienable.

Fichte approached the question of Rights from a different angle. Jefferson and other members of the Anglo-American tradition argued that human individuals are endowed by their Creator with Rights. Fichte argued that Rights do not have a divine origin; he insisted that Rights are constructed by human beings themselves. He claimed that Rights are products of social evolution. First, Rights originate in social interaction within human societies. Second, they evolve over time; Rights are products of an organic evolution that takes place within a distinct society or nation over time. Rights are, in short, products of human History.

Since Rights are products of an organic evolution particular to distinct societies, they cannot be universal. Also, Rights can hardly be inalienable – and, Fichte might add, anyone with eyes in his or her head will easily observe that in many societies citizens are not granted any Rights, and that in societies which *do* grant their citizens' Rights, these Rights are in fact routinely violated.

Fichte, in other words, agreed that Right was a principle that underlies order in civilized societies. However, he did not see Rights as given by God; he argued that they were developed by Man. Rights are not given to all people, but to citizens – or rather, Rights are encased in law and guaranteed by the state. Right, concludes Fichte, is a mark of civilization. Rights ensure that all human beings may live a decent life in a good society. And societies which have evolved Rights can rightfully impose the idea of Rights on other societies that do not yet have it.[17]

Fichte, France, and Prussian Politics
Fichte arrived in Jena in 1793. These were unsettling times. Just before his arrival the French Revolution had shaken all of Europe, inspired rebellious demands of reform in several countries and frightened the established elites. At this unsettling moment Fichte arrived in Jena and expressed his views about citizens' Rights and the role of the state in society. Soon after, the French Revolution

entered its most radical phase. Many of its initial sympathizers got cold feet and turned away. Fichte was not among them.

Fichte defended the republican ideals of the Revolution in lectures and pamphlets. This was at first popular with the Jena students – his auditorium often overflowed; students stood on ladders at the windows to hear him. But his principled stands and strident manners also attracted the hostile attention of Conservative monarchists who were already alarmed by international events. When the Revolution erupted in a reign of terror and bloodshed and Fichte continued to defend its moral principles, he came across as a democrat and a Jacobite.[18] Students turned away from him. The university administration got tired of him. When Fichte in 1798 published a radical treatise on religion, *On the Basis of our Belief in a Divine World-Order*, his goose was cooked. In 1799 he was charged with atheism and asked to leave. He left Jena in 1800 and settled in the Prussian capitol of Berlin.

At about this time Napoleon rose to power in France. Fichte was shocked by Napoleon's behavior. He saw him as a traitor to the Revolution. He condemned Napoleon for having betrayed the values of the Revolution and making them serve his ambitions of power and military expansion.

Fichte observed the European scene. He wrote comments and made speeches that sought to make sense of current events. He published a proposal for economic reform, *A Closed Commercial State* (1800). It was a deeply political work which began where his *Science of Knowledge* and his *Foundations of Natural Right* had ended: With the claim that all human beings have a right to live a decent life. But now Fichte went further; he argued that to secure this right, it is necessary to establish a foundation of material well-being. This is best achieved by establishing a division of labor in society. Fichte then acknowledged, alluding to the social philosophy of Plato, that such a division will give rise to different social classes and to strife and conflict in society. However, to ensure that the relationship among the social classes is marked by harmony rather than conflict, the state must intervene to regulate social relations. For only the state can have a full overview of society and the common good, argued Fichte. And only the state will have the authority to regulate the social division of labor for the benefit of all.

The basic role of the state, according to Fichte, is to ensure the rights of its citizens. The Germans, however, had a problem: they had no proper state. The Germans were politically fragmented, divided among several hundred small states. However, argued

Fichte, they were culturally unified; they possessed a common language and constituted a *Volk*. But he also recognized that no culture could long survive without political unity. He therefore looked forward to the establishment of a united German *Reich*.

The main function of such a *Reich* would be to coordinate the German *Volk*, manage its culture, regulate its social division of labor, and harmonize its class relations. The *Reich* should also protect the citizens. This meant defending them against military threats – first and foremost against France. But it also meant protecting the German economy against foreign trade – among other things restricting the activities of the German mercantile class which were easily influenced by foreign commercialism. Finally, the *Reich* should educate the nation. It should articulate its culture, consolidate the identity of the German nation into a self-conscious *Volk*. It should then shield the *Volk* against the corrupting influences of foreign impulses.[19]

A Closed Commercial State has been largely neglected by posterity. That is a pity, for it presents a clear view of the nature of the state and of state responsibilities. Fichte argues, like British and American Enlightenment authors, that the basic purpose of the state is to protect the innate Rights of Man. But Fichte distanced his argument from that of the liberal, Anglo-American representatives of the Enlightenment. Where the Enlightenment philosophers would begin their discussion of Rights by assuming a rational individual, Fichte began by discussing the necessary preconditions of Rights. Where the Enlightenment *philosophes* were preoccupied with the role played by human Reason, Fichte was preoccupied by the effects of human social interaction. Where the liberal theorists wanted to secure the Rights of the citizens by reducing the role of the state in society, Fichte argued that the Rights of citizens could be strengthened only by enhancing the role of the state.

Fichte and the Stages of Political Evolution

Fichte had no teaching job in Berlin. He wrote books and taught privately. Increasingly he was concerned with educating the public. He made open lectures on philosophical topics as well as on current affairs. Times were uncertain, topics were plentiful, and Fichte had his hands full. For Napoleon's armies fought in Austria and in Italy – and won important victories (near Marengo in June 1800 and outside Naples in March 1801).

In 1801 Napoleon returned to Paris. Here he initiated sweeping reforms designed to reestablish domestic order in France after a decade of revolution and war. Then he wrote a new constitution, followed by a comprehensive new civil code – the *Code Napoléon*. These legal reforms undid the most radical measures of the revolution while retaining many of its fundamental reforms.[20] Finally, in 1804 Napoleon declared himself Emperor of France.

Fichte observed these events and tried to place them in a larger historical framework. In 1803 he held a series of lectures in which he laid out the main lines of European politics. In his speeches, which were collected and published as *The Characteristics of the Present Age* (1806), Fichte argued that History unfolds according to a distinct pattern or plan, and interpreted Napoleon's actions in the light of this larger, historical evolution.

Fichte identified five historical stages in the evolution of political society. The first stage was a period marked by individual of freedom – a condition reminiscent of Rousseau's state of nature – which Fichte called the "State of Innocence". It was undermined by inequality and corruption and gave way to a stage marked by the loss of both rights and freedom – a stage which saw the rise of authoritarian government. A third stage followed, marked by the decay of absolute authority and the advent of increasing freedom – not *real* freedom, Fichte emphasized, but "empty freedom": meaningless liberties that amounted to little but licentiousness and arid intellectual posturing.

Napoleon represented this third, still-degenerate stage of pseudo-freedom, argued Fichte. This third stage would, however, soon be replaced by a fourth, more progressive stage marked by the establishment of new laws based on Reason. This would in turn initiate the transition to a fifth and final stage: an entire new social order of Liberty and Reason. Only then should "the purpose of this Earthly Life be attained, its end become apparent, and Mankind enter upon the higher spheres of Eternity."[21]

Fichte and Napoleon

Fichte's theory resembles Herder's. Both authors develop theories of historical change marked by an organic evolution from one stage of human interaction to the next. Both authors begin with an initial stage of innocence and natural liberty that is followed by decline. After an evolution marked by corruption, vanity and authoritarian rule, the declining trend is reversed, and a new development begins marked by increasing freedom and humanity.[22]

But there are also differences between the two thinkers. One of them is that Herder's theory focuses on culture, whereas Fichte directs his attention towards principles of government and other political aspects of human society. Another is that Herder addresses the cultural evolution of humankind, whereas Fichte directs his attention more closely towards the political development of France and Germany. A third telling difference is that Fichte's argument is marked by a greater sense of urgency. There is in Fichte's argument a shrill sense of great stakes – of the human/German condition getting rapidly worse, of time running out, and of a sense that it may soon be too late to act and remedy a deteriorating situation.

This sense of urgency was apparent in a new series of speeches that Fichte delivered in 1806, in the wake of a new wave of French military offensives. Napoleon invaded Germany and demanded Germans to place themselves under his protection. Prussia's King Frederick "the Great" found this intolerable and decided to teach Napoleon a lesson. It was, in fact, Napoleon who taught King Frederick a lesson: the Prussian army suffered a quick and catastrophic defeat outside the city of Jena, proving the King's military self-confidence self-delusional.[23] Napoleon's soldiers then proceeded to occupy Berlin and to impose the *Code Napoléon* on the conquered German lands.

The Germans reacted viscerally to Napoleon's imposition. They rose up in protest against the universal pretentions of the French. They reached back to Herder's arguments of cultural pluralism and the uniqueness of all nations. Against Napoleon's general proclamations they hurled their own, alternative doctrine of German particularism. In opposition to the general French concepts of *peuple* and *patrie*, they posed the particular Prussian notions of *Volk* and *Nation*. They argued that all cultures were products of unique processes of historical evolution, and that each nation was marked by a distinct language that carried forth the culture of a distinct *Volk*. They insisted that foreign institutions and ideas could not be transplanted unchanged from one country onto another.

Fichte sharpened these arguments and formulated them in a series of speeches which he delivered under the title *Addresses to the German Nation*. These speeches were charismatic and emotional. They expressed a particular hatred for Napoleon and a general contempt for the French – and were popular with the Prussian audience. But the speeches were also set in a larger, theoretical framework: Fichte encased them in the stage-theory that he had developed three years previously.

He began by arguing that history is moving fast, that during only a couple of years, History had made the transition from its third to its fourth stage – from the stage of "Completed Sinfulness" to the stage of "Progressive Justification". Prussia, he continued, had brought disaster upon itself. The German people – not just its rulers – had developed its materialism and its vanities to an extreme limit of decadence and had, as a consequence, been rewarded by moral and military catastrophe in the form of French occupation. However, Fichte continued, this indignity did not spell total hopelessness for the Prussian *Volk*. Napoleon's all-conquering armies had brought the corrupt Prussian regime to collapse; but he had also placed the Germans before a choice: they could *either* accept the dictates of the conquering power and build a nation according to Napoleon's degenerate plans, *or* they could choose to undergo a spiritual renewal and build a new German nation.

For Fichte the choice was simple. He warned strongly against accepting the universal principles laid down in the *Code Napoléon*– first, because this would mean submitting to an inferior culture –degenerate, corrupt and impure; second, because it would destroy the German *Volk* and its German culture – a culture which, according to Fichte, was superior to all other cultures. Furthermore, submission would destroy that culture forever. By invoking the threat of *völkish* extinction, Fichte rallied the Berliners to work for a spiritual renewal, to extricate the German nation from the third stage of "Complete Sinfulness" and lift it to the fourth stage of "Progressive Justification" and thus become "on the spot what we ought to be in any case: Germans."[24]

If the Germans performed a spiritual renewal they would enact their true *Volksgeist* and redeem themselves. In addition, they would be the pioneers of a new political order and lead the way into the next stage of History – not only for Germany, but for other nations, too. The stakes were high. If Germany failed, the promise of a new world would slip away. In other words, it was not only the fate of the German *Volk* that hung in the balance, but the future of the entire world was also at stake. And only the German *Volk* could save it.[25]

The implication was clear: the German *Volk* was not only unique; it was also purer and more authentic than other *Völker*. And as if that was not enough, the German *Volk* also had a decisive role to play in world history. It had a unique mission of, first, pulling itself out of the historical stage of sin and corruption, and then of lifting the world itself up to the higher stage of "Progressive Justification."

Post-Kantian and anti-Enlightenment thought: Herder, Fichte and after

Immanuel Kant wrote his main works during the 1780s and early -90s. His philosophy was based on *à priori* principles, and he worked hard to make his system logically consistent and all-encompassing. Kant's political theory, then, is part of a greater philosophical whole.

Kant's philosophical system represented an enormous intellectual feat. It was widely admired and exerted an immense influence. His *Aufklärung* dominated the curricula in German philosophy departments for many decades after his death in 1804. But there were also thinkers who criticized Kant and who presented alternative philosophical systems. His own students Hamann and Herder were among the first.

Whereas Kant developed his philosophy under the impact of the Enlightenment, his immediate successors wrote under the impact of the French revolution and the Napoleonic Wars. As long as the ideals of the Revolution were alive and well, these events provided inspiration for rethinking basic questions about the nature of the authority of the state and the Rights and Duties of the citizens.

However, after Napoleon made himself Emperor in 1804, and launched new, ambitious military adventures in Europe, a wave of deep disillusion washed across the supporters of the Revolution. Political themes faded from philosophical discussions and metaphysical themes emerged in their stead. In the early 1800s German philosophy quickly slid into abstract discussions of ontology and theology.[26] This turn towards the abstract and the metaphysical was followed up by Fichte's students and successors, most famously by Hegel, one of the most complex and abstract of the German post-Kantian philosophers, but also one of the most influential.

The Themes of the post-Kantian philosophers.

Kant and his students lived and worked at a time of upheaval; a time when established truths and religious certainties were being eroded by new critiques but before new certainties emerged. The philosophical flowerings of Kant's immediate successors, with their holistic approaches and the construction of vast systems that tried to capture the human experience in its totality, were formed during a transition from religiously anchored to scientifically informed doctrines of knowledge.

Hamann, Herder, Fichte and other post-Kantian thinkers were influenced by many factors – by old theological beliefs as well as new Enlightenment ideas, by waves of revolution and war, by the formation of a new German states, and by a rising consciousness of a unique, German nation. They pursued a variety of questions and produced works of great diversity. Yet, in spite of their differences, there are some common themes that blaze through their works. First of all, they were students of Kant. They were deeply influenced by his philosophy, but they also developed reservations toward his philosophical system and dared to criticize it. Second, they were patriots. They worked at a time when Königsberg was influenced by British trade and by French militarism. They opposed both.

Quite aware of the influence of foreign interference in Prussia, they cultivated German values, and worked to identify the spirit of the German nation. Hamann was driven in this quest by a deep skepticism toward British commerce and Fichte by a staunch opposition towards all things French. Herder delved into the German past to find the unadulterated spirit of the German nation.

Herder worked along lines suggested by Hamann, who opposed the tendency of English and French Enlightenment thinkers to identify universal values and general principles. Hamann rejected the Enlightenment cultivation of Reason, arguing that there are other sources of knowledge than sense-perception and Reason – such as *Ahnung*, instinct and divine inspiration. Hamann and Fichte both rejected the notion of universal values. Fichte protested the idea of universal reason and disagreed with the idea of universal Rights – arguing that these were products of British and French history. Herder, who observed that humanity was divided by God into an almost infinite number of different languages, each carrying the culture of a distinct *Volk*, emphasized the value of the particular and the local.

Hamann, Herder, and Fichte all pursued ideas of linguistic diversity and cultural pluralism. They entertained the idea that each language has its own logic and grasps reality in a unique way. Haman and Fichte relied on theology to explain this diversity; Herder fashioned a secular argument that emphasized natural environment and historical and social context. Geographic location, natural conditions, climate, migration, the collective experiences of a people... these are some of the factors that affect the evolution of language, society and culture of a distinct *Volk*. Both Herder and Fichte emphasized evolution as a central concept in the analysis of societies and cultures. To explain any social phenomenon fully, it would be necessary to trace its historical evolution, they both argued.

There are, however, a couple of decisive differences between these two thinkers: Whereas Herder traced the evolution of the unique German culture from a distant past, Fichte was concerned that the German nation should realize its authentic and unique identity in the future. Also, whereas Herder respected each culture as unique and valuable in itself, Fichte began to differentiate among cultures, to rank them, and to argue that some were more authentic and worthy than others. Whereas Herder discussed the cultures of the world on the basis of equality, appreciating the contribution of each to the rich diversity of humanity, Fichte created a hierarchy of cultures, and placed the German culture on top as the most genuine, authentic, and uncorrupted. But by doing this, Fichte entangled himself in contradictions. On the one hand he protested the universalism of the Enlightenment *philosophes* and of Napoleon; on the other, he posited a universalism of his own. In the *Addresses to the German Nation* (a nation which did not exist at the time), Fichte argued that the unique cultural capacities of Germans held the key to the regeneration of the entire human race. "If you sink", Fichte told his audience in his concluding address, "all humanity sinks with you, without hope of future restoration".[27]

Concluding thoughts

The writings of Hamann, Herder and Fichte launched arguments that foreshadowed approaches and themes of German thought for decades to come – themes that in turn would affect political thinking and moral philosophy in other parts of the world as well. First, there was their emphasis on language and culture. This would be picked up by other thinkers and, thanks to elaborations by Jacob and Wilhelm Grimm (1785-1863 and 1786-1859, respectively), revolutionized the science of linguistics.

Second, there was the emphasis on History. Herder pioneered "historicism", a mode of analysis that seeks to explain social phenomena in evolutionary terms and that places great importance on a specific context – such as geographical location, historical period, language, and local culture. Herder's organic definition of a nation as produced by a specific historical evolution under specific circumstances, contrasted sharply with the French understanding of a nation in contractual terms as citizens unified by an agreement on political norms and social values. In Germany, History quickly became a central component in the study of society and culture and, thanks to scholars like Leopold von Ranke (1795-1886), soon evolved into a scientific field in its own right.

Third, there was the logic of dialectics. It was noted by Kant but thanks to the elaborations of Fichte, it emerged around the turn of the century as a German alternative to the reason-based, cause-and-effect logic that evolved hand in hand with the natural sciences in Britain and France. It was an approach which suited the strong German predilection for historical reasoning and grand theories of social evolution.

Finally, there was the German emphasis on the authentic community of the nation and the evolution of the *Volk*. It was a reaction against the British and French influence and provided a German alternative to the British and French understanding of national identity – an evolutionary alternative to the reason-based, contractual understanding of the Enlightenment *philosophes*.

These ideas emerged in a politically weak and divided nation. It is tempting to interpret them as a philosophical self-defense fashioned by an intellectual community that felt threatened by neighboring Atlantic states that were more politically and economically modern and more expansionist. From their collective efforts sprang a "German ideology" that sought to define the German "spirit" as different from and better than that of the foreign intruders.

Hamann, Herder and Fichte agreed that the German culture had more spiritual depth than the materialist Western powers. Fichte fashioned an extreme version of this claim, charging Germany's more powerful Western neighbors for being calculatingly rational and wanting in soul. Germany, he averred, possessed a greater knowledge of human reality than they. This attitude went hand in hand with an attack on Western soullessness – on British commercialism, French militarism – and on the arrogant claim to universality that was inherent in the Western presumption of superiority. Hamann, Herder, and, especially Fichte countered the Western claims to universality and superiority with a doctrine of cultural relativism. They constructed local ideals and romantic glorifications of indigenous roots, linguistic authenticity, and cultural purity. And they touted a dialectical alternative to the linear reason of Western science.[28] These arguments packed a powerful political punch. They were soon elaborated by subsequent German thinkers – among them Hegel and Marx – and transformed left-wing and radical ideologies. Later, they were disseminated beyond Germany and Western Europe – first to the Russian intelligentsia, then to intellectuals in other parts of the world. Themes that were developed by Hamann, Herder and Fichte in early 18th-century

Königsberg, reverberated through British and French colonies during the mid-20th century. Champions of national liberation would criticize their colonial masters for commercialism, militarism, and cultural insensitivity, extolling their own cultural inheritance to be more spiritual, more profound, and more authentic than the corrupt powers of the West.[29]

Notes

1   Kant's critiques would eventually become the famous trilogy *Critique of Pure Reason* (1781), *Critique of Practical Reason* (1788) and *Critique of Judgement* (1790).
2   Cf. John 1:1
3   Cf. Genesis 11:1-9
4   This argument is elaborated in Theodore von Laue, *The Revolution of Westernization*. (Oxford and New York: Oxford University Press, 1987)
5   See, Robert A. Sparling, *Johan Georg Hamann and the Enlightenment* (Toronto: University of Toronto Press, 2011)
6   F. M. Barnard, *Herder's Social and Political Thought: From Enlightenments to Nationalism* (Oxford: Clarendon Press, 1965).
7   Friedrich Meinecke, *Historicism: The Rise of a New Historical Outlook*. (London: Routledge & Kegan Paul, 1972).
8   Peter Watson, *The German Genius* (New York: Simon & Schuster, 2010), p. 261.
9   Ibid.
10   It also predisposes man for religion. Herder acknowledges that Man possesses an immortal soul.
11   Herder praised Ossian's Songs – a collection of folk songs that were supposedly incredibly ancient and recently discovered in Scotland by a James Macpherson. He was embarrassed when it was later disclosed that Mr. Macpherson had written the songs himself to exploit the fashionable interest in ancient folk literature for fame and money. *Selection from correspondence on Ossian and the songs of ancient peoples* (1773).
12   Immanuel Kant, "Reviews of Herder's Ideas of the Philosophy of the History of Mankind" in Hans Reiss (ed.), *Kant. Political Writings*. (Cambridge: Cambridge University Press, 1991 [1785]), pp. 201-21.
13   Herder's second volume took the opportunity to attack Kant's "Idea for a General History from a Cosmopolitan Point of View" (1784), which was built around a notion of historical progress towards steadily more rational systems of government.

14 When he, at the age of 8, one day demonstrated total recall of that day's sermon in a local church, one of the local noblemen was so impressed that he decided to sponsor the education of this remarkable young man.

15 Thomas Seebohm, "Fichte's Discovery of the Dialectical Method" in Daniel Breazedale and Tom Rockmore, eds. *Fichte: Historical Contexts/Contemporary Controversies* (Prometheus Books, 1994), p. 17.

16 If he had agreed, he would hardly have bothered to write his big book on the *Foundations of Natural Right* to explain the nature and function of the phenomenon.

17 Fichte might take exception to Jefferson's listing of Rights as including Life, Liberty and Happiness – Happiness would especially raise his rankles (although he might recognize that Jefferson really had "property" in mind, and prefer not make a big point out of it). He would, however, disagree with the notion that these three Rights are unique and universally valid. Fichte might agree that freedom and property are important Rights, but he might also think of other important Rights – among them the right to employment, which he would see as an important precondition for a decent life...

18 His crusading attitude is captured in the title of books such as, *Contribution designed to compel the Judgement on the Public on the French Revolution* (1793) and *A Report, Clear as the Sun, for the General Public on the Real Essence of the Latest Philosophy: An Attempt to compel the Reader to Understand* (1801).

19 Fichte sought to clarify some of these arguments in a pamphlet of 1801: *A Report, Clear as the Sun, for the General Public on the Real Essence of the Latest Philosophy: An Attempt to compel the Reader to Understand.*

20 The new constitution had no bill of rights, for example, but it guaranteed the inviolability of homes and as well as liberties of the individual. It centralized the administration of the country by placing local government in the hands of centrally appointed prefectures, and reformed the fiscal system.

21 Johann G. Fichte, *Characteristics of the Present Age.* (London: Trüber, vol 2 in Popular Works, 1889). See also Fichte, Johann G. *Addresses to the German Nation.* Cambridge: CUP (2008) (edited by Gregory Moore)

22 The labels that Fichte gave to his five different historical stages are telling: 1) The "State of Innocence", followed by 2) the "State of Progressive Sin" and 3) the "State of Completed Sinfulness" – which would correspond to the present state of affairs. This third stage would then give way to 4) the "State of Progressive

Justification", followed by 5) the "State of Completed Justification and Sanctification".

23   When Prussia's army was mobilized against the French forces, Fichte volunteered to accompany the Prussian troops as orator or lay preacher. His request was politely rejected. He was told that this was a time for speaking with acts rather than with words, and that rhetoric ought to be saved and employed after the Prussian victory.

24   Fichte 12th address, p. 155, in Fichte, *Addresses to the German Nation*, edited by Gregory Moore (Cambridge Texts in the History of Political Thought, 2008)

25   Ibid., 14th address, p. 196.

26   Even Fichte began, towards the end of his career to explore the true nature of the thing-in-itself, write about the Spirit as Absolute Ego and to equate this Ego with the Christian God.

27   Fichte, *Addresses*, p. 196.

28   See e.g., von Laue, *The World Revolution of Westernization* [Note 4], pp 37ff.

29   Cf. ibid.

4

Hegel, Revolution, and the Rule of Law[1]

Sabrina Ramet

Summary: Georg Wilhelm Friedrich Hegel was one of the philosophic giants of the nineteenth century. Well versed in both ancient and more recent philosophical tracts, he rejected the individualism of Hobbes and Locke, as well as their notion that the state was an agency set up in the first place to protect life and property, and, drawing inspiration from Aristotle, outlined a vision of the state as an agency bound, in the first place, to protect the weak and the powerless. Hegel further rejected Kant's individualistic ethics and counseled that ethical behavior had to be understood as taking place in a social context, with real duties toward other people. For Hegel, an individual had rights and duties within the context of the family, in the community, and, as a citizen, vis-à-vis the state. He emphasized the network of duties in which each individual finds himself, urging political moderation and concern for the good of the entire community.

Hegel was a towering figure in nineteenth century philosophy, offering a vision of a world moving steadily in a progressive direction, toward greater freedom and ever greater understanding. It was an inspiring vision. But it was his methodology, combining geneticism, that is, a search for the origins of phenomena, and monism, the understanding that all facets of socio-political life are interconnected, with the dialectical method, a method which emphasized the interaction of opposing factors in producing change, which influenced some of his contemporaries the most. Among those who were influenced by Hegel's questions and methodology was Karl Marx, and even today Hegel continues to have lingering influence, albeit often indirect, in the way scholars approach questions of historical, cultural, and political change.

In turning to Hegel, one encounters one of the most problematic and controversial thinkers of all time.[2] While Hobbes, Rousseau, and for that matter Plato, as well as others, have seen their share of controversies, in the case of Hegel, commentators have argued over the most basic points, including:

■   Whether Hegel was a democrat or an authoritarian;

■   Whether Hegel should be seen as part of the liberal tradition or not;

■   Whether Hegel is politically on the "left" (secular, pro-working class) or on the "right" (clerical, pro-establishment);

■   Whether his methodology ("dialectical monism) is inherently "progressive" and whether it can be somehow "separated" from his substantive points and conclusions;

■   And even whether he should be understood as an "idealist" or as a "realist", or as standing somehow outside or above this dichotomy.

This last controversy is a bit surprising, given the intensity of Hegel's attack in *The Phenomenology of Mind* on Kant's idealism.

The French Revolution and the wars which it spawned constituted a watershed in European history and confronted political thinkers with the necessity of rethinking fundamental questions about political life. The French Revolutionary Wars, in which the Holy Roman Empire and Prussia were allied with countries fighting against revolutionary France, lasted from 1792 to 1802, while the Napoleonic Wars, which followed, lasted from 1803 to 1815. In 1819, Hegel wrote to a colleague,[3] that in his 40 years he had seen too much fear and plenty of (dashed) hopes, and hoped for a time when the fears which had engulfed the continent would dissipate.[4] It would have been impossible for anyone thinking seriously about politics in his day to have avoided reflecting upon the relationship between revolutionary aspirations and war. For Hegel, witnessing 23 years of virtually continuous conflict, war appeared to be a predictable, and in that sense "normal", recourse for states unable to resolve serious differences by peaceful means.[5]

But, in spite of its destructiveness, war was also regenerative, according to Hegel. "War has the higher significance," he wrote in *Philosophy of Right*,

> that by its agency, as I have remarked elsewhere, "the ethical health of peoples is preserved in their indifference to the stabilization of finite institutions; just as the blowing of the winds preserves the sea from the foulness which would be the result of a prolonged calm, so also corruption in nations would be the product of prolonged, let alone 'perpetual', peace."[6]

War also served to unite the citizens of a state the most firmly around the state.

But the French Revolution also unleashed the ill-famed Reign of Terror in which, between 27 June 1793 and 27 July 1794, some 1,285 persons were guillotined in Paris. In their quest for freedom, the French revolutionaries had let loose a "rage and fury of destruction," as Hegel put it in *The Phenomenology of Mind*.[7] Indeed, in his chapter on "Absolute freedom and terror", Hegel used the expression "absolute freedom" in a disparaging way, reflecting on how "absolute freedom puts itself on the throne of the world, without any power being able to offer effectual resistance."[8] The French revolutionaries had proclaimed *liberté, egalité, fraternité*, and, Hegel noted, in the quest for "absolute freedom all social ranks or classes, which are the component spiritual factors into which the whole is differentiated, are effaced and annulled."[9] But, Hegel would argue later in *Philosophy of Right*, "Men are made unequal by nature...To oppose to this right a demand for equality is a folly of the Understanding which takes as real and rational its abstract equality and its 'ought-to-be'."[10]

His Intellectual Development

Georg Wilhelm Friedrich Hegel (1770-1831) read widely in the works of *classical antiquity* (not only Plato, Aristotle, and Thucydides, but also Sophocles, whose play, *Antigone*, he translated into German) and of *The Enlightenment* (including Hobbes, Locke, Kant,

Feder, Sulzer, Mendelssohn, and Montesquieu – indeed "the whole tradition of the Enlightenment").[11] In reading Kant, the young Hegel was impressed by Kant's thesis "that it is not possible to know 'things-in-themselves' or things as they really are."[12] Hegel was also influenced by Kant's demonstration of the limits of human reason.[13] But already in his early years, Hegel did not find Kant's appeal to the categorical imperative sufficient, either to induce ordinary people to be moral or to guide people with any certainty to behavior which would be recognized as moral. On the contrary, Kant's approach to morality struck Hegel as hopelessly formalistic and ultimately leading to moral subjectivism.[14] We shall return to Hegel's criticism of Kant below, in the section devoted to Natural Law.

The young Hegel was also exposed to the ideas generated in classical Greece, both through the works of Schiller and Goethe (especially the latter's *Iphigenie)* and through his exposure to the writings of Aristotle, which he read in the original Greek.[15] In time he would embrace the Greek thinker's emphasis on the weight to be placed on the mores of the community – a position which represented an explicit repudiation of Kant's individualistic ethics.

In 1801, he was named Privatdozent at the University of Jena. The French Revolution was, by then, far advanced, and in the years 1806-1813, Hegel was broadly sympathetic to the principles for which the Napoleonic army was purportedly fighting. No German nationalist, he endorsed the decision taken at the Congress of Vienna (in 1814) not to establish a unified Germany. For him, the challenge to be met was not unification but political modernization; it was in this spirit that he expressed satisfaction with the reformed states of Bavaria, Württemberg, and Prussia, after the close of the Napoleonic Wars.

Both in his attitude to the Napoleonic code and in his response to German political reforms, Hegel was guided by his belief that the Enlightenment (especially Lockean) concept of the state which served, in the first place, to preserve property, however defined, was simply inadequate. Already in this period, in his manuscript, *The German Constitution* (1802),[16] Hegel shifted the emphasis from the protection of property to the organization for "common action and common defence." Eventually, in *Reason in History*, Hegel would define the state, or at least the progressive state, as the natural order of things, and insist that humankind realized the fullest freedom by operating within the legal framework of a strong state – a proposition which surely seemed self-evident in the revolutionary times in which he lived.

If the question of religious toleration may be seen as a barometer of left versus right, then, at least on this issue, Hegel was gravitating to the left. On this subject, he wrote that "...in religion at least an identity might have been thought necessary, but...[s]imilarity of religion has no more prevented wars or united peoples into a state than dissimilarity of religion has in our day rent the state asunder."[17] In fact, Hegel emphasized that the state's control and regulation of the lives of citizens should be limited to what is necessary for it to function and for the defense of the homeland.

In March 1807, the same year that his *Phenomenology of Mind* was published, he moved to Bamberg to assume the post of editor of the local newspaper, *Bamberger Zeitung*. Marriage in 1811 was followed by the publication of *Die Wissenschaft der Logik* (The Science of Logic) in three volumes (1812-1816).[18] At this point, he received offers of a post from the universities of Berlin, Erlangen, and Heidelberg. He chose Heidelberg; the major achievement during the years he spent in Heidelberg was the publication of his *Enzyklopädie der philosophischen Wissenschaften im Grundriß* (Encyclopedia of Philosophical Science in Outline) in 1817.[19] Then, in 1818, he accepted a renewed offer from the University of Berlin and moved to Berlin, where he lectured on the philosophy of history, the history of philosophy, the philosophy of religion, and aesthetics until his death in 1831. In 1821, came publication of his *Grundlinien der Philosophie des Rechts*, published in English under the title *The Philosophy of Right*. Hegel's last political work was his essay, *On the English Reform Bill*, published in 1831.

In August 1831, Berlin was hit by a cholera epidemic. Hegel left the city and took up temporary residence in Kreuzberg. When the school year began in October, Hegel returned to Berlin but, on 14 November of that year, he passed away. The official diagnosis was that he had died of cholera. At the funeral ceremony held at the University of Berlin, Philip Konrad Marheineke, one of the speakers, "likened Hegel's death to Christ's leaving the terrestrial realm in order to return to the ethereal heights of the spiritual kingdom."[20]

Hegel and Natural Law

Hegel "was engrossed in the reading of Kant...when the French Rev-olution broke out," and Hegel would subsequently define his own position on morality, in part, in response to Kant's framework.[21] As early as 1802, Hegel published an essay on Natural Law in the *Kritisches Journal der Philosophie,* assaying a critique of Kant's moral rationalism and of British empiricism (as expostulated among others by Locke and Hume. In this essay, Hegel described what he considered "the breakdown of traditional Natural Law theories."[22] The heart of the problem, for Hegel, was what to make of the allegedly supreme authority of conscience and how to reconcile this with the claim of the state to political supremacy. Kant had confronted the problem head-on and had adopted the solution favored by Richard Hooker: i.e., where the government issues an immoral order, the individual should choose passive disobedience and, if need be, martyrdom; rebellion and revolution were ruled out. Hegel considered this solution of the problem inadequate. He believed there were at least two problems with Kant's formulation. The first was that Kant's categorical imperative can guide individuals only to consid-er what they, subjectively, believe would be universalizable. However, this pure subjectivity could actually result in actions which would be widely considered immoral, and could have injurious results.[23] The second problem was that the appeal to the categorical imperative as the criterion for moral judgment elevates individual judgment above the rules and expectations of the community in which the individual lives, which, in Hegel's view, could only lead "to hatred of the law, to the destruction of the ethical community and to the ruin of the public order in which the law is supposed to function."[24] Now, having critiqued previous efforts to grapple with Natural Law, Hegel proceeded to lodge ethical life not in personal morality, let alone in religiosity, but in civic-mindedness, which is to say that, for Hegel, virtue consisted in an orientation toward the good of the community and an attention to one's concrete duties – to one's family, one's local community, and one's state – quite a difference from Kant's individual-centered categorical imperative!

The Phenomenology of Mind (1807)

Turgid in its prose and often defiantly obscure, *The Phenomenology of Mind (Die Phänomenologie des Geistes)* is Hegel's greatest masterpiece. In this work, one sees Hegel torn between his fear "that history is essentially catastrophic"[25] and his hope that history would provide a stage for a growth in humankind's awareness of its potentials and moral resources, and evolution of steadily more progressive forms of political association. It was, thus, with a retrospective glance to Hobbes (whose political philosophy Hegel reviled), that Hegel closed the *Phenomenology* by constructing history as "...at once the recollection and the Golgotha of Absolute Spirit, the reality, the truth, the certainty of its throne, without which it were lifeless, solitary, and alone."[26]

In his *Phenomenology*, he poured scorn on both German idealist Friedrich Wilhelm Joseph Schelling (1775-1854) and Kant, calling the latter's moral system "lifeless" while finding a tendency in Schelling to lead his converts into "...the night in which, as we say, all cows are black – that is the very naïvete of emptiness of knowledge."[27] Against these antagonists, Hegel promised to sketch a path to a higher truth, understood as a "bacchanalian revel, where not a member is sober."[28]

The French Revolution, as Hegel understood it, was sparked, among other things, by a widespread desire for what he termed "universal freedom". But universal freedom – or perhaps one might say, the drive to establish universal freedom – can "produce neither a positive achievement nor a deed; there is left for it only negative action."[29] Moreover, by shattering the pre-existing social order and proclaiming a doctrine of popular sovereignty in which "the people" were expected to speak with a single voice, the revolutionaries opened the way for the use of terror against those who disagreed with their policies.[30] In this regard, Hegel's fear of the consequences of the disintegration of political order was not so different from Hobbes', even if his solution was entirely different. On the other hand, Hegel differed from Hobbes and Kant in viewing war as not only unavoidable but also salutary, insofar as it induced individuals to think as citizens and to fight to protect the community. But revolution was another matter, because, unlike interstate war, it did not unite citizens in a common cause, but divided them. Revolution, thus, inexorably resulted in a fluidity in, and uncertainty about, social mores, a breakdown in consensus about the business of politics, and a condition in which violence, even against innocent bystanders, could not be excluded. Accordingly, in a passage striking both for its directness and for its clarity, Hegel reflected that, insofar as the aspiration toward "universal freedom" is associated with revolution,

> [t]he sole and only work and deed accomplished by universal freedom is therefore *death* – a death that achieves nothing, embraces nothing within its grasp; for what is negated is the unachieved, unfulfilled punctual entity of the absolutely free self. It is thus the most cold-blooded and meaningless death of all, with no more significance than cleaving a head of cabbage or swallowing a draught of water.[31]

The reference to the "draught of water" was inspired by the not-so-uncommon practice, in French revolutionary times, of carrying out mass executions by drowning.[32] As for the cabbage heads – as Hegel saw – the revolutionaries experienced no more anxiety or remorse in guillotining those they came to view as enemies of the people than they had in chopping cabbage!

The problem with universal freedom, as understood by the French revolutionaries, was that it was conceptualized outside the framework of an ethical community, as if the individual should be seen as floating above the community, a law unto himself. Hegel would return to the legacy of the French Revolution in his *Philosophy of Right*, declaring there that

> [Rousseau] takes the will only in a determinate form as the individual will, and he regards the universal will not as the absolutely rational element in the will, but only as a 'general' will which proceeds out of this individual ... The result is that he reduces the union of individuals in the state to a contract and therefore to something based on their arbitrary wills, their opinion[s], and their capriciously given express consent...For this reason, when these abstract con-

clusions came into power, they afforded for the first time in human history the prodigious spectacle of the overthrow of the constitution of a great actual state and its complete reconstruction ab initio on the basis of pure thought alone, after the destruction of all existing and given material...and the experiment ended in the maximum of frightfulness and terror.[33]

Hegel, indeed, had welcomed the Revolution initially, but recognized that it had ended in disaster, indeed in the transformation of the First Republic into the Empire established by Napoleon Bonaparte.

Hegel followed developments not only in Europe but also in Saint-Domingue, a French colony in the Caribbean, where black slaves launched a 15-year-long rebellion in 1791, finally establishing the independent state of Haiti in 1805.[34] Coming just two years after the French revolutionaries had unfurled a banner calling for liberty and equality, the Caribbean rebellion drove home the point that calling "the Rights of Man" universal and demanding universal equality could only be hypocritical unless liberty and equality were extended to all humans, regardless of race or color.[35] In fact, the section on "Lordship and Bondage" in *The Phenomenology of Mind* was inspired, at least in part, by events transpiring in Saint-Domingue.[36] Thus, in writing that "it is solely by risking life that freedom is obtained,"[37] Hegel was thinking precisely of the "life-and-death struggle"[38] taking place in the Caribbean. In a passage which has puzzled some readers because of the abstract way it was formulated, Hegel wrote:

> ...just where the master has effectively achieved lordship, he really finds that something has come about quite different from an independent consciousness. It is not an independent, but rather a dependent consciousness that he has achieved....But just as lordship showed its essential nature to be the reverse of what it wants to be, so, too, bondage will, when completed, pass into the opposite of what it immediately is: being a consciousness repressed within itself, it will enter into itself, and change round into real and true independence.[39]

Transposing this into the Caribbean context, it becomes clear that, insofar as the slave-holding class made itself dependent on slavery for its wealth,[40] its consciousness of itself as the dominant class was indeed dependent on holding the slaves in subjection. In this way, while "the master...gets the enjoyment" from this relationship, as Hegel put it, the master finds that his "consciousness... is mediated with itself through another consciousness."[41]

The Philosophy of Right (1821)

By the time Hegel assumed his post at the University of Berlin (in 1818), he had completely turned his back on the Enlightenment notion that the state should serve to protect property, which is to say, to protect the propertied classes. On the contrary, for Hegel, it was the state's duty to function as the protector of the weak and the propertyless. In *The Philosophy of Right* (PR), Hegel championed the rule of law, which he believed was gaining ground in Europe. Skeptics notwithstanding, it was not Hegel's intention to portray the Prussian monarchy as the highest embodiment of reason and the rule of law. Rather, his purpose in writing PR was to ground morality in the social context and to explain why freedom presumed and required the rule of law. On his view, moral behavior can only be understood to mean behavior consistent with a community's moral consensus. On the surface, this might seem to imply moral relativism. But this is not the point. Rather, the point is that no individual should presume to construct a private morality from scratch, ignoring the moral consensus: such an approach can have disastrous consequences.[42]

It was precisely here that Kant had erred, according to Hegel. By uprooting moral judgment from social context and appealing to the formulaic categorical imperative, Kant left it to each individual to decide for him- or herself whether a particular choice or action could be universalizable. The result was that Kant allegedly opened the door to extreme subjectivism in both moral and political decision-making.[43] Bearing in mind that the political order (the state) was the guarantor of the community, and that it was only within a community that any person could realize his or her full potential, Hegel drew two inferences: first, patriotism, understood as loyalty to the community, had high ethical value; and second, freedom, in the sense in which we normally understand it, is possible only within a state operating according to the rule of law (a nomocracy). (When one considers the most likely alternatives – whether an anarchic society characterized by rivalry between plundering warlords or a dictatorship operating without any legal protections or a theocracy, in which self-designated prophets impose their vision of the will of God on everyone or a plutocracy in which the rich rule a state constructed to function as their agent – nomocracy looks preferable, especially for those who might not be associated with the ruling elites.)

Hegel was also committed to the idea that real equality had to include more than mere equality before the law. Accordingly, he championed progressive taxation as a device which might serve to promote economic equality. Yet, at times, Hegel's notion of the state seems utterly elusive. Consider, for example, the following passage from *The Philosophy of Right*:

> What is of the utmost importance is that the law of reason should be shot through and through by the law of particular freedom, and that my particular end should become identified with the universal end, or otherwise that state is left in the air. The state is actual only when its members have a feeling of their own self-hood and it is stable only when public and private ends are identical. It has often been said that the end of the state is the happiness of the citizen. That is perfectly true. If all is not well with them, if their subjective aims are not satisfied, if they do not find that the state as such is the means to their satisfaction, then the footing of the state itself is insecure.[44]

On the face of it, it might appear that Hegel's call for public and private ends to be rendered identical could be realized only at the expense of the individual. But the emphasis should, it seems to me, be placed on Hegel's notion that the purpose of the state is to foster "the happiness of the citizen" – a formulation not so remote from Jefferson's appeal to "life, liberty, and the pursuit of happiness" – and on his affirmation that "the law of reason should be shot through and through by the law of particular freedom" by which Hegel appears to have meant that the laws of the state should safeguard the particular freedom of each individual – an assertion which betrays agreement with, if not a debt to, Spinoza. But what is this happiness? Hegel tells us – in Charles Taylor's paraphrase – that "...the happiest, unalienated life for man, which the Greeks enjoyed, is [one] where the norms and ends expressed in the public life of a society are the most important ones by which its members define their identity as human beings."[45] Happiness, in brief, consists in contentment with the norms and ends expressed in public life.

This formulation already points to Hegel's conviction that the state did not exist merely, or even primarily, to serve the interests of individuals. In paragraph 258 of *Philosophy of Right*, Hegel reject-ed the Lockean idea that the ultimate purpose of the state could be reduced to protecting property and securing personal freedom, a notion which, he thought, confused the state with civil society. Where Hobbes and Locke had described the state as a contract be-tween the sovereign and his subjects, Hegel argued that "the state is not a contract at all; nor is its fundamental essence the uncondi-tional protection and guarantee of the life and property of mem-bers of the public as individuals."[46] Rather, its main function was to guarantee the ethical life of the community – which is say that people behave in accordance with the moral law and respect their duties to each other.[47] Social contract theory (in which connection he mentioned also Rousseau[48]) was founded on an atomistic view of society, offering not so much a false interpretation as one that is only partial. In Hegel's view, "the Enlightenment... sees the world only as a heap of objects, open to human scrutiny and use; it does not see it also as manifestation, the emanation of reason."[49] This, in turn, provides a clue as to the affinity of liberalism for a utilitar-ian-materialist perspective on the world. But, married to an atom-istic model of free enterprise – under the slogan of "the invisible hand" – social contract theory ends in self-contradiction. On the one hand, it preaches that laissez faire economics allows each indi-vidual maximum autonomy to chart his or her own course. But, on the other hand, each individual operates within a system to which s/he contributes only minor input, a system which is the product of competition rather than of vision ("will" in Hegel's terminology).

In Hegel's view, thus, an individual is actually less free in a laissez faire system than s/he is in a society in which the state, acting on behalf of all citizens, fashions rules which operate in the interest of all.[50]

Like many persons in his era, Hegel believed that religion was "an integrative factor in the state"[51] and could condition people to ethical behavior. Hence, it is not surprising to find him suggest, in *Philosophy of Right*, that "...the state should even require all its citizens to belong to a church", though he immediately adds, "*a* church is all that can be said, because since the content of a man's faith depends on his private ideas, the state cannot interfere with it."[52] Thus, the state cannot be confessional, and state neutrality in matters of religion is upheld. In this, he rejected Rousseau's appeal to a civic religion. Indeed, in an early essay, Hegel had declared that "nothing is more intolerable than publicly employed guardians of morals."[53] While he would adopt a more friendly disposition toward Christianity in PR, he had rejected, in his early writings, any doctrines which claimed to "transcend reason without contradicting reason,"[54] and seemed, if anything, to admire the Olympian religion of classical Greece.

But Hegel insisted that there could be no tolerance for the non-performance of civic duties, even if the recalcitrants should justify their non-performance in terms of their religious faith. Here Hegel appeared to be criticizing those religious sects which objected to public oaths, to the performance of military service, and so forth. Hegel's criticism was direct and harsh:

> Those who 'seek guidance from the Lord' and are assured that the whole truth is directly present in their unschooled opinions, fail to apply themselves to the task of exalting their subjectivity to consciousness of the truth and to knowledge of duty and objective right. The only possible fruits of their attitude are folly, abomination, and the demolition of the whole ethical order, and these fruits must inevitably be reaped if the religious disposition holds firmly and exclusively to its intuitive form and so turns against the real world and the truth present in it in form of the universal, i.e., of the laws...[55]

Yet, like Rousseau, Hegel saw the ethical life of the community realized within the framework of the state; for both thinkers, either religious associations support the state (in which case they are to be evaluated positively) or they undermine the state (in which case they do not deserve to be tolerated and indeed, should not be tolerated). Hegel was quite explicit on this point, telling us:

> ...the state is not a [mere] mechanism but the rational life of self-conscious freedom...On the other hand, the doctrine of the church is not purely and simply an inward concern of conscience. As doctrine it is rather the expression of something, in fact the expression of a subject-matter which is most closely linked, or even directly concerned, with ethical principles and the law of the land. Hence, *at this point the paths of church and state either coincide or diverge at right angles.*[56]

The Philosophy of History (1830-1831)

Hegel's point of departure in *The Philosophy of History* was that the world operates according to rationally comprehensible principles. It followed, for him, that "in world history, things have come about rationally."[57] This did not mean that people should be presumed to act rationally or even that some ultimate rational purpose is served by people's irrational actions. What it meant, for Hegel, rather was that one could understand politics and history in terms of certain scientific laws – which had the consequence that political science could be possible. And yet, Hegel's meaning was not limited to that. In fact, he also wanted to suggest that, in some larger sense, history unfolds in accordance with a rational principle, and hence he wrote that "world history...has proceeded rationally,...it represents the rationally necessary course of the World Spirit, the Spirit whose nature is indeed always one and the same, but whose one nature unfolds in the course of the world."[58] Hegel at once connected this point of view with that of the pre-Socratic philosopher Anaxagoras,[59] whom he credited with first having viewed reason as a guiding principle in world affairs.

He then asked what is the purpose of history and answered that its purpose was the development of the idea of freedom. Indeed, these two ideas – freedom and reason – are linked in the state, which Hegel described as "that actuality in which the individual has and enjoys his freedom," although he immediately qualified this by adding, "but only as knowing, believing, and willing the universal."[60] For Hegel, it made no sense to talk of either freedom or duty outside an ethical order, which is to say, outside a community. Hence, "[t]he right of individuals to be subjectively destined to freedom is fulfilled when they belong to an actual ethical order, because their conviction of their freedom finds its truth in such an objective order."[61] Moreover, it is in duty that "the individual finds his liberation...from dependence on mere natural impulse...[and] from the indeterminate subjectivity which...remains self-enclosed and devoid of actuality."[62] What he meant more specifically was that it is through "the mutual constraint of all" that "a small space of liberty for each" is assured and that, therefore, "law, morality, the State, and they alone, are the positive reality and satisfaction of freedom."[63] But if law is the foundation of freedom and the realization of the purpose of history, then one is entitled to ask whether any kind of law will do, and any kind of state, or whether some laws are better than others. His answer is predictable, viz., that those laws are best where the state comes the closest to realizing reason in its codes. He therefore wrote that "The laws of ethics are not accidental, but are rationality itself."[64] As already emphasized, Hegel did *not* claim that the Prussian state was the highest embodiment of rationality. Indeed, Hegel advocated the use of trial by jury and the idea that all citizens be eligible for civil service – features not found in Prussia at the time.[65]

Hegel's viewpoint was explicitly teleological, with history seen as a gradual but steady ripening of knowledge, morality, and freedom. Thus, as he put it in *Philosophy of Right*,

...world history is not the verdict of mere might, i.e., the abstract and non-rational inevitability of a blind destiny. On the contrary, since mind is implicitly and actually reason, and reason is explicit to itself in mind as knowledge, world history is the necessary development, out of the concept of mind's freedom alone, of the moments of reason and so of the self-consciousness and freedom of mind. This development is the interpretation and actualization of the universal mind.[66]

In one of his most famous passages, directed against Kant, Hegel expanded on his vision of law based on reason. Here he offered a vision of the state as

> ...the externally existing, genuinely moral life. It is the union of the universal and essential with the subjective will, and as such it is *Morality*. The individual who lives in this unity has a moral life, a value which consists in this substantiality alone...[This means that the individual's] particular will has no validity...What counts is the common will.[67]

Even more controversially, as already noted, Hegel added that the state did not exist to serve individuals, and that he would prefer to say that the state is "the end" and the citizens its means! But then he immediately cast this formulation aside, noting that the end-means formula was misleading; instead, he now suggested that "All the value man has, all spiritual reality, he has only through the state."[68] This passage has given rise to various misconstruals of Hegel as an authoritarian. But such misreadings of Hegel depend upon a misunderstanding of what Hegel meant by the word "Staat" (state). As Z. A. Pelczynski, Leon Goldstein, and Kenneth Westphal have noted, Hegel used the term "Staat" with a much broader meaning than what we customarily mean by "the state"; in his usage, the term referred alternatively to the political state (the government), to civil society (the citizens collectively), and to the "ethical community", which is to say the society as a shared culture. By "civil society", Hegel meant "a system of public authorities and autonomous bodies existing to further the private interests of individuals or their more or less organization groups...[and] also a network of spontaneous, private relations established within the framework of the law by individuals pursuing their particular ends."[69] What Hegel had in mind, thus, in emphasizing "the state" was to stress what Aristotle had previously stressed, viz., that people fulfil themselves within a community and derive their culture from that community; Hegel's originality here consisted in his further argument that it was only through the cultural and political ties achieved in a state community that a people could aspire toward a higher level of freedom in the fullest sense.[70] It followed that notions of freedom which emphasized individual preferences were misguided; true freedom meant only the possibility to live in a moral way.[71] And this, in turn, meant that one could be free only if one participated, through informed give and take, in determining the moral standards of the society. By contrast, ignoring the moral views of others or defiantly doing as one pleases could not be a route to any real freedom (as Raskolnikov discovered in Fyodor Dostoyevsky's novel, *Crime and Punishment*).

But again, there could be misunderstanding in stressing the common will and thus Hegel added the caution that one should not refer anything to "the people". Hegel did not believe in the Enlightenment notion of popular sovereignty, viewing sovereignty rather as a facet of the state itself. As he had remarked earlier in *The Philosophy of Right*, sovereignty, in his view, "...is the strictly individual aspect of the state, and in virtue of this alone is the state *one*...Hence this absolutely decisive moment of the whole is not individuality in general, but a single individual, the monarch."[72] A constitution, accordingly, is embodied in the monarch and does not reflect the conscious choices and preferences of a people, according to Hegel, but should be seen rather as a measure of the level of "the people's spiritual development."[73]

Hegel and Liberal Democracy

In *Philosophy of Right*, Hegel stated explicitly his skepticism about the notion that popular election of representatives would conduce to a government working in the best interests of the people generally. In his view, people are simply too ignorant to be trusted to pursue their own interests and are inclined to "irrational, barbarous, and frightful" behavior.[74] This led him to conclude that "it is not essential that the individual should have a say as an abstract individual entity [in the affairs of government]; on the contrary, all that matters is that his interests should be upheld in an assembly which deals with universal issues."[75] At the same time, in a passage which may reflect some inconsistency on Hegel's part or perhaps merely some subtlety on his part, he referred, in his essay "The English Reform Bill", to "...the right of the people to participate in public affairs...The exercise of this right is a lofty duty."[76] It should be stressed, however, Hegel's political vision did admit of rights and he allowed that people were under no obligation to respect bad laws or institutions (provided that they did not judge the laws on an individual basis). Insofar as Hegel viewed historical progress in terms of a widening vision of human freedom, it followed that people are free only when they recognize the laws of their community as rational and appropriate. For Hegel, "[a] practice or law is rational, and commands our commitment, if it is part of a system of ethical life that is (1) coherent and (2) functional and enduring, and (3) if we are 'at home' in this system of ethical life."[77] The notion of *home* is crucial here and refers to the community's consensus, or perhaps, better said, *general sense,* that the laws and institutions of the state reflect the values of the community "in a system of ethical life that promotes freedom" and are broadly speaking rational (which is to say, not obviously irrational, whether in the Aristotelian sense of working solely in the interests of the ruling elite or in a more commonsensical understanding of what constitutes irrationality).[78] Where that is not the case and where the laws and institutions serve as instruments of oppression – as in the France of King Louis XVI or the French colony of Saint-Domingue – then, for Hegel, "the poor have...a right to rebel against the order which prevents the realization of their freedom."[79]

To understand Hegel's response to the notion of mass participation in political life, it is critical once again to remember that he was writing during and immediately after the French Revolution and its attendant wars. On the positive side, Hegel saw that the French Revolution marked the first occasion in European history when there was a recognition of "the right of all citizens to have their welfare needs met and their personality respected, and with this the right of all human beings to be free."[80] He thus justified non-compliance, resistance, and even rebellion when the state and its laws were unjust and when such actions were necessary in order to put the state (the community and its laws) on a rational footing. But, in spite of its role in making people aware of their rights and in spurring European states to rethink their politics, the French Revolution was a failure, in Hegel's view. As already noted, he recoiled at the terror which that revolution unleashed, blamed Rousseau's writings for having played a "pernicious role" in the revolution, and concluded that the whole notion of popular sovereignty was profoundly dangerous.[81] Yet, late in life, reflecting on the French Revolution, Hegel commented, with words that sound somewhat nostalgic, "A sublime feeling ruled that time, an enthusiasm of the spirit thrilled through the world, as if we had finally come to the real reconciliation of the divine with the world."[82] This musing, whatever else it reveals, confirms once again that Hegel cannot be construed as a conservative in the nineteenth-century understanding of that term.

Against the individualism which he identified with the French Revolution and with Kant's moral philosophy, Hegel posited an organic conception of the state, in which customs, traditions, and ethical life were accorded their place. On this point, he looked to the ancient Greek polis as a model of a society in which there was no diremption between the ethics of the community and the ethics of the individual. Against the notion of mass participation in politics, Hegel advocated a constitutional monarchy with limited popular participation but with government working in the interests of the people. To be sure, Hegel supported the establishment of an Estates Assembly, but his idea was that this would be a consultative rather than a legislative body, affording its deputies the possibility of informing themselves about the affairs of state and offering reflections for the executive to consider.[83] Moreover, Hegel did not want to see such deputies elected as he feared that popular elections would only encourage people to promote their ostensible short-term and particular interests over the interests of the community as a whole.[84] Hegel was, thus, no advocate of democracy. But he was no advocate of authoritarianism either, if, by that term we may understand a system in which a monarch or despot rules in his own interest and without regard to the laws of the land. Hegel was a legitimist, who believed that the monarch should succeed to the throne according to the rule of primogeniture,[85] and, far from advocating that the law could be set aside, he urged that the monarch rule within the framework of the constitution and the law. He could be described as an advocate of nomocracy and of legitimate government (as he understood legitimacy), and as hostile to irrational rule, which he equated both with authoritarianism and with mass participation democracy. In this context, it is worth stressing that Hegel *explicitly* called for the separation of Church and state,[86] and that he, likewise explicitly, endorsed the principle of the separation of powers, championed earlier by Montesquieu. "Amongst current ideas," he wrote in PR,

> mention may be made...of the necessity for a division of powers within the state. This point is of the highest importance and, if taken in its true sense, may rightly be regarded as the guarantee of public freedom....[However,] if the powers (e.g. what are called 'Executive' and the 'Legislature') become self-sufficient, then *as we have recently seen on a grand scale*, the destruction of the state is forthwith a *fait accompli*.[87]

A few pages later, Hegel acknowledged his debt by writing that "here again, as in so many places, we must recognize the depth of Montesquieu's insight in his now famous treatment of the basic principles of...government."[88]

Again, Hegel insisted that both the laws and the judicial system itself be comprehensible to the citizens,[89] that the laws be published and enforced,[90] that provision be made for public education,[91] and that individuals have not only duties to the state but also rights against it.[92] Addressing the issue of poverty, he argued that the best solution was to provide work for the poor, although, to the extent that that might not be possible, they should be supported either by public resources or by having "the burden of maintaining them at their ordinary standard of living...directly laid on the wealthier classes."[93]

But what about liberalism? Here the debate remains lively. It is clear that Hegel defended the rule of law and individual rights.[94] He advocated the separation of Church and state with religious tolerance (within some limits),[95] and one may even find a passing reference to respect for the harm principle.[96] But he imbued these terms with his own meaning and gave them a weighting which is different from, let us say, the Lockean heritage or the Kantian legacy; moreover, he placed these principles within a framework radically different from that of classical liberalism. Furthermore, although he paid tribute to the importance of individual rights, such rights were set in a context in which the individual's duties to the state received equal stress. Again, as we have already seen, Hegel rejected the social contract theory of the state. One of the problems with social contract theory is the notion of the contract itself, which suggests that people may opt in or out, whereas in reality people are born into a state and, unless they emigrate, do not make the decision to opt in or out of one or another state, and even for those immigrating into a state they choose, such immigrants are not in a position to negotiate a contract with that state. Closely connected to this is the assumption, which Hegel attributed to social contract theorists, that the purpose of political association is the promotion of the interests of individuals.[97] In Hegel's mind, this construal of the state was utterly unacceptable; against this individualistic concept of the state he argued that the state, when founded on the rule of law and when committed to the aforementioned core liberal values, had a value in its own right, even to the extent that we might consider the state to be a kind of ethical community.[98] This meant, as we have seen, that the protection of private property could *not* be construed as a purpose of the state. In his view, it was precisely due to the overemphasis on individual rights and especially the right to accumulate property that the American Republic had gone off track. As he saw it, the culture of the American people was characterized by "the endeavour of the individual after acquisition; commercial profit, and gain; [and] the preponderance of private interest," with the individual devoting himself "to that of the community only for [his] own advantage."[99]

Hegel also rejected the classical liberal theory of natural rights which – erroneously in his view – argued that such rights could exist prior to or outside the framework of civil society.[100] To Hegel's mind, such a concept of rights was unutterably abstract. This led directly to a third objection which Hegel registered against liberalism, especially in its Kantian incarnation, viz., that the kind of morality which it encouraged referred only to good intentions and was not grounded either in the customs and practices of the community or in a recognition of the network of concrete relations of obligation in which any person finds him- or herself. Again, for

Hegel, social contract liberalism encouraged excessive attention to rights and insufficient attention to duties – Kantian theory notwithstanding. Thus, for Hegel, "It is uncultured people who insist most on their rights, while noble minds look on other aspects of the thing."[101] A fourth error committed by classical liberalism, according to Hegel, was that it posited (as per John Locke's *Second Treatise*) that, in establishing a state, people gave up their natural right to punish offenders; for Hegel, however, to the extent that people have a right to respond to offenses outside the framework of the state, that right takes the form of a right to revenge, not a right to punish, since punishment is, strictly speaking, a function of an organized political authority.[102] A fifth error, of which Hegel found Hobbes and Locke guilty, was that they had attempted to derive rights from needs[103] – i.e., to derive an "ought" from an "is" (a derivation generally considered impossible by philosophers). The final error committed by classical liberalism is the argument that the state limits people's natural freedom and autonomy. According to Hegel, the relationship of the state to freedom is precisely the opposite of what he thought classical liberalism supposed, in that the state is the prerequisite of human freedom and the agency through which freedom may be achieved and guaranteed. And in considering freedom, Hegel placed especial emphasis on a person's freedom to choose his or her line of work.

But for all of Hegel's criticism of Locke and Kant, as well as Hobbes and Rousseau, some scholars have argued that it does not automatically follow that Hegel should be seen as outside the liberal tradition. There are at least two other possibilities. The first, argued by Steven Smith, is that Hegel might be seen as having articulated a position midway between liberalism and its critics.[104] The second, argued by F. R. Cristi, is to view Hegel as having argued for a conservative strain of liberalism,[105] a strain which, to use terminology favored by Hegel's translators, both "cancels and preserves" the most basic elements of the liberal tradition. In Cristi's view, the monarch is an essential linchpin of liberalism in Hegel's system in that the monarch serves as a barrier to the revolutionary chaos which modern civil society might otherwise throw up. What both of these perspectives share is a recognition that Hegel was responding to the challenge posed by the French Revolution as well as to the theories of Montesqueiu, Locke, and Kant and wanted to improve on their theories, safeguarding values which these earlier thinkers had considered important. Hegel had considerable esteem for Montesquieu's *The Spirit of the Laws,* which he described as "immortal".[106] But Hegel had some reservations concerning Montesquieu's call for a strict separation of powers, believing that the competition between the Estates-Assembly (the legislature) and the Directorate (the executive) in the first phase of the French Revolution had proven destructive.[107] For Hegel,

> The fundamental characteristic of the state as a political entity is the substantial unity, i.e. the ideality, of its moments.... That is to say, sovereignty depends on the fact that the particular functions and powers of the state are not self-subsistent or firmly grounded either on their own account or in the particular will of the individual functionaries, but have their roots ultimately in the unity of the state as their single self.[108]

Although there is no suggestion that Hegel was thinking of the young American Republic, it is clear that his perspective on the separation of powers was very different from that of Jefferson and Madison.

A third possibility, which is entirely compatible with Smith's interpretation, is to construe Hegel as emphasizing the social contexts (family, community, state) in which people find themselves. This reflects the brunt of Hegel's charge against Kant who, in his view, sketched out a moral theory in which the individual is called upon to act on the basis of rational consistency and respect for other people, but in which no account is taken of the fact that there are social mores presented ready-made to people already as they grow up.[109] In Hegel's view, duties "...are far less a product of deliberate reflection than of social and cultural development."[110] Hegel, thus, emerges as a champion of reformed monarchism – a formula which saw some currency beginning with the reigns of the liberal Habsburg monarchs Maria Theresa and Joseph II in the late eighteenth century and which continued to be considered viable in some quarters well into the nineteenth century.

Hegel's Importance

To view Hegel only through the lenses of those who responded to him – whether Feuerbach and the other Young Hegelians, or Marx and Engels, or the so-called Old Hegelians – is to trivialize him. Hegel's importance, indeed his greatness, must be sought in the corpus of work he left behind, including in his success in grappling with the issues of his day. Here one finds a vision of history as progress in knowledge and growth in moral understanding – ideas which he inherited from Immanuel Kant – but also a vision of a flowering of human freedom to be achieved not by stripping away the functions of the state (a strategy which could only harm the most vulnerable sectors of society), but by refining its normative framework so that politics should become less and less about the rule of men and women, and more and more about the rule of law, with such law corresponding to the moral consensus and level of progress achieved by the given society. What Hegel bequeathed to the world was, in short, an alternative vision of political life – a vision of political life which rejected the notion that the state should be seen "as a necessary evil to be endured for the sake of civil peace and the enjoyment of private goods"[111] and emphasized rather the fact that human freedom itself is realized only within the context of the *Rechtsstaat*. I find myself in agreement, thus, with Steven Smith's conclusion that "Hegel's chief accomplishment has been to show that the state and community are not just a precondition for, but [also] a dimension of, freedom."[112] For the state, properly understood, "...is ultimately a meeting of minds, since it depends on a common cultural history and a sense of civic identity...[and is charged with] the positive function of promoting a way of life."[113]

Notes

1   This chapter was originally published in *Eastern Review*, Vol. 9 (December 2020), pp. 11-31.

2   Among classic and noteworthy works on Hegel, one may mention (in chronological order): Joachim Ritter, *Hegel und die französische Revolution* (Frankfurt-am-Main: Suhrkamp Verlag, 1965); Z. A.

Pelczynski (ed.), *Hegel's Political Philosophy – problems and perspectives* (Cambridge: Cambridge University Press, 1971); Shlomo Avineri, *Hegel's Theory of the Modern State* (Cambridge: Cambridge University Press, 1972); Charles Taylor, *Hegel* (Cambridge: Cambridge University Press, 1975); Judith N. Shklar, *Freedom and Independence: A Study of the Political Ideas of Hegel's Phenomenology of Mind* (Cambridge: Cambridge University Press, 1976); Reinhardt Albrecht, *Hegel und die Demokratie* (Bonn: Bouvier Verlag Herbert Grundmann, 1978); Charles Taylor, *Hegel and modern society* (New York: Cambridge University Press, 1979); Allen W. Wood, *Hegel's ethical thought* (Cambridge: Cambridge University Press, 1990); Frederick C. Beiser (ed.), *The Cambridge Companion to Hegel* (Cambridge: Cambridge University Press, 1993); and Alan Patten, *Hegel's idea of freedom* (Oxford: Oxford University Press, 1999) . Among recent, noteworthy books dealing with Hegel, one may mention (in alphabetical order): Susan Buck-Morss, *Hegel, Haiti, and Universal History* (Pittsburgh, Pa.: University of Pittsburgh Press, 2009); Renato Cristi, *Hegel on freedom and authority* (Cardiff: University of Wales Press, 2005); Frederick Neuhouser, *Foundations of Hegel's Social Theory: Actualizing Freedom* (Cambridge, Mass.: Harvard University Press, 2000); Robert B. Pippin, *Hegel's practical philosophy: Rational agency as ethical life* (Cambridge: Cambridge University Press, 2008); Robert B. Pippin, *Hegel on Self-Consciousness: Desire and death in The Phenomenology of Spirit* (Princeton, N.J.: Princeton University Press, 2011); Steven B. Smith, *Hegel's Critique of Liberalism: Rights in Context* (Chicago: University of Chicago Press, 1989); Charles Taylor, *Hegel* (Cambridge: Cambridge University Press, 2008); and Charles Taylor, *Hegel and Modern Society* (Cambridge: Cambridge University Press, 2015).

3   Georg Friedrich Creuzer (1771-1858).

4   Ritter, *Hegel und die französische Revolution*, p. 18.

5   G. W. F. Hegel, *Philosophy of Right* [hereafter, PR], trans. by T. M. Knox (London & Oxford: Oxford University Press, 1967), p. 24 (section 334).

6   *Ibid.*, p. 210 (section 324), quoting from his own "Über die wissenschaftlichen Behandlkngsarten des Naturrechts". The reference to perpetual peace is a critical allusion to Kant's essay on that subject.

7   G. W. F. Hegel, *The Phenomenology of Mind* [hereafter, PhM], trans. by J. B. Baillie (New York: Harper & Row, 1967), p. 604.

8   *Ibid.*, p. 601.

9   *Ibid.*, p. 601.

10   Hegel, PR, p. 130 (section 200).

11   Avineri, *Hegel's Theory*, p. 1.

12   John Inyang, "Hegel's Idea of the Absolute and African Philosophy", in *Complementary Reflection*, at http://www.frasouzu.com/Issues%20 and%20Papers%20Hegel%20The%20Absolute%20and%20 African%20Philosophy.htm [accessed on 15 August 2011].

13 Linda Alcoff, "Continental Epistemology", in Jonathan Dancy, Ernest Sosa, and Matthias Steup (eds.), *A Companion to Epistemology*, 2nd ed., Vol. 4 (Chichester: Wiley-Blackwell, 2010), p. 287.

14 Walter A. Kaufmann, "Hegel's Early Antitheological Phase", in *The Philosophical Review*, Vol. 63, No. 1 (January 1954), p. 6.

15 *Ibid.*, p. 14; and Alfredo Ferrarin, *Hegel and Aristotle* (Cambridge: Cambridge University Press, 2004), p. 395.

16 Hegel began work on "The German Constitution" and worked on it intermittently until 1802, leaving it unfinished. The manuscript was published after Hegel's death. – Z. A. Pelczynski, "An Introductory Essay", to *Hegel's Political Writings*, trans. by T. M. Knox (Oxford: Clarendon Press, 1964), p. 13.

17 G. W. F. Hegel, *The German Constitution*, in *Hegel's Political Writings*, pp. 158-159.

18 G. W. F. Hegel, *Hegel's Science of Logic*, trans. by A. V. Miller (London: Allen & Unwin, 1969 – reissued by Humanity Books of New York).

19 Wiedmann, *Georg Wilhelm Friedrich Hegel* , p. 59.

20 Shlomo Avineri, "Hegel Revisited", in *Journal of Contemporary History*, Vol. 3, No. 2, Reappraisals (April 1968), p. 135.

21 Pelczynski, "An Introductory Essay", p. 29. See also Richard Kroner, *Von Kant bis Hegel*, 2 vols. (Tübingen: Mohr, 1921, 1924). By the same author: "God, Nation, and Individual in the Philosophy of Hegel", in *Philosophy and Phenomenlogical Research*, Vol. 2, No. 2 (December 1941), pp. 188-198.

22 Avineri, *Hegel's Theory*, p. 83.

23 Thomas Mertens, "Hegel's Homage to Kant's Perpetual Peace: An Analysis of Hegel's 'Philosophy of Right'", in *The Review of Politics*, Vol. 57, No. 4 (Autumn 1995), p. 668.

24 *Ibid.*, p. 670.

25 George Lichtheim, "Introduction to the Torchbook Edition", in Hegel, PhM, p. xxi.

26 Hegel, PhM, p. 808.

27 *Ibid.*, p. 79. Regarding "lifeless", see p. 108.

28 *Ibid.*, p. 105.

29 *Ibid.*, p. 604.

30 Robert Wokler, "Contextualizing Hegel's Phenomenology of the French Revolution and the Terror", in *Political Theory*, Vol. 26, No. 1 (February 1998), p. 43.

31 Hegel, PhM, p. 605, Hegel's emphasis.

32 Details in James Schmidt, "Cabbage Heads and Gulps of Water: Hegel on the Terror", in *Political Theory*, Vol. 26, No. 1 (February 1998), pp. 8-10.

33 Hegel, PR, p. 157 (section 258).
34 Susan Buck-Morss, "Hegel and Haiti", in *Critical Inquiry,* Vol. 26, No. 4 (Summer 2000), pp. 833—835.
35 Hegel relied, in part, on the monthly journal *Minerva* for information about political developments worldwide and coverage of the Haitian rebellion in *Minerva* was especially thorough during the period from fall 1804 to the end of 1805, precisely at the time when Hegel, a regular reader of *Minerva,* was fully absorbed with the writing of *The Phenomenology of Mind.* It is likely, thus, that his famous phrase, "the owl of Minerva flies at dusk", refers not only to the Roman goddess of wisdom but also to the journal, and, in suggesting that wisdom might "fly" only at dusk, he had in mind that people respond to crises in a wise way only when the crisis has reached the point where it is almost too late. Humanity's belated and still hesitant response, in the 21st century, to the perils associated with global warming and the destruction of the environment and its species may serve as an illustration of what Hegel had in mind by this reference.
36 Buck Morss, "Hegel and Haiti", pp. 842-854; see also Buck-Morss, *Hegel, Haiti, and Universal History.*
37 Hegel, PhM, p. 233.
38 *Ibid.,* p. 232.
39 *Ibid.,* pp. 236-237.
40 Buck, Morss, "Hegel and Haiti", p. 847.
41 Hegel, PhM, p. 234.
42 Steven B. Smith, "What is 'Right' in Hegel's Philosophy of Right?", in *American Political Science Review,* Vol. 83, No. 1 (March 1989), pp. 4-5; and Terry Pinkard, "Freedom and Social Categories in Hegel's Ethics", in *Philosophy and Phenomenological Research,* Vol. 47, No. 2 (December 1986), pp. 222-223.
43 Mertens, "Hegel's Homage to Kant's Perpetual Peace", p. 670. See also Pedro Ramet, "Kantian and Hegelian Perspectives on Duty," in *Southern Journal of Philosophy,* Vol. 21, No. 2 (Summer 1983), pp. 281-299.
44 Hegel, PR, p. 281 (addition to section 265).
45 Taylor, *Hegel,* p. 383.
46 Hegel, PR, p. 71 (section 100).
47 Taylor, *Hegel and Modern Society,* p. 86.
48 Hegel, PR, p. 157 (section 258).
49 Taylor, *Hegel,* p. 401. I have modified the text, moving "only" from its original position just before "sees".
50 *Ibid.,* p. 405.
51 Hegel, PR, p. 168 (section 270).

52   *Ibid.*, p. 168 (section 270).
53   *Hegels theologische Jugendschriften, nach den Handschriften der Kgl. Bibliothek in Berlin*, ed. by Herman Nohl (Tübingen and Frankfurt/ Main: Minerva, 1907), p. 45, as quoted in Kaufmann, "Hegel's Early Antitheological Phase", pp. 7-8.
54   *Hegels theologische Jugendschriften*, p. 53, as quoted in Kaufmann, "Hegel's Early Antitheological Phase", p. 8.
55   Hegel, PR, p. 167 (section 270).
56   *Ibid.*, p. 170 (section 270), my emphasis.
57   G. W. F. Hegel, *Reason in History* [extract from *The Philosophy of History*], trans. by Robert S. Hartman (Indianapolis: Bobbs-Merrill Co., 1953), p. 11.
58   *Ibid.*, p. 12.
59   See also Hegel, PhM, p. 114.
60   Hegel, *Reason in History*, p. 49.
61   Hegel, PR, p. 109 (section 153).
62   *Ibid.*, p. 107 (section 149).
63   Hegel, *Reason in History*, p. 50.
64   *Ibid.*, p. 50.
65   Thom Brooks, "No Rubber Stamp: Hegel's Constitutional Monarch", in *History of Political Thought*, Vol. 28, No. 1 (Spring 2007), p. 92.
66   Hegel, PR, p. 216 (section 342).
67   Hegel, *Reason in History*, p. 50, Hegel's emphasis.
68   *Ibid.*, p. 52.
69   Z. A. Pelczynski, "The Hegelian conception of the state", in Pelczynski (ed.), *Hegel's Political Philosophy*, p. 10. See also Kenneth Westphal, "The basic context and structure of Hegel's *Philosophy of Right*", in Beiser (ed.), *Cambridge Companion*, pp. 256-261; and Leon J. Goldstein, "The Meaning of 'State' in Hegel's Philosophy of History", in *The Philosophical Quarterly*, Vol. 12, No. 46 (January 1962), pp. 61-66.
70   Esperanza Durán De Seade, "State and History in Hegel's Concept of People", in *Journal of the History of Ideas*, Vol. 40, No. 3 (July-September 1979), p. 370. See also Alfred Ferrarin, *Hegel and Aristotle* (Cambridge: Cambridge University Press, 2007).
71   Hegel, *Reason in History*, p. 55; and Neuhouser, *Foundations of Hegel's Social Theory*, p. 249.
72   Hegel, PR, p. 181 (section 279).
73   Hegel, *Reason in History*, p. 60.
74   Hegel, PR, p. 198 (section 303).
75   Hegel, PR, as quoted in Mark Tunick, "Hegel on Justified Disobedience", in *Poliical Theory*, Vol. 26, No. 4 (August 1998), p. 517.
76   Hegel, "The English Reform Bill", in *Hegel's Political Writings*, p. 318.

77 Tunick, "Hegel on Justified Disobedience", p. 522.
78 See *Ibid.*, pp. 517—526; quoted extract on p. 526.
79 Dieter Henrich, "Vernunft in Verwirklung", paraphrasing Hegel and as quoted in Tunick, "Hegel on Justified Disobedience", p. 529.
80 Tunick, "Hegel on Justified Disobedience", p. 524.
81 J.-F. Suter, "Burke, Hegel, and the French Revolution", in Pelczynski (ed.), *Hegel's Political Philosophy*, pp. 55-56, 62.
82 Hegel, *Collected Works*, as quoted in Taylor, *Hegel*, p. 424 (Taylor's translation).
83 Westphal, "The basic context and structure", p. 261.
84 *Ibid.*, p. 261.
85 Cristi, *Hegel on freedom and authority*, p. 12.
86 Hegel, PR, p. 173 (section 270).
87 *Ibid.*, p. 175 (section 272), my emphasis.
88 *Ibid.*, p. 177 (section 273).
89 Peter G. Stillman, "Hegel's Civil Society: A Locus of Freedom", in *Polity*, Vol. 12, No. 4 (Summer 1980), p. 630. See also Hegel, PR, p. 138 (section 216).
90 Hegel, PR, p. 142 (section 224).
91 *Ibid.*, p. 148 (section 239).
92 *Ibid.*, p. 161 (section 261).
93 *Ibid.*, p. 150 (section 245).
94 See Allen W. Wood, "Hegel's ethics", in Beiser (ed.), *Cambridge Companion*, p. 221. See also Hegel's comment, "individuals have duties to the state in proportion as they have rights against it." -- PR, p. 161 (section 261).
95 Hegel, PR, pp. 167-168, 173 (section 270). See also Walter Jaeschke, "Christianity and Secularity in Hegel's Concept of the State", in *Journal of Religion*, Vol. 61, No. 2 (April 1981), pp. 127-145, especially pp. 129-131, 134, 142.
96 See Hegel, PR, pp. 206-207 (section 319).
97 Neuhouser, *Foundations of Hegel's Social Theory*, p. 176.
98 Smith, *Hegel's Critique of Liberalism*, pp. 145-147.
99 Hegel, *The Philosophy of History*, trans. & ed. by T. M. Knox (Oxford, 1962), p. 85, as quoted in G. A. Kelly, "Hegel's America", in *Philosophy & Public Affairs*, Vol. 2, No. 1 (Autumn 1972), p. 6.
100 Steven B. Smith, "Hegel's Critique of Liberalism", in *American Political Science Review*, Vol. 80, No. 1 (March 1986), pp. 122-123.
101 Hegel, PR, p. 235 (addition 23 to para. 37).
102 Peter G. Stillman, "Hegel's Critique of Liberal Theories of Rights", in *American Political Science Review*, Vol. 68, No. 3 (September 1974), p. 1090.

103 Smith, *Hegel's Critique of Liberalism,* pp. 68-70.

104 Smith, "Hegel's Critique of Liberalism", p. 121 (abstract).

105 F. R. Cristi, "Hegel's Conservative Liberalism", in *Canadian Journal of Political Science / Revue canadienne de science politique,* Vol. 22, No. 4 (December 1989), pp. 717-738.

106 Cristiana Senigaglia, "Verfassungseinheit und Gewaltenausgleich: Hegels Auseinandersetzung", in *Parliaments, Estates and Representation,* Vol. 27, No. 1 (November 2007), p. 39.

107 *Ibid.,* p. 47.

108 Hegel, PR, pp. 179-180 (sections 276, 278).

109 Terry Pinkard, "Freedom and Social Categories in Hegel's Ethics", in *Philosophy and Phenomenological Research,* Vol. 47, No. 2 (December 1986), pp. 221-222; and Smith, *Hegel's Critique of Liberalism,* pp. 71-72.

110 Smith, *Hegel's Critique of Liberalism,* p. 72.

111 *Ibid.,* p. 135.

112 *Ibid.,* p. 233.

113 *Ibid.,* p. 233.

5

Friedrich Schleiermacher – theologian, moral philosopher, and German patriot

Sabrina Ramet

Summary: Best known for his work on theology, Friedrich Schlei-ermacher was also deeply concerned with issues of moral philoso-phy and undertook a critique of Immanuel Kant's work. In Schlei-ermacher's view, Kant's account of moral reasoning was flawed because it failed to take moral feeling into account and also be-cause it ignored the differences in moral thinking across societies and between individuals. Schleiermacher defended the separation of Church and state and advocated the moral equality of women with men. He argued that constitutional monarchy was the sys-tem best suited to safeguarding the rights and interests of people.

Friedrich Schleiermacher (1768-1834) was the most important Ger-man Protestant theologian of the nineteenth century. Regarded as the father of modern liberal theology, he immersed himself in pol-itics in the era of Prussia's war with Napoleon, translated most of Plato's dialogues into German, developed a theory of the state as a community arising from the shared traditions of a people,[1] and promoted "a radical separation of state and Church," arguing that through its association with state authorities, the spirituality of the Church was damaged.[2] He provoked conservative clerics by treat-ing the anthropomorphic image of God as no more than a useful device, by deriving religion from feeling rather than from abstract concepts or doctrines,[3] by insisting that any presentation of Chris-tian doctrine is relative to its time,[4] and, perhaps above all, by seek-ing, as Kant had before him, to divorce morality from religion.[5]

An Independent Thinker and German Patriot

Friedrich Daniel Ernst Schleiermacher was born in Breslau (today's Wrocław) on 21 November 1768. His father was an army chaplain of the Reformed (Calvinist) Church and both parents came from families of clergymen. From 1783 to 1785, he attended a school run by the Moravian Brethren (Herrnhuters), a Pietist order, at Niesky. It was during the years spent there that he developed a lifelong interest in ancient Greek philosophers. In 1785, his father enrolled him in the Moravian seminary at Barby, in Saxony-Anhalt. But after two years, bridling at the dogmatic views of the Moravians, Schleiermacher persuaded his father to allow him to leave the seminary[6] and he enrolled instead at the University of Halle. He sat for his first exams in Reformed theology in 1790, receiving grades of "very good" or "excellent" in every subject except dogmatics, a field in which he would later make a mark. During the years 1790-1793, he worked as tutor in the household of Count Dohna of Schlobitten.

He took his second set of theological exams in 1794 and, upon successful completion, was ordained a minister of the Reformed Church, and appointed to serve as assistant pastor in Landsberg-an-der-Werthe. While in Landsberg, he read Friedrich Jacobi's *Letters about the Teaching of Spinoza (Briefe über die Lehre des Spinoza)*, which had been published in 1785. From this time, he nurtured a keen interest in the philosophy of Dutch philosopher Benedictus de Spinoza (1632-1677). In September 1796, he moved to Berlin, taking up a position as chaplain at the Charité hospital and home for the aged. Following his arrival in Berlin, he had an active social and intellectual life, visiting salons hosted by Jewish women and associating with writers of the Romantic school. His ecclesiastical superiors disapproved of these associations, as well as his publication of unorthodox views about religion and, perhaps especially, of a love affair he carried on with a married woman. Among the writings of which his superiors were critical were his 1799 publication, *On Religion: Speeches to its cultured despisers (Über Religion. Reden an die gebildeten unter ihrer Verächtern)* – discussed below – and his *Soliloquies (Monologen,* 1800) in which he dared to champion individuality and self-discovery. In this rebellious work, Schleiermacher recorded "...there dawned upon me what is now my highest intuition. It became clear to me that each human being should express *[darstellen]* humanity in his own manner in a unique mixture...[7] Later, in the same work, the young pastor mused, "Oh, if people only knew how to employ fantasy, this power of the gods, which alone sets the spirit free and carries it far beyond all coercion and limitation, and without which their horizon remains so narrow and dreadful."[8] It was at this point that Schleiermacher announced his break with Kant. Where Kant had postulated transcendental freedom, in which moral choices could be made without regard to personal circumstances or sheer necessity or, for that matter, psychological predispositions, Schleiermacher, having steeped himself in Kant's writings, now rejected Kant's approach, arguing among other things that moral judgments followed from the moral agent's character and, thus, should not be seen as the outcome of some "transcendental" rational calculation.[9] For Schleiermacher, all of the foregoing factors needed to be taken into account and set the framework within which an individual confronted moral choices.[10] Where Kant had placed his emphasis on the role of reason in ethics, Schleiermacher's professor at the University of Halle, Johann August Eberhard (1739-1809), underlined the importance of moral feeling, thus rendering moral choice instinctual.[11] Schleiermacher was convinced by Eberhard's argument. Furthermore, in *Soliloquies,* he criticized Kant for having neglected the importance of individual differences in affecting moral choices,[12] And where Kant had emphasized the moral law and duty, Schleiermacher underlined the value and power of love. Shortly after the publication of *Soliloques,* Schleiermacher set to work on *Outlines of a Critique of Previous Ethical Theories (Grundlinien einer Kritik der bisherigen Sittenlehre)*, published in 1803. In this work, Schleiermacher criticized Kant and Fichte, while showing his partiality for Plato and Spinoza and mounting the argument that all past ethical systems remained incomplete. Among other things, he faulted them for having failed to undertake a serious investigation of love and friendship, although Aristotle devoted some attention to three kinds of friendship in his *Eudemian Ethics.*

The following year, Schleiermacher was offered and accepted an appointment as an Extraordinary Professor at the University of Würzburg. But Würzburg lay in largely Catholic Bavaria, and

Schleiermacher had misgivings about moving to a Catholic king-dom.[13] Although the appointment served as a recognition of his scholarly accomplishments, Schleiermacher hoped to find an alternative that would allow him to remain in Prussia. He therefore appealed to King Friedrich Wilhelm III to offer him a position in Prussia. It was in this way that an offer was extended to Schleiermacher to assume a professorship of theology and philosophy at the prestigious University of Halle, where he had studied earlier. He was the first Reformed theologian at a faculty dominated by Lutherans, and he was at the time still an enthusiast for Romantic idealism. The Romantics, in brief, held that people were fundamentally good and stressed the value of individual differences. At first, his Lutheran colleagues kept their distance, but this changed over time and, in 1805, he was promoted to Ordinary Professor of Theology. That same year he brought out his *Christmas Celebration (Die Weihnachtsfeier)*, in which he abandoned his earlier equation of religion with feeling and intuition, now referring to it simply as feeling, specifically as a feeling that God is present in us.

In 1806, Napoleon's troops took control of Halle and the university was shut down. Schleiermacher lost his living quarters and some of his possessions. In 1807, he moved back to Berlin, although this city too was occupied by French troops at the time. In autumn of that year, he wrote to his sister, "I want, as long as I can, to seek the German fatherland where a Protestant can live and where Germans rule."[14] In the months from January to June 1808, he delivered almost 20 sermons, addressing the issues of the day. In particular, he used his sermon on 24 January 1808, presented in Berlin's Trinity church, to lend his support to the economic and political reforms being introduced by Baron Karl vom und zum Stein, who served as prime minister of Prussia 1807-1808. R. C. Raack recounts:

> While Schleiermacher wisely based his appeal for progress on [an appeal to] tradition, his effort from the pulpit was in substance revolutionary. It was the first of a series of such reform sermons which definitely aligned Schleiermacher and his influential pulpit with the reform party in the Prussian state...Schleiermacher was to take up the same reform theme again in support of the introduction of elected gov-

ernments in the cities and the liberation of the church from state control.[15]

Indeed, already in *On Religion,* he had called on the state to take control of most of the schooling then being supervised by the Church.[16]

Through his political sermons, he was drawn into a covert conspiracy against the French occupation. He became involved in the conspiratorial Charlottenbund Verein and, in late August 1808, he made a trip to Königsberg, where the King had taken up temporary residence, on assignment from the anti-French plotters.[17] Although Schleiermacher was not able to see the King, he did meet with Queen Louise and Baron Stein, among others, and used the occasion to promote his ideas about political reform, including regarding Church-state relations in Prussia. Then, in July 1809, Schleiermacher received an appointment to serve in the section for public instruction under the minister of education, Wilhelm von Humboldt (1767-1835). The task at hand was to organize a new University of Berlin to replace the now-shuttered University of Halle; the Friedrich Wilhelm University of Berlin, as it was called at the time, opened its doors in October 1810. He was to serve as dean of the theological faculty at that university four times (1810-1811, 1813-1814, 1817-1818, and 1819-1820), as well as serving as rector of the university during 1815-1816. He lectured on the theory of the state six times between 1808 and 1833.[18] Even while serving as dean, the ever-energetic Schleiermacher tried, during 1813-1814, to secure an appointment as field chaplain to the Prussian army; although he was not successful in this application, he showed his patriotism by drilling with the Berlin militia (the *Landsturm).* He also took on the editorship of the *Preussischer Correspondent,* a newspaper which had been set up in June 1813 to serve as the organ of the Prussian state. When he used that vehicle to criticize the Prussian government in 1813 for having signed an armistice with France, he was forced to resign from the editorship.[19]

Meanwhile, Schleiermacher had pinned his hopes on the University of Berlin promoting Prussian patriotism among the young. He soon despaired of this hope but, in any event, wanted to stimulate *German* consciousness across the various German states, preparatory to forging eventually a united Germany. Schleiermacher was nothing if not a passionate German nationalist. Accordingly, when the occasion arose on 18 October 1818 to commemorate the fifth anniversary of the Prussian victory at the Battle of Leipzig, Schleiermacher used the pulpit to deliver a scathing reprimand of Prussians who had allegedly lacked the will to resist the French, calling them traitors. In effect, he was declaring that, during the French occupation and the struggle to regain alienated Prussian territory, the King and most of those still in positions of authority in 1818 had let the Prussian and German people down. Because of his outspoken criticism, it was "only in 1824...that he no longer feared being dismissed because of his political beliefs."[20]

In his later years, he lectured on psychology and aesthetics, while continuing to lecture on theology and working on his major work on systematic theology, *The Christian Faith (Der christliche Glaube)*, published in 1821-1822 and in a revised edition in 1830-1831. His relations with the King remained uneasy until 1831, due in part to differences concerning Church-state relations. As early as 1804, Schleiermacher brought out a report, anonymously, on the relations of the Protestant Church to the Prussian state. The war with Napoleon resulted in a long delay in the government taking up the philosopher's proposal, which included support for the unification of the Lutheran and Reformed Churches in a single Protestant Church. Then, on 17 September 1814, the King restarted discussion of a *Unionskirche* and appointed a committee to study the question of the potential unification of the two Protestant religious bodies. Although Schleiermacher favored union, he criticized the committee for prioritizing liturgical reform over reform of ecclesiastical government. He was especially critical of the King's stated intention to retraditionalize the liturgy. Meanwhile, when Baron Karl von Altenstein, appointed Minister of Culture in 1817, undertook to impose a common liturgy on the newly created Evangelical Church – the formation of which Schleiermacher had welcomed – the theologian/philosopher/Prussian patriot attacked Altenstein's formula for not furthering German national consciousness. Altenstein became increasingly fed up with Schleiermacher's German nationalism and pressed the King to dismiss him from the faculty of the University of Berlin. However, Prince Wittgenstein, who had the King's ear, saved Schleiermacher from losing his university post. The King made few compromises and imposed his new liturgy in 1829. There were, however, two concessions:

Schleiermacher was allowed to face the congregation rather than the altar while praying, and was freed from the requirement to make the sign of the cross and to recite the Apostles' Creed. At the end of this long period of struggle with the King there was a reconciliation of sorts, [with] the King awarding Schleiermacher the order of the Red Eagle (third class) in July 1830.[21]

Personal rivals also played a part in this fraying of relations with the court and an edict of banishment was prepared, though never enacted. He delivered his last sermon on 2 February 1834 and his last university lecture on 6 February. He died from inflammation of the lungs a few days later. He had made so great an impact that an estimated 20,000 to 30,000 people joined in his funeral procession through the streets of Berlin.[22]

Moral and Religious Thought

Influences on Schleiermacher's moral and religious thought included: Plato, most of whose dialogues he translated into German[23]; Kant, whose major works he studied carefully before finally rejecting Kant's excessively – in his view -- rational approach to moral choices, which, among other things, he felt devalued inherent moral instinct[24] and the importance of individual differences; Spinoza, albeit assimilating his understanding of the secular thinker initially through Friedrich Heinrich Jacobi's critical account[25]; Friedrich Schlegel (1772-1829), a prominent Romantic and champion of individualism; Friedrich Wilhelm Joseph von Schelling (1775-1854), alongside Fichte and Hegel one of the three most influential German Idealist thinkers; and Johann Gottfried Herder (1744-1803), whose *God: Some conversations* (1787), defended a modified version of Spinoza's thought.[26] In terms of negative influences, which is to say thinkers to whose writings he felt a need to respond, one may mention not only Kant, after the passage of some time, but also Fichte; Schleiermacher criticized both for suggesting that reason alone could be determinative in ethical questions.[27]

Early Writings, 1788-1800. In his early writings, Schleiermacher grappled with the problem of freedom. He understood, just as Spinoza had, that this was a crucial precondition for moral choice, and distinguished between two limits on freedom: constraint and necessity. Constraint, such as being incarcerated, limits, if it does not eliminate, the possibility of moral choices. But necessity is another matter. Some choices can be, in practice, necessary – such as the choice to save someone who is drowning. But the choice and the consequent action are, nonetheless, free. The philosopher sometimes referred to necessity as constituting determinism and, in turn, argued that determinism, or necessity, is always present in moral choices.

The earliest surviving essay from Schleiermacher's pen is his 1788 *Notes on Aristotle*. In those notes, the pastor reflected that moral feeling, by itself, is no guarantee that a person acts morally.[28] That same year, Schleiermacher obtained a copy of Kant's *Critique of Practical Reason* and began to study it closely. This resulted in the composition of several works not published in Schleiermacher's lifetime: *On the Highest Good* (1789), in which he drew inspiration from Plato and Aristotle and rejected Kant's appeal to his categorical imperative; *Notes on Kant* (1789), in which the author held that reason by itself "cannot provide adequate motivation for pursuing the good"[29]; *On What Gives Value to Life* (1792-1793), in which Schleiermacher first registered his objection to the notion of uniformity in ethics, choosing rather to defend "the value of diversity or individuality even in the moral sphere" and thus "not only a (moral) distinctiveness of different human societies vis-à-vis the human species as a whole...but also a (moral) distinctiveness of the individual vis-à-vis his society"[30]; and *On Freedom* (1790-1793), in which he rejected Kant's notion of a noumenal realm.[31] There followed two essays on Spinoza, written during 1793-1794: *Spinozism (Spinozismus)* and *A Brief Presentation of the Spinozist System (Kurze Darstellung des Spinozistischen Systems)*; these latter two essays figured as a transition to the 'neo-Spinozist' views reflected in *On Religion*.

On Freedom. Julia Lamm has judged that *On Freedom* was probably the most important of his early works on moral philosophy.[32] In this work, Schleiermacher stated that his purpose was to elucidate Kant's theory of freedom.[33] In fact, while accepting Kant's claim that virtue and happiness should not be seen as conjoined,[34] the pastor now moved further away from Kant, denying the reality of transcendental (or absolute) freedom as postulated by Kant. No one is transcendentally free, Schleiermacher argued; there are always conditions (such as one's employment) and situations which impose necessity, thus figuring as forms of determinism, in Schleiermacher's language. But this was a soft determinism which did not entail predictability or exclude freedom.[35] He distinguished between necessity and compulsion and, while defining freedom as the "absence of compulsion",[36] he insisted that one could not understand moral agency unless one took determinism/necessity into account.

Schleiermacher's central argument in *On Freedom* was that a person's moral choices are rooted in his or her character, albeit shaped by circumstances and, through one's choices, one can shape and develop one's character. Thus, each decision or action either builds and reinforces one's character or erodes a person's natural proclivities, thus modifying the agent's character. In the absence of constraint, people enjoy some measure of freedom, but, Schleiermacher wrote, it would be a mistake to think that a feeling of complete freedom is necessary for moral life.[37] Indeed, according to Schleiermacher, "only God...can be thought to enjoy transcendental freedom in the sense defined by Kant's *Critique of Pure Reason:* 'a faculty of causality without necessary connection with what has gone before.' Such freedom can never apply to human beings."[38]

On Religion. In 1799, Schleiermacher brought out his *On Religion,* a radical reassessment of Christianity, which sent shock waves through theological circles.[39] The book rankled conservative churchmen including his immediate Church supervisor, Fr. S. G. Sack, who pressed the author to revise his work. A second edition, substantially revised, came out in 1806. In this edition, his concept of religion centered on feeling, not instinct; he also reworked his discussion of the relationship of religion to morality for the second edition. But his references to God seemed to his critics to smack of pantheism.[40] In this second edition, Schleiermacher responded more to Fichte than to Kant. But there were several features which rendered the second edition as controversial as the first. To begin with, he continued to insist on separating religion and morality, whereas conservative churchmen insisted that without Christianity one could not conceive of morality. Second, his rejection of portrayals of God in human form threatened the way in which churchmen had communicated with the faithful. Third, he was sharply critical of people who yearned for posthumous personal immortality. And fourth, he continued to reject the idea of miracles properly understood; what might appear at first glance to be miraculous should be understood, rather, in terms of natural causation.[41] As for the charge of pantheism, as Julia Lamm explains,

> Schleiermacher was obviously sensitive to charges of pantheism and Spinozism and tried to distance himself from both. Nevertheless, he did not dismiss either out of hand; indeed, he argues in the Introduction to the *Glaubenslehre* for an acceptable form of pantheism which comes close to his own interpretation and adaptation of Spinoza.[42]

Further revisions led to the publication of a third edition of *On Religion* in 1821. In this edition, he continued to trim away elements of Romantic exuberance, continuing thus with edits already undertaken for the second edition. Neither in the second edition nor in the third did he repudiate any of the substantive arguments he had offered in the first edition. But the significant modifications in the second and third editions were driven above all by Schleiermacher's desire not to be misunderstood and to make his points as clearly as possible. Even so, some of his formulations here confused his commentators. For example, what is one to make of his demand that "...belief must be something different from a mixture of opinions about God and the world?"[43] Did he mean to equate religious belief with sheer acceptance of the teachings of the (Protestant) Church? That seems unlikely, given his further claim that the "outward form" of religion is not identical with its "true nature".[44] "True religion," he tells us, "is sense and taste for the Infinite," adding, "Each religious person fashions his own asceticism according to his need, and looks for no rule outside of himself, while the superstitious person and the hypocrite adhere strictly to the accepted and traditional, and are zealous for it, as for something universal and holy."[45] Lest anyone miss the point, Schleiermacher, an ordained minister, took direct aim at the authority of his Church, declaring, "…those dogmas and doctrines…that many consider the essence of religion…are not necessary for religion…Miracle, inspiration, revelation, supernatural intimations – much piety can be had without the need of any one of these conceptions."[46] He went further yet, contrasting the "true church" with the "visible church".[47] As for Church-state condominium, Schleiermacher declared himself opposed to any form of union between Church and state, arguing at one point that an established Church is prone to corruption.[48]

The Protestant Church, of course, preached a certain code of conduct, basing it on the Ten Commandments in the first place but also on sayings attributed to Jesus of Nazareth, for example in the Sermon on the Mount. But Schleiermacher challenged his own Church head on:

> It has never seriously been my opinion that the doctrine of ethics should everywhere be one and the same. It will suffice, if I here adduce what is universally accepted. It appears to me that morality never can be everywhere the same, as all times witness that it never has been…Nor can its content be the same, even if everyone who dealt with ethics set out from pure humanity, for he only sees it through the medium of his age and his personality. Wherefore, any doctrine of morals of universal application can contain only the most general truths in formulas of varying worth. Hence the universal application is always rather apparent than real.[49]

Later moral writings, 1812-1813

Lectures on Philosophical Ethics – the ethical dimension. In his later years, Schleiermacher viewed ethics as a *descriptive* science, rather than a normative one. Accordingly, he argued, practitioners in the field of ethics should study and document how people actually live and behave, taking into account all societies.[50] Already in his *Value of Life,* Schleiermacher had turned away from Kant's focus on specific moral decisions and his employment of the categorical imperative in order to raise the more "fundamental question…, How ought I to live? Or, What should my life be like?"[51]

He returned to this notion in his *Lectures* of 1812-1813, noting that "Everything which has become moral is a good, and the totality of that [process is]...the highest good. The objective depiction of the ethical is therefore the depiction of the highest good."[52] He credited the ancients with having understood "the good" but expressed regret that in his time there was little evidence of such understanding. It seemed self-evident to Schleiermacher that the highest good embraced all the virtues and that an individual striving to embody the highest good would need to embody all the virtues.[53] Duty, then, should not be limited to calculations about specific moral decisions (as per Kant) but should be seen as associated with the highest good. Indeed, he emphasized, "...the highest good can only come into being as a result of actions which are in accordance with duty."[54] In his *Soliloquies*, Schleiermacher had written that "...each human being is meant to present humanity in his own way, in his own mixture of its elements"[55] – a clear endorsement of individuality if not also of originality. In his *Lectures*, Schleiermacher remained true to this principle, stating: ""We can only regard an action as being in accordance with duty if it develops out of the human being himself, from the moral urge within him; for otherwise it is either his own but sensory, or else moral but not his own."[56]

Political Thought

Although Schleiermacher never wrote a political treatise as such, his promotion of German unification, his patriotic speeches during the war with Napoleonic France, his role as a "secret agent" on a mission to Königsberg, his proposal for the reform of Church-state relations, and his engagement in the founding of the Friedrich Wilhelm University of Berlin (known today as Humboldt University) all document his serious engagement with the political issues of his day. He advocated national self-determination on the argument that "cultural and linguistic unity" provided a firm foundation for state-building. Accordingly, he considered social contract theory to be at best misleading. Moreover, he did not need to appeal to a supposed contract in order to advocate a limited state, although it is of some interest that his motivation here was his desire to guarantee conditions in which people could cultivate and develop their individuality. This, in turn, was limited to his defense of what he called "free sociality" – what we would call people's right to an autonomous private sphere not under state control.[57] In this connection, he defended also the autonomy of religious life and academic life, and favored constitutional monarchy as the system most conducive to developing common consciousness among the citizens.[58] He understood that the more inequality one finds in a given state, the less democratic it will prove to be.[59] Liberal in both his theology and his political views, he was ahead of most of his contemporaries in advocating gender equality, although he does not seem to have envisioned *political* equality for women.[60]

Finally, in his *Lectures on the Teaching about the State (Vorlesungen über die Lehre vom Staat)*, Schleiermacher outlined what he considered the most basic functions (duties) of the state:

[First,] the state guarantees freedom and movement, which means that the individual has certain key freedoms including the right to travel within and outside of the state. [Second,] the state will defend the individual against the whole, which means that the individual's rights are to be safeguarded against any massive intrusion by the state. [And third,] the state guarantees the basic subsistence of each individual. *This...means that no individual will be left destitute and that the state will provide an appropriate safety net.*[61]

This third function was challenged by advocates of a minimal state who, in Schleiermacher's words, mistakenly "believe that the best of states is one that gives least evidence of its existence." On the contrary, Schleiermacher considered the state "the greatest achievement of human art, by which man *[Mensch]* should be raised to the highest level of which he is capable."[62]

Lectures on Philosophic Ethics—Politics.

We have seen in the chapters devoted to Kant and Hegel that these philosophers wrestled with the tension between obligations under the moral law and obligations to the state, the duties associated with citizenship and civic-mindedness. Schleiermacher addressed this issue explicitly in his *Lectures*, declaring, "The genuine civic disposition...consists here merely in this: if a man regards something as necessary to the general good, he shall attempt to implement it even if this means staking his own existence on it."[63] *Vaterlandsliebe* – love of one's fatherland – thus should assume the highest priority, according to Schleiermacher. In the context of the foregoing assertion and reflecting on the French occupation of a part of Prussia, the pastor-professor extended the sense of duty toward one's fellow (Prussian) countrymen to the national territory. "Essentially, people and soil belong together," he said in his *Lectures*, "and for this reason the soil is the first object, for everyone, of the force of attraction exercised by love, so that a people must always feel it to be theft when it forfeits some part of the soil it originally inhabited."[64] Lest he be misunderstood, Schleiermacher set forth the clear maxim that an individual citizen is not bound to obey immoral commands.[65] On the other hand, in his posthumously published *Christian Ethics (Christliche Sittenlehre)*, discussed below, the author suggested that, if one obeyed orders from political authorities, in the process committing actions which seemed to be or were morally wrong, the individual would bear no guilt, because of the obligation associated with citizenship.[66] Consistently, Schleiermacher ruled out conscientious objection, because it would allow that an individual, "not himself having magisterial authority," might pass judgment on the state.[67] Thus, even the passive disobedience allowed by Kant is specifically excluded by Schleiermacher.

At the time he was writing, social contract theory, promulgated by the English philosophers Hobbes and Locke, and in a different form by the French philosopher Rousseau, exerted increasing influence. For Schleiermacher, the notion that one could imagine the state as justified by virtue of an implicit – let alone explicit – contract with its citizens was an absurdity. To his mind, "such a contract would have to arise by force of persuasion, but force of that kind can never be present in the individual where there is no urgent need." Moreover, if one could find somewhere a state founded on the basis of a contract, such cannot last, because mere self-interest on a wide scale is no substitute for *Vaterlandsliebe*.[68]

When it came to religious freedom, Schleiermacher drew a fine distinction. On the one hand, "To the extent that the individual is at the same time a part of scholarly and religious organizations he is right to demand that, since the state does not engage in these processes, it should not prevent him from engaging in them himself."[69] On the other hand, Schleiermacher ruled that "There is no necessity for the state to grant the same civil rights to the adherents of every religion."[70] Finally, the theologian tried to strike a balance between overly critical and overly enthusiastic appraisals of the Church. "There is a negative view of the church," he wrote,

> analogous to that of the state, which suggests that it is merely an institution devoted to the repression of the passions...
>
> There is also an excessively positive view which posits the church as the absolute ethical community and subordinates both state and knowledge to it.[71]

Christian Ethics (Christliche Sittenlehre).

Published posthumously in 1843, Schleiermacher's *Christian Ethics* further developed some of the political themes already presented in the *Lectures*. He refused to countenance conscientious objection, judging that refusal to fight for one's country was nothing less than mutinous. Again, the obligations of a citizen to a state which betrayed the expectations of its citizens drew his attention. For Schleiermacher, the state should be understood in terms of a constitutional order and its laws. When the state tramples on the legal order, "...there is no longer a state, but [only] an eruption of raw power."[72] The difficulty, he acknowledged, was to determine, with a reasonable degree of confidence, if and when a given state had become a rogue state. Moreover, for one group of citizens to decide that another group of citizens should be seen as "enemies of the state" involves huge risks, including that of "regress back to the state of nature."[73] Summing up his views on rebellion in a manner reminiscent of Kant, he wrote

> ...if subjects break the contract [the laws], magistrates have the right to punish them. However, if magistrates break the contract, they cannot be punished by the[ir] subjects: in that case the whole contractual status would be overthrown and a situation of chaos [would be] established; this means that the task can only be to produce an entirely new order.[74]

Schleiermacher was probably thinking of Protestant states, including the various German Protestant states, when he wrote that

"Christianity pronounces the government, including every valid authority in the state, to be a divine institution."[75] Accordingly, disobedience to state authorities must be accounted disobedience to a divinely sanctioned institution, and hence, "when disobedience against the law is ongoing, the state must respond in order to prevent its own dissolution."[76] Finally, taking aim at the rampant colonialism of his time, and perhaps implicitly at John Locke's defense of colonialism,[77] Schleiermacher rejected the alleged right of European states to take possession of lands belonging to other peoples on the pretext of "civilizing" them.[78]

Schleiermacher's Importance

In his 1984 book, *Die Philosophie Schleiermachers*, Gunter Scholtz wrote that

> Whether [Schleiermacher] is a 'great' or [a] 'minor' philosopher, an original thinker or merely a disciple and syncretist, or only a theologian – about all this there is no common sense, not even concerning in which philosophical school or orientation to locate him.[79]

I have tried to suggest, in the foregoing pages, that Schleiermacher developed a clear moral theory and spelled out a clear political vision; moreover, alongside his universally recognized, major contribution to Protestant theology, he also engaged himself in debates on topics which preoccupied other thinkers of his time, including the legitimacy and extent of state authority, the obligations of citizens, the moral status of rebellion, and the proper balance in Church-state relations. Taking the foregoing into account, I believe that he fully belongs in the company of Immanuel Kant and Georg Wilhelm Friedrich Hegel.

Writing in 1941, Richard Brandt held that "It is agreed on all sides that Schleiermacher has been the most important figure in Protestant theology since the time of the Reformation."[80] For Wilhelm Windelband, Schleiermacher's most significant philosophical work was in the field of ethics, while, among those who have advocated for Schleiermacher's importance, perhaps no one has done as much as his biographer and fellow philosopher Wilhelm Dilthey (1833-1911).[81] Finally, Schleiermacher offered a liberal perspective on politics by urging a vision of comprehensive equality, and defied religious conservatives by rejecting anthropomorphic representations of God, suggesting that religion was centered on feeling (not doctrine) and by urging his fellow Christians to think for themselves on matters regarding religion and morality.

Notes

1   Friedrich Schleiermacher, *Lectures on Philosophic Ethics*, trans. from German by Louise Adey Huish (Cambridge: Cambridge University Press, 2002), p. 24.

2   Miriam Rose, *Schleiermachers Staatslehre* (Tübingen: Mohr Siebeck, 2011), p. 191.

3   Julia A. Lamm, *The Living God: Schleiermacher's theological appropriation of Spinoza* (University Park, Pa.: Pennsylvania State University Press, 1996), p 103.

4   Friedrich Schleiermacher, *Selections from Friedrich Schleiermacher's Christian Ethics*, ed. and trans. by James A. Brandt [hereafter, *Christian Ethics*] (Louisville, Kentucky: Westminster John Knox Press, 2011), pp. 23-24.

5   On this point, see Richard B. Brandt, *The Philosophy of Schleiermacher: The development of his theory of scientific and religious knowledge* (Westport, Conn.: Greenwood Press, 1968, 1971; reprinted from New York: Harper & Row, 1941), p 95.

6   Horace L. Friess, "Introduction" to *Schleiermacher's Soliloquies*, trans. by Horace Leland Friess (Chicago: The Open Court Publishing Co., 1926), p. xvii.

7   As quoted in Brent W. Sockness, "Schleiermacher and the Ethics of Authenticity: The 'Monologen' of 1800", in *The Journal of Religious Ethics*, Vol. 32, No. 3 (Winter 2004), p. 495.

8   As quoted in *Ibid.*, p. 504.

9   John P. Crossley, Jr., "The Ethical Impulse in Schleiermacher's Early Ethics", in *The Journal of Religious Ethics*, Vol. 17, No. 2 (Fall 1989), p. 15.

10 Gerald N. Izenberg, *Impossible Individuality: Romanticism, revolution, and the origins of modern selfhood, 1787-1802* (Princeton, N.J.: Princeton University Press, 1992), p. 44.

11 Albert L. Blackwell, "Editor's Introduction" to Friedrich Schleiermacher, *On Freedom,* trans., annotated, and introduced by Albert L. Blackwell (Lewiston/Queenston/Lampeter: The Edwin Mellen Press, 1992), p. v.

12 Frederick C. Beiser, "Schleiermacher's ethics", in Jacqueline Mariña (ed.), *The Cambridge Companion to Friedrich Schleiermacher* (Cambridge: Cambridge University Press, 2005), pp 60-61.

13 Zachary Purvis, "Quiet War in Germany: Friedrich Schelling and Friedrich Schleiermacher", in *Journal of the History of Ideas,* Vol. 76, No. 3 (July 2015), p. 388. See also Albert L. Blackwell, "Three New Schleiermacher Letters Relating to His Würzburg Appointment of 1804", in *The Harvard Theological Review,* Vol. 68, No. 3/4 (July-October 1975), pp. 333-356.

14 As quoted in R. C. Raack, "Schleiermacher's Political Thought and Activity, 1806-1813", in *Church History,* Vol. 28, No. 4 (December 1959), p. 379.

15 *Ibid.,* p. 380.

16 Jerry F. Dawson, *Friedrich Schleiermacher: The evolution of a nationalist* (Austin: University of Texas Press, 1966), p. 76.

17 Raack, "Schleiermacher's Political Thought", p. 381.

18 Theodore Vial, "Schleiermacher and the state", in Mariña (ed.), *The Cambridge Companion,* pp. 269-270.

19 Raack, "Schleiermacher's Political Thought", p. 386.

20 Dawson, *Friedrich Schleiermacher,* p. 143.

21 Vial, "Schleiermacher and the state", p. 282.

22 See Robert P. Scharlemann, "Friedrich Schleiermacher", *Britannica Online Encyclopedia,* at https://www.britannica.com/print/article/52757, p. 3 of 3 [accessed on 1 August 2020]; also Michael Forster, "Friedrich Daniel Ernst Schleiermacher", *Stanford Encyclopedia of Philosophy,* first published on 17 April 2002; substantive revision on 8 August 2017, at https://plato.stanford.edu/entries/schleiermacher/, p. 3 of 30 [accessed on 2 August 2020].

23 See *Schleiermacher's Introductions to the Dialogues of Plato,* trans from German by William Dobson (Cambridge and London: Pitt Press & John William Parker, 1836; reissued by Forgotten Books in 2012).

24 Brent W. Sockness, "The Forgotten Moralist: Friedrich Schleiermacher and the Science of Spirit", in *The Harvard Theological Review,* Vol. 96, No. 3 (July 2003), p. 346.

25 Forster, "Friedrich Daniel Ernst Schleiermacher", p. 2 of 30.

26 *Ibid.*

27 Burkhard Biella, "Bildung der Öffentlichkeit. Nachdenken mit Schleiermacher über Staat, Gesellschaft, Religion und Erziehung",

in Elke Ariëns, Helmut König, and Manfred Sicking (eds.), (Bielefeld: Transcript Verlag, 2011), p. 205; and Günter Meckenstock, "Schleiermachers Auseinandersetzung mit Fichte", in Sergio Sorrentino (ed.), *Schleiermacher's Philosophy and the Philosophical Tradition* (Lewiston/Queensland/Lampeter: The Edwin Mellen Press, 1992), pp. 27-46, esp.- pp. 33-36, 44-49-

28 Julia A. Lamm, "The Early Philosophic Roots of Schleiermacher's Notion of Gefühl, 1788-1794", in *The Harvard Theological Review*, Vol. 87, No. 1 (January 1994), p. 72.

29 *Ibid.*, p. 78.

30 Forster, "Friedrich Daniel Ernst Schleiermacher", p. 18 of 30.

31 Albert L. Blackwell, *Schleiermacher's Early Philosophy of Life: Determinism, freedom, and phantasy* (Chico, Calif.: Scholars Press, 1982), p. 34.

32 Lamm, "Early Philosophic Roots", p. 81.

33 Schleiermacher, *On Freedom*, p. 4.

34 Blackwell, "Editor's Introduction", p. viii. See also chapter 2 in this volume.

35 Louden, "Introduction" to Schleiermacher, *Lectures on Philosophical Ethics*, p. xiii; and C. Jeffery Kinlaw, "Freedom and Moral Agency in the Young Schleiermacher", in *The Review of Metaphysics*, Vol. 58, No. 4 (June 2005), p. 843.

36 Schleiermacher, *On Freedom*, as quoted in Kinlaw, "Freedom and Moral Agency", p. 850.

37 Schleiermacher, *On Freedom*, p. 68.

38 Blackwell, "Editor's Introduction", p. xi.

39 See Richard R. Niebuhr, *Schleiermacher on Christ and Religion: A new interpretation* (New York: Charles Scribner's Sons, 1964), p. 32.

40 Lamm, *The Living God*, p. 58; and Brandt, *The Philosophy of Schleiermacher*, pp. 173-176.

41 Lamm, *The Living God*, pp. 67, 71, 87-88, 90, 133.

42 *Ibid.*, p. 167, n30.

43 Friedrich Schleiermacher, *On Religion: Speeches to its cultured despisers*, 3rd ed., trans. from German by John Oman (New York/San Francisco/London: Harper Torchbooks, 1958), p. 31.

44 *Ibid.*, p. 33.

45 *Ibid.*, pp. 39, 62.

46 *Ibid.*, p. 87 (punctuation modified).

47 *Ibid.*, p. 212.

48 *Ibid.*, pp. 167, 181.

49 *Ibid.*, pp. 261-262.

50 Robert B. Louden, "Introduction", to Friedrich Schleiermacher, *Lectures on Philosophic Ethics*, p. xxv.

51 *Ibid.,* p. xiv, quoting from Julia Annas, *The Morality of Happiness* (New York: Oxford University Press, 1995), p. 27.
52 Schleiermacher, *Lectures on Philosophic Ethics,* p. 11.
53 *Ibid.,* pp. 11, 101.
54 *Ibid.,* p. 124.
55 As quoted in Louden, "Introduction", p. xix.
56 Schleiermacher, *Lectures on Philosophic Ethics,* p. 124.
57 Jeffrey Hoover, "Friedrich Schleiermacher's Theory of the Limited Communitarian State", in *Canadian Journal of Philosophy,* Vol. 20, No. 2 (June 1990), p. 247; and Rose, *Schleiermachers Staatslehre,* p. 112.
58 Rose, *Schleiermachers Staatslehre,* p. 118; and Hoover, "Limited Communitarian State", p. 254.
59 Christopher Adair-Toteff, "Schleiermacher and the state", in *History of European Ideas,* Vol. 46, No. 3 (2020), p. 30.
60 Rose, *Schleiermachers Staatslehre,* pp. 125, 209; and Friedrich Schleiermacher, *Idee zu einem Katechismus der Vernunft für edle Frauen,* as summarized in Louden, "Introduction", p. xvii.
61 Adair-Toteff, "Schleiermacher and the state", p. 304 (my emphasis).
62 *Schleiermacher's Soliloquies,* p. 59.
63 Schleiermacher, *Lectures on Philosophic Ethics,* p. 77.
64 *Ibid.,* p. 77.
65 *Ibid.,* p. 130.
66 Schleiermacher, *Christian Ethics,* p. 93.
67 *Ibid.,* p. 93; and Schleiermacher, *Lectures on Philosophic Ethics,* p. 92.
68 Schleiermacher, *Lectures on Philosophic Ethics,* pp. 71-72.
69 *Ibid.,* p. 75.
70 *Ibid.,* p. 74 n3.
71 *Ibid.,* p. 91.
72 Schleiermacher, *Christian Ethics,* p. 90.
73 *Ibid.,* p. 89.
74 *Ibid.,* p. 89.
75 *Ibid.,* p. 89.
76 *Ibid.,* p. 85.
77 On this point, see Barbara Arneil, *John Locke and America: The Defence of English Colonialism* (Oxford: Clarendon Press, 1996; reprinted, 1998).
78 Schleiermacher, *Christian Ethics,* pp. 94, 96.
79 As quoted in Sockness, "The Forgotten Moralist", p. 326.
80 Brandt, *The Philosophy of Schleiermacher,* p. 299.
81 Wilhelm Windelband, *Lehrbuch der Geschichte der Philosophie* (1892), as cited in Sockness, "The Forgotten Moralist", p 330; and Wilhelm Dilthey, *Leben Schleiermachers,* Vol. 1 (Berlin: Druck und Verlag von Georg Reimer, 1870).

6

The Young Hegelians in an Age of Radicalism

Sabrina P. Ramet

Summary: The Young Hegelians were distinguished from the Old Hegelians not only by difference in age but also by the fact that, while the Old Hegelians subscribed to conservative views about Christianity and politics and were focused on preserving and building on Hegel's substantive analysis, the Young Hegelians tended to be liberal or radical and were inspired by Hegel's opening up of new ways of thinking. Several of them, who were associated with the Young Hegelians at least temporarily – specifically Bruno Bauer, Ludwig Feuerbach, Max Stirner, and David Friedrich Strauss – broke with traditional Christianity, with Bauer, Feuerbach, and Stirner arguing that Christian religion had exerted a negative influence on humanity. Most of the Young Hegelians called themselves "Die Freien" (the Free Ones) and met regularly at Hippels Weinstube in downtown Berlin. There they debated the sundry issues thrown up by the French Revolution, especially as interpreted by Hegel. But the radical ideas discussed at the Weinstube were part of a larger continent-wide philosophical transformation, which saw the emergence of anarchism (Proudhon, Bakunin, Kropotkin), advocacy of rule by scientists (Henri de Saint-Simon), advocacy of free love (Barthélemy Prosper Enfantin), and perspectivism (as Nietzsche's denial of the existence of any objective reality came to be called). The nineteenth century was, thus, a century during which both philosophy and politics were radicalized. It was a century characterized by both bitterness and hope, a confidence in progress (however defined), and recurrent optimism. More than that, it was a century very much under the influence of Hegel's ideas.

Nineteenth-century thinkers tended to be utopians and sketched out visions which often had little relation to what was possible. Thus, we find Saint-Simon wanting to put scientists in charge of politics, Ludwig Feuerbach believing that as long as people were religious they would be alienated (and, presumably, miserable), and anarchists plotting to abolish the state, the Church, and the police, and organizing society on the basis of direct cooperation among people and decision-making through councils in which all adults would take part.

Although the French Revolution was suppressed, it had sown ideas of liberty, equality, and fraternity (or solidarity), had placed Reason above God, and had conjured up visions of people organizing their own lives according to their own ways of thinking. It had also conjured up the notion of *citizenship,* thereby opening a potential gulf between what it means to be a good person and what it means to be a good citizen. This set the stage for the emergence of several strands of radical politics after 1815. Radical politics was further encouraged, in some instances, by the continuing development of science and by the optimism which scientific innovation inspired in some quarters. And then there was the influence of Hegel, who challenged his students and admirers to think in new ways. Among the results were Saint-Simon's effort to reconcile a reconstructed form of Christianity with science, Feuerbach's radical humanism, Max Stirner's nihilist egoism which seemed to celebrate only Stirner himself, and the collectivist anarchism associated with Proudhon, Bakunin, and Kropotkin (see Box 6.1).

The Count Claude Henri de Rouvroy de Saint-Simon (1760-1825)

Saint-Simon loomed large in his day, earning him a reputation as a champion of rule by science – an idea which lives on even today.[1] Born in Paris on 17 October 1760, into a noble family, he received his first military commission at the age of 17. In 1779, when he was 19, he was sent to America, as part of the Touraine Regiment, to fight shoulder-to-shoulder with the American revolutionary army. Later, in 1785, he visited Holland and, in 1786, became involved in a murky plot to drive the English out of India. Nothing came of this scheme, however. In 1787 he made his way to Spain where he found the Spanish government entertaining the idea of constructing a canal from Madrid to the sea; Saint-Simon, flushed with money, was ready to lend the Spanish government the funds it needed to carry out this project, but the French Revolution broke out before plans could be finalized, and Saint-Simon hurried back to France.

In September 1793, four years into the French revolution, Saint-Simon formally abdicated his noble titles. It was about this time that he began devising various constitutional programs and dabbling in mathematics, science, psychology, and the social doctrines of the ideologues. In 1801, he married Mlle. de Champgrand, but soon thereafter he heard that Madame de Stael, renowned for her brilliant intellect, had lost her husband. Saint-Simon now divorced de Champgrand, with whom he had agreed, prior to their marriage, that either partner might leave the marriage at any point. He travelled to Coppet, Switzerland, where de Stael lived and proposed to her with the following words, "Madame, you are the most extraordinary woman in the world, as I am the most extraordinary man; together we would undoubtedly have an even more extraordinary child."[2] De Stael, however, was more interested in the novelist and political commentator Benjamin Constant, and declined Saint-Simon's offer of marriage.

Saint-Simon maintained an active social life, entertaining intellectuals, artists, politicians, and other prominent people in his salon.[3] In the course of the early years of the nineteenth century, his finances deteriorated, but in 1814 his family granted him a small annuity in exchange for his renunciation of any claim to a portion of the ancestral estate. Now, at age 54, he set aside his scientific projects to devote himself to writing political tracts. Earlier in life, he had been regarded by many as a "crackpot", but now he won a new respect and gained "admittance into the circle of liberal economists and publicists identified with Jean-Baptiste Say and Charles Dunoyer."[4] Saint-Simon gradually emerged as a champion for the French bourgeoisie and launched a series of periodical publications which circulated during the last decade of his life.

Toward the perfection of civilization

Like his contemporary, Hegel, Saint-Simon was a great optimist and believed that humankind was heading inexorably toward a better social and political system than it had had up to then. He once described his own task in life – one might even say destiny – in these words: "To study the course of the human mind, in order to work for the perfection of civilization."[5] In his view, ideas were the driving force in history and, before a new system of government could be attempted, it was first necessary to develop the ideas for such a government in a systematic way. As he put it, "...the new political system of Europe must be the outcome of the new philosophy."[6] But that did not mean that any scheme could be applied at any time; on the contrary, ideas which might be offered prematurely could not succeed. The education of the populace was, in his view, a key limiting factor. And hence, he concluded, citing the Habsburg emperor Joseph II as an example, that a sovereign who tried to enact legislation and reforms for which people were not prepared could expect to provoke opposition.[7] It followed, for Saint-Simon – echoing Montesquieu – that political institutions should be useful to society, but also in tune with the people's thinking and culture.[8]

Saint-Simon's orientation bears comparison with that of his contemporary Jeremy Bentham (1748-1832). Like Bentham, he believed that "the happiness of nations is the only and exclusive goal of the body social."[9] It was, moreover, in an entirely utilitarian spirit that Saint-Simon urged that "one cannot be truly happy except by searching for one's happiness in the happiness of one's neighbour" – in an explicit appeal to what it means to be a good person -- so that interests come to be seen as mutual, rather than conflictual.[10] And hence, it was imperative to "organize human society in the way most advantageous for its felicity" on the principle that governance "should work for the happiness of the governed."[11]

At this point, Saint-Simon took a leap into the religious realm, urging that Christianity embrace utilitarianism (rather than Natural Law or Divine Law) as its guiding principle. Calling for the fashioning of a new Christianity which would embrace utilitarian doctrine, he also imagined the priesthood of his imagined Church as a scientific body of men who would apply scientific principles to the faith. His religious revisionism entailed a rethinking of Natural Law, emphasizing its roots in Reason, now to be refined by scientific investigation. This notion also reveals Saint-Simon's quasi-religious view of scientists. While Europe was convulsed by revolutionary and counterrevolutionary violence, Saint-Simon called on Europeans to establish a "scientific priesthood" which "would end the moral crisis of the age and…give impetus to a vast expansion of scientific knowledge."[12] He seemed to have an optimistic view of scientists. His admiration of science hit a crisis as the violence in Europe escalated in 1812-1813, however, and Saint-Simon suffered a nervous breakdown. Among other things, he was deeply disappointed in the apparent indifference of the scientific world to the slaughter going on around them. It was as he recuperated from his nervous collapse that Saint-Simon hit on the idea to urge priests to become scientists, so that they would bring their moral orientation into their scientific work. This solution also addressed the growing rivalry between science and religion, in Saint-Simon's view.

Saint-Simon came to embody the spirit of the Restoration in his acceptance of the view, popularized by Joseph de Maistre and Louis Viscount de Bonald, that social inequality was natural and even desirable. But from this initial premise – that inequality was natural and good – Saint-Simon drew the corollary that social policy should encourage, reinforce, and deepen all sorts of inequality, including class inequality. With his faith in science and industrial management, Saint-Simon slid into a form of libertarianism, arguing that, with qualified scientists and industrial managers in charge, society could dispense with government in the traditional sense; in its place, the scientific-industrial complex would assume the functions of government, as a kind of government by experts.[13]

In his last work, *Nouveau Christianisme* (The New Christianity), published in 1825 on the eve of his death, Saint-Simon, who had already begun to talk about love as a social bond for harmony in society, asserted that all of Christianity could be summed up in one sentence: "all men should behave towards each other as brothers."[14] To Saint-Simon's mind, religious teachings had arisen in an effort to provide answers to questions to which science was now providing better answers. But, he wrote, "the sciences now begin to supplant every other branch of knowledge; and the great industrious combinations tend more directly to the amelioration of the condition of the poor, than any of the measures hitherto taken by the temporal or spiritual power."[15] Up to then, Christianity had promised that happiness could be found in heaven, which is to say, after death. But Saint-Simon wanted Christianity to work toward bringing happiness to people in this life. This was the task to which he believed his "New Christianity" was well suited. Indeed, he promised, "the adoption of New Christianity will accelerate the progress of civilization more than could be done by any general measure."[16] His optimistic faith in humanity seemed to be restored as he confidently asserted that "[t]he human race has never ceased to progress,...to increase its knowledge and to perfect its civilization."[17]

But Saint-Simon was fully aware that his Christian revisionism involved an assault on the traditional theology and dogmas of the Church. Indeed, he admitted as much on his deathbed, when he mournfully told those of his disciples who had gathered to pay their last respects that religion had shown that it was "no longer in harmony with the progress of positive science."[18]

Saint-Simon's liberal roots

Friedrich Engels' *Socialism: Utopian and Scientific*, written between January and March 1880, cast Saint-Simon as a utopian socialist, alongside François Fourier (1772-1837) and Robert Owen (1771-1851). Although Engels conceded that the three visionaries aspired to liberate all humanity, and not just the proletariat, the label "utopian socialist" cast Saint-Simon in a curious and misleading light. In fact, Saint-Simon had something in common with Marx and Engels. For one thing, Saint-Simon spoke in terms of reorganizing property so that it would serve the general interest of society as a whole; moreover, he saw that "the bourgeois[ie], who made the revolution and directed it in their [own] interest,...have forced themselves into the governing class so that today the *industriels* must pay the nobles as well as the bourgeois[ie]."[19] Furthermore, he reproached the feudal constitution prevalent in Europe "... because it operates entirely to the advantage of the governors and to the detriment of the governed."[20]

But the differences between Saint-Simon and the two socialists is far greater than these superficial similarities. For one thing, when Saint-Simon used the term "bourgeois", he had in mind the governing classes of civil servants and political managers who figured as an intermediate stratum between the lingering noble classes and the *industriels;* and, in using the term *industriels*, Saint-Simon had in mind all those involved in production, whether factory owners or their employees.[21] Thus, the problem, for Saint-Simon, was not any class conflict between capitalists and proletariat, as Marx and Engels believed, since, in the French reformer's view they had common interests. The problem, rather, was a phenomenon of historical lag, in which a nation which had reached the "industrial" stage of development was still subject to a government which was "feudal" in character.[22]

Saint-Simon himself declared that what he wanted to see was "the peaceful establishment of the liberal regime."[23] But he wanted to refine and improve liberalism, so that "all institutions" would be "directed toward the aim of the amelioration of the moral and physical well-being of the poorest class," so that "all classes of society and all nations [might] prosper with the greatest rapidity possible."[24] To his mind, the English political system was the "least vicious" among European regimes,[25] and accordingly he sketched out a plan to transform England into a state which would correspond to his vision. As he drafted it, the House of Commons would be redesigned as a Chamber of Resolution, composed of the leading industrialists in the country; attached to it would be two advisory bodies (modelled in their powers on the British House of Lords). These were the Chamber of Invention, made up by technicians and artists, which would be authorized to make proposals to the Chamber of Resolution, and the Chamber of Examination, composed of scientists, empowered to review bills which had been proposed or were under consideration.[26]

Saint-Simon's importance

Saint-Simon was one of the first writers to argue that scientists should operate largely without external restraint and provide the leadership to guide society. It was, after all, Saint-Simon who addressed a letter to scientists in 1803 with these words:

> Scientists, artists, look with the eye of genius at the present state of the human mind; you will see that the sceptre of public opinion has fallen into your hand; grasp it with vigour! You can create happiness for yourselves and for your contemporaries; you can preserve posterity from the evils from which we have suffered and from those which we still endure; all of you, subscribe![27]

In this way, Saint-Simon anticipated some of the arguments offered by libertarians in the twentieth century.

Saint-Simon had a wide-ranging influence on sundry thinkers in the nineteenth century. Among others, Hegel read *The Globe,* an organ of the Saint-Simonians, in his last years, and advised his students to acquaint themselves with the French thinker's writings. Hegel's followers (the Old Hegelians) were impressed by Saint-Simon's realization that economic progress was leading to the impoverishment of industrial workers.[28] Fichte's thought also reflected the influence of Saint-Simon, among others,[29] as did also Nietzsche's thinking. Indeed, when Nietzsche wrote about socialism, he had in mind Saint-Simon's version.[30] In his native France, Saint-Simon set forth ideas which would be picked up by Proudhon. Among other things, Proudhon assimilated Saint-Simon's ideas about social evolution and about government as an administration of things. "Both Saint-Simon and Proudhon view man as essentially a producer, and production as the supreme power in the state. Both make much of economic forces and laws... Both contrast science with the social power of man, to the advantage of the former."[31]

Edward Gans, whose lectures Karl Marx attended in Berlin, "was impressed by the ideas of Saint-Simon," and, in writing *The Communist Manifesto*, Marx himself would be inspired by the Frenchman's periodization of history.[32] For that matter, Saint-Simon's commitment to science also exerted a certain influence on Marx.[33] Finally, mention should be made of Saint-Simon's influence on John Stuart Mill, who "recognize[d] the importance of the St. Simonian contribution to sexual equality" and saw in Saint-Simon's writings a powerful indictment of tyranny.[34]

The Saint-Simonian Movement

At the time of Saint-Simon's death, Olinde Rodrigues (1795-1851), a banker who had embraced Saint-Simon's program of social reform, and his friend, Barthélemy Prosper Enfantin (1796-1864), a famously dashing young man, founded the review, *Le Producteur*, in which they assailed the idea of competition, arguing in favor of mutual aid societies. A Saint-Simonian movement grew up around these two men and Saint-Amand Bazard (1791-1832), a French socialist. By 1829, Enfantin was acknowledged as one of the leading figures in the movement, which was regularly attracting about 200 women to its lectures by 1830. In 1831, Bazard left the movement. By this point, Enfantin was embracing liberal views about sexual freedom and Rodrigues, who considered Enfantin's views extreme, left the movement in protest in 1832, declaring himself Saint-Simon's true disciple. In the meantime, Enfantin had resigned his job as cashier and was devoting himself to organizational work, setting up branches in some of the more important cities of France. As of 1832, Enfantin claimed to have a following of 40,000 converts to the gospel of "free love" and he declared that he had been chosen by God to lead the movement. He also sent out emissaries in search of a "female messiah" who would "save the world from prostitution as Jesus saved it from slavery."[35] Then, in 1832, some of these women launched their own newspaper – *La femme libre* [The Free Woman] – arguing that "The woman question is fundamentally connected to that of women workers."[36] Enfantin increasingly promoted an androgynous view of God and sanctioned levels of promiscuity which apparently exceeded what some of the movement's followers could readily accept. Indeed, Enfantin gained a certain notoriety, and the movement's meetings "...were often disrupted by hoodlums hired by prominent citizens who feared that the cult would seduce their young."[37] But the movement survived these attacks to become a potent influence in nineteenth-century France.

Where love had been largely de-sexualized in Saint-Simon's thought, figuring for the most part as love of humanity, for the Saint-Simonians, and especially for Enfantin, love meant free love, the liberation of the passions. Indeed, in 1831, Enfantin turned the master on his head by proposing to found a new religion based on a vision of a future where neither sexual inhibitions nor jealousy would be found and where monogamy would be optional. For the Saint-Simonians, the struggle for women's equality and the liberation of sexual passions were two sides of the same coin; they deplored the Judaeo-Christian tradition's abhorrence of sex and relegation of women to second-class status.

But the Saint-Simonians did not lose sight of the master's high valuation of science, although they no longer believed, as the master had, that science and industry could regulate themselves. On the contrary, they believed that extreme competition had proven to be damaging both to the economy as a whole and to ordinary workers. Deploring this extreme competition, which they interpreted as a symptom of moral crisis, the Saint-Simonians evoked an idealized picture of medieval Europe, imagining it as an age dominated by love, chivalry, faith, and duty. For them, thus, the ideal was an (imagined) age "in which spiritual and religious authority were spontaneously respected, [and] in which there was no conflict, no opposition, no contradiction, no dissension."[38] The analysis of the roots of the crisis in turn suggested the solution, viz., a complete overhaul of the educational system to emphasize love. And this, in turn, also entailed a repudiation of revolutionary militancy, since class conflict did not provide a path to a flowering of love. Ultimately, however, the French government considered all this talk about love to be potentially dangerous and applied repressive measures; by the end of the 1830s, the movement had been largely suffocated.

The Young Hegelians ("Die Freien")

After Hegel's death in 1831, among those who wanted to continue his legacy were those who emphasized its more conservative features (the so-called "Old Hegelians" or "Right Hegelians") and those who focused, rather, on the radical potential of his dialectical methodology (the so-called "Young Hegelians" or "Left Hegelians"). Some of the latter – numbering a few of Hegel's former students and admirers – met on a regular basis at Hippels Weinstube on the Friedrichstrasse in downtown Berlin in the early 1840s. There, amid clouds of tobacco smoke and to the accompaniment of round after round of alcoholic beverages, they discussed Hegel's ideas and methodology as well as their own diverse theories of social transformation. Morality – what it means to be a good person or a good citizen – was never far from their thoughts. They called themselves "Die Freien" (the free ones).[39] Their leading members were the following:

■ **Bruno Bauer** (1809-1882) played the central role in organizing this group of unlike-minded philosophical comrades and subscribed to left-wing views briefly, but then came to believe in the moral and political superiority of absolutist monarchy, feeling that ordinary people could not be trusted to determine their own future. At one point, he hoped that tsarist Russia would lead Europe out of political darkness to the higher bliss of monarchical absolutism, before embracing Bismarck's Germany as Europe's destined savior. Beginning in the 1840s, he began writing that the story of Jesus of Nazareth, as it has come down to us, is a myth, forged by fusing elements from Jewish, Greek, and Roman sources. Among other things, by a careful study of relevant texts, he showed that the New Testament writers borrowed heavily from Seneca the Younger (4 BCE-65 CE), the Roman dramatist and Stoic philosopher. As early as 1838, with his book, *The Religion of the Old Testament,* Bauer turned his back on monotheism. In this volume, he denigrated Judaism, while exalting the ancient Olympian religions. He argued that it was high time to break with all forms of monotheism and abolish the hegemony of religious organizations.[40] By 1842, Bauer was lashing out at the liberal state, demanding that both Judaism and Christianity be suppressed as a precondition for establishing guarantees for civil rights. In his view, "in the unfree Christian state there are no true civil rights."[41]   There followed his choleric anti-Christian tirade, *Christianity Unmasked,* in which he characterized Christianity as "the religion *par excellence* of hatred, exclusiveness, and self-love."[42] After this, by late 1844, Bauer was under siege from Christians, Jews, and liberals.

Bauer was *sui generis*[43] in that he blended political positions associated with the Old Hegelians with the atheist and anti-Christian views associated with the Young Hegelians. Certainly, his admiration for absolute monarchy associated him with the conservative Old Hegelians and, after breaking with the circle of Die Freien, of which he had been the acknowledged leader,[44] he brought out his *Complete History of the Partisan Fights in Germany during the Years 1842-1846* (Charlottenburg, 1847), in which he polemicized against Young Hegelian ideas.[45]

In the 1840s, the issue of citizenship for Jews resurfaced. Earlier, Prussian constitutional thinking had reflected the viewpoint of Friedrich Julius Stahl, who held that Christian baptism was sufficient for Jews to enjoy all the rights of citizenship. But in the 1840s, Bruno Bauer joined Hermann Wagener in rejecting this liberal view, holding rather "that Jews and Germans were so intrinsically different in their history and character that the Jews could never truly become part of the German state."[46]   In the judgment of David Friedrich Strauss, "Bauer was a scoundrel in every possible respect."[47]

■ **Arnold Ruge** (1802-1880), by contrast, who also came regularly to Hippels Weinstube, was a classical liberal, committed to the building up of liberal democracy. He published a number of plays, translated ancient Greek texts, and briefly joined Karl Marx in editing the *Deutsch-Französische Jahrbücher*, a publication based in Paris. In 1850, in the wake of the failure of the 1848 revolution, he moved to Brighton, England, where he earned a living as a teacher and writer. Ruge, "while ultimately denying any truth to Christian claims, continued to make Christianity a central theme...and never totally denied its positive human significance."[48]

■ **Ludwig Feuerbach** (1804-1872) was raised Protestant and, in his early years, was a devout Christian. In 1823, he matriculated at the theological faculty of the prestigious University of Heidelberg. He later defended his doctoral dissertation at the University of Erlangen, subsequently lecturing on the history of modern philosophy and publishing three books in that area in the years 1833-1838.[49] His theological training notwithstanding, as early as the 1820s, Feuerbach was equating religion with spiritual enslavement.[50]

In 1841, Feuerbach brought out his *Essence of Christianity*, which, in its first edition, had clear political content, alongside its overt anti-religious message. He came under pressure from the authorities and police searched his home in April 1843. Feuerbach beat a retreat, issuing a largely depoliticized second edition in 1843,[51] adding a favorable reference to Martin Luther by way of legitimizing his nonetheless critical interpretation of

Christianity.[52] A third, equally depoliticized edition followed in 1849. Even so, Feuerbach's critique of Christianity remained strident through all three editions, in which he articulated his notion that Christianity was fostering forms of self-alienation among people, by attributing all goodness in the world to God. He championed a new humanism, in which people would subscribe to a secular morality and reject organized religion. In his earlier work, *Thoughts on Death*, he had argued that the widespread Western emphasis on the immortality of the personal soul had originated in the Reformation. For Feuerbach, this belief in personal immortality

> ...is the central result of a mistaken position concerning the relationship between individual existence and its environment...[But] if it can be proved that the individual human totally ends at the close of his natural life here, then human sights can be lowered back to realistically attainable ideals, to sharing in the goals of *this* life. Collapse the imagined beyond, and religious humanity will be able to accept the real restrictions on the life of the individual and at the same time give back to this life its real value.[53]

■ **David Friedrich Strauss** (1808-1874), like Feuerbach, obtained his professional training in theology – first at the theological seminary in Blaubeuren and later in Tübingen. It was during his years at the University of Tübingen, 1827-1830, that Strauss read Schleiermacher's *Glaubenslehre* and met with friends to discuss Hegel's *Phenomenology of Mind*. Upon completing his theological studies at Tübingen, he was appointed to serve as assistant pastor in Kleiningersheim near Ludwigsburg. Subsequently, in summer 1832, he was appointed as an assistant lecturer in the theological college in Tübingen.

It was then that he undertook to write what proved to be one of the most controversial books published between the end of the Napoleonic Wars in 1815 and the outbreak of continent-wide revolutionary upheavals in 1848 – his *Life of Jesus Critically Examined*. Strauss had hoped for an enthusiastic response from "serious and enlightened men of all persuasions as a liberation from the fetters of dogmatism and as a basis for the revitalization of the true essence of the Christian faith."[54] In this book, he debunked the notion that Jesus of Nazareth was divine, describing him, rather, as merely a very virtuous man. This argument was a natural complement to Feuerbach's argument but cost Strauss his teaching post. Instead of seeing his work celebrated, he found himself the target of sharp attacks.[55] In 1835, he was transferred to Ludwigsburg, where he worked briefly as a professor's substitute. The following year, he resigned from service and went into retirement in 1836.

He brought out a second edition of *The Life of Jesus* in 1836, albeit with no significant revisions but with some additional material. This was followed by a third edition, in which he "conceded many points to his critics."[56] With this, he hoped to regain a position in academia. In the years 1836-1839, liberal supporters in Zürich made three attempts to secure a position for him at their university. Local conservatives blocked his appointment the first two times but, on the third effort, an offer was drawn up to appoint Strauss Professor of Dogmatics and Church History at the University of Zürich. But his book had made too big a splash and intense pressure from the public now resulted in the revocation of the provisional offer. Denied this rehabilitation, Strauss now prepared a fourth edition (published in 1840), restoring the radical analysis of the first edition.[57]

The Life of Jesus attracted admirers among Left Hegelians. Yet his argument "that the accounts of the Gospel literature were in large part myth, not history, and thus that Jesus could not be historically verified as the God-man of orthodox faith"[58] attracted enemies. As if that was not enough, his book was seen as threatening to the political order of his day.[59]

■ **Friedrich Engels** (1820-1895), Marx's collaborator, was an occasional visitor to gatherings of Die Freien at Hippels Weinstube. Although it would be wrongheaded to call him a Young Hegelian, he did associate with some of the leading Young Hegelians and his reading of Hegel's works would influence his own thinking. A convinced socialist, he rejected outright the arguments of Bruno Bauer and Arnold Ruge, but had considerable sympathy for Feuerbach's diagnosis of what was wrong with Christian religion. Like Marx, however, Engels felt that Feuerbach was describing only one of a set of interlocking problems and that, in any event, his solution was completely inadequate. Feuerbach seemed to look to education to lead people out of Plato's cave; Engels, like Marx, felt that only socialist revolution would suffice. (For further discussion of Marx and Engels, see the following chapter.)

■ **Kuno Fischer** (1824-1907),[60] **Moses Hess** (1812-1875),[61] and **Edgar Bauer**, Bruno's brother, were also part of this circle, as was **Max Stirner** (1806-1856), a quiet, pipe-smoking teacher at a girls' school, whose real name was **Johann Caspar Schmidt** and whose magnum opus, *Der Einzige und sein Eigenthum*, appeared in October 1844. Stirner and Bruno Bauer were lifelong friends.

Max Stirner (1806-1856)

Stirner was born in Bayreuth, to lower-middle-class Lutheran parents. His father died when he was 6 months old; his sister died when he was 6 years old; and his mother was declared insane when he was 29 and was committed to a mental hospital in Berlin (in 1835). At age 20 he enrolled at the University of Berlin in the faculty of philosophy, and attended lectures by Hegel, Schleiermacher, and Philip Marheineke, a Protestant preacher and professor of philosophy. Due to financial problems, as well as his mother's deteriorating mental condition, he finished his formal studies at the University of Berlin only in 1834, at the age of 28.

He married in 1837, five months after the death of his stepfather, but his wife died a year later, giving birth to a stillborn child. In 1839, he was hired to teach history and literature at a respectable girls' school; it was his first and only secure job. While employed there, he began to associate with "the free ones", in 1841. He published an interesting essay in April 1842, entitled *The False Principle of Our Education*, arguing against rote memorization and urging that people be encouraged, instead, to think critically.[62]

At Hippels Weinstube, Stirner met Marie Dähnhardt, one of "the free ones", and in October 1843, they married. By this point, Stirner was busy writing *Der Einzige und Sein Eigenthum* (The Ego and his Own). Published in October 1844, the book argues that morality, law, and religion are all lies, and defends the proposition that people might do as they please. He resigned his teaching job the same month that the book was published, and a period of financial hardship began. Nor was the book popular, except among a few people on the philosophical fringe, and he was subjected to repeated attacks. Then, in April 1846, Dähnhardt left Stirner, who struggled to make ends meet by doing some translation work. Stirner actually spent two brief periods in a debtors' prison in Berlin during 1853-54, and in June 1856, died from a fever resulting from being stung by a winged insect.[63]

The Ego and His Own.

Stirner's principal purpose in *The Ego and His Own* was to attack the ideas expressed by his associates at Hippels Weinstube, and thus one finds attacks on liberalism, humanism, monarchism, socialism, religion, and even the notion of respect for the law, although his criticisms of his friend Bruno Bauer were mild and did not affect their friendship. Needless to say, Stirner's book had no use for notions of a good person or a good citizen. Feuerbach, on the other hand, was placed at the center of Stirner's critique, with Stirner dismissing the author of *The Essence of Christianity* as a "pious atheist".[64]

Stirner was not an anarchist, however, because he had no interest in developing any sort of vision of a better world. Stirner is best understood as a nihilist, because, as he freely admitted, nothing had any value for him. He was particularly intent on criticizing morality itself. Thus Stirner wrote, "The moral man is necessarily narrow in that he knows no other enemy than the 'immoral' man... Therefore the moral man can never comprehend the egoist."[65]

Egoism may be understood as doing as one pleases. But Stirner, who had declared himself against all principles, did not want to be thought to be championing freedom which, in his view, was never more than freedom from some particular oppression and which, inevitably, included, in his view, the acceptance of a new "dominion". Nor was he prepared to agree that some states might be better than others. On the contrary, Stirner insisted:

> Every state is a *despotism*, be the despot one or many...If one were even to conceive the case that every individual in the people had expressed the same will, and hereby a complete 'collective will' had come into being, the matter would still remain the same. Would I not be bound today and henceforth to my will of yesterday? My will would in this case be *frozen*. Wretched *stability*! ...So in the state-life I am at best...a bondsman of myself.[66]

In taking this view, Stirner was clearly repudiating Hegel's thesis that a high level of freedom can be realized only within a state community. Moreover, Stirner broke with more than 2,000 years of Western philosophical tradition by claiming that it was possible to have rights without duties. Traditionally, philosophers understood right as the entitlement to the performance of a duty, i.e., the necessary corollary of the statement, "I ought". But for

Stirner, right was to be derived from will, from the statement, "I want". He was quite explicit on this score: "Owner and creator of my right, I recognize no other source of right than – me, neither God nor the state nor nature nor even man himself with his 'eternal rights of man', neither divine nor human right."[67] This passage seemed to allow that Stirner might be recognizing that individuals generated their own rights, but a few pages later he excluded this possibility by rejecting the concept of right altogether. "I want" was all that is left. Arriving, finally, at the end of his dead-end, one reads a passage in which one may easily imagine Stirner shouting, "Of what concern to me is the common weal?....The *people* is dead! Up with *me!*"[68]

In the 1890s, there were briefly some "Stirnerite" currents in parts of Germany, and the "spirit of Stirner" may be thought to have resurfaced in European punk in the 1970s and early 1980s. But Stirner's nihilism is a philosophical dead-end. Indeed, Stirner happily trumpeted that his philosophy was a dead-end, though he believed that the same could be said of all other philosophies. Its importance lies in this, that his nihilism represents a "boundary point" demarcating a particular extreme, that he spelled out the premises of "moral nihilism" as an alternative to other approaches, and that, within the context of Western philosophy, he took the "realist" position to its limit, advocating pure self-indulgence without regard to norms or to the needs of others.

Anarchism

The anarchists start with outrage – outrage at inequality of wealth and power above all and outrage at social injustice. Beyond that, what anarchists share in common is a profound and deep-seated faith in humankind and a conviction that it is government which is ultimately responsible for most of the social ills plaguing society. Anarchists further share the Aristotelian conviction that people are communal by nature, concluding that solidarity and mutual assistance were natural instincts, obstructed only by the state and its sundry institutions, laws, and instruments.[69] Russian anarchist Pyotr Kropotkin even wrote a book urging the proposition that all species, including humankind, were naturally inclined to mutual assistance.[70]

But if the state and the police were the great enemies, what should take their place after they are overthrown? Judging from the experiences of the Paris Commune of 1871 and the Spanish

Republic in 1936 (especially in Barcelona), it appears that anarchists thought in terms of something like direct democracy, although they did not use that term, rather than representative democracy, and in terms of general cooperation in administration. Proudhon, the best-known French anarchist, thought in terms of a future in which workers' communes and workers' cooperatives would operate on the basis of shared labor, shared profits, and complete equality. Anarchists tended to be hostile to differences in wealth, to Churches, and to warfare in general, as well as to nationalism. Anarchists were also deeply hostile to traditional notions of democracy, for several reasons:

1. They rejected the concept of popular sovereignty, championing instead a notion of sovereignty of the person.[71]
2. They felt that the sovereignty of a person could not be "represented".
3. Their commitment was, in the first place, to freedom, specifically the freedom of each individual.

Pierre-Joseph Proudhon (1809-1864)

A professional revolutionary and political publicist, Proudhon is best known today for his book, *What is Property?*, first published in 1840. Pierre-Joseph Proudhon was born in Besançon in 1809 to a working class family. Educated at the Collège Royal in Besançon, Proudhon read tirelessly – especially works of political philosophy. Among the books he read were Montesquieu's *The Spirit of the Laws*, which left him unimpressed, and Rousseau's *Social Contract*, which inspired him. He also read the works of Grotius, Sieyès, Thomas Reid, Kant, Hegel, and Giambatista Vico. He took profuse notes on these books, interspersing his notes with comments reflecting his profound outrage with the social system as it existed. In 1848, when continent-wide revolution broke out, he was elected to the National Assembly of France, but later, after the establishment of the Second Republic (1848-1852), he was briefly imprisoned. He married Euphrasie Piégard in 1849, when he was 40. He died in Paris in 1864, at the age of 55.

What drove Proudhon was outrage at injustice and a desire to see justice promoted and served. He was also convinced that humanity had always striven for justice.[72] Proudhon was a professional revolutionary and, like fellow professional revolutionaries Bakunin, Marx, Malatesta, and Lenin, he spent more time criticizing the social evils which he wanted to remedy than outlining his solution. What is, however, abundantly clear is that Proudhon believed that unjust inequalities of wealth were sown into the very system of property itself, so that it made sense, in his view, to describe property as theft; this meant that, to the extent that government existed to protect property systems, it served to protect systems of theft. It followed, for Proudhon, that, in order to end social injustice, one had to do away with government itself. Because citizenship signified membership in and respect for a state, there was, for Proudhon – as for other anarchists – no such thing as a "good citizen".

But Proudhon also rejected Marxist-style communism as a false solution, accusing the communists of introducing a theory of property into the very foundations of their program. The only difference between so-called "property" systems and communist systems, according to Proudhon, was that in the latter the community was said to be the owner of all property. Communism promised, of course, to liberate people, but instead, Proudhon charged, it imposed a demand for "passive obedience, irreconcilable with a conscious will" and promoted mediocrity by providing equal rewards for mediocre performance and for excellent performance.[73]

Against these systems, Proudhon envisioned a just society based on the recognition of three fundamental rights: the liberty of the individual, equality, and security. In his eyes, it was obvious that "...we are associated for the sake of liberty, equality and security, we are not associated for the sake of property; thus, if property is a natural right, this natural right is not social but anti-social."[74] Later, he added two more principles which must be central to anarchist society – law and proportionality. Law may come as a surprise, because we often think of law as the product of government, but what Proudhon had in mind was Natural Law, which he described as "the application of a moral principle."[75] Natural Law was not to be understood as an abstract maxim, however, but as a set of moral imperatives operating within a context of sociability, in which a mother feels a natural sentiment for her child and a healthy person feels a natural sympathy for a sick person.

The abolition of government was necessitated not merely on moral grounds, however, but also on economic grounds and, as already suggested, for the sake of the security of citizens. But his emphasis on sociability is only one of a number of clues as to his vision of what would follow a successful anarchist revolution. Rejecting the faith in the perfectibility of humankind to which Marx subscribed, Proudhon was convinced that there would always be a need for a coordinative mechanism which could fashion policies for the community (again, unlike Marx and Engels, who anticipated the eventual withering away of the state). But coordination could be accomplished directly; in Proudhon's view, "human reason is sufficient to enable interdependent individuals and groups to discover mutually acceptable bases for common action."[76]

Mikhail Bakunin (1814-1876)

For many, Bakunin is the quintessential anarchist, denouncing the state, the police, and the Church, getting involved in international revolutionary activity, and escaping from prison. Bakunin was the third of 10 children born into a well-to-do gentry family. At age 14, he went to St. Petersburg to begin training for and service in the Russian military. He received his commission as an officer, but, seven years later, he left the military. He then spent some years in Moscow, where he began reading the works of Hegel; at the time, he was deeply influenced by Hegel's works; about this time, he also read Feuerbach and found the German thinker's argument about religion convincing.[77] But he later repudiated Hegelianism and all of German philosophy as "the spiritual opium of all those who thirst for action and are condemned to inactivity."[78] He later moved to Berlin, where he shared an apartment with Ivan Sergeyevich Turgenev, who would later gain fame as the author of *Fathers and Sons* and other novels. He participated in the Prague insurrection in 1848, in an insurrection in Dresden in 1849, and in the Polish insurrection of 1863, and, in 1866, he founded the International Brotherhood, a secret revolutionary organization, in Naples. The governments of Europe considered Bakunin dangerous. At one time or another, he was expelled from France, sentenced to death in Saxony, sentenced to death in Austria, imprisoned in St. Petersburg, and exiled to Siberia.

Bakunin was, by this point, coming to the conclusion that, far from being the embodiment of ethical life, as Hegel had claimed, the state was the greatest enemy of humankind and needed to be smashed. In Bakunin's view, religion functioned to legitimate state authority, among other things by justifying various forms of repression and inequality. As a result, in the effort to destroy political repression, it would be necessary also to destroy the institutions which served to inculcate habits of obedience to state authorities, above all the Churches. Further, his reflections on the French Revolution had made Bakunin aware that revolutions could be derailed by ambitious leaders; in that event, anti-state revolution might end by establishing new state authorities, thereby nullifying their entire rationale. His solution was to demand that the "...future organization of society should be carried out entirely from below upwards, by the free association and federation of the workers."[79]

In 1864, he joined the First International, where he vied with Marx for leadership of the international revolutionary movement. Their relations became acrimonious and strains involved much more than a mere clash of ambitions. Specifically, Bakunin charged that Marx's thinking and organizational strategy would lead not to liberation but to tyranny. In *Statism and Anarchy*, his major work, Bakunin wrote specifically, "By education and by nature [Marx] is a Jacobin, and his favourite dream is of a political dictatorship."[80] Bakunin thought that it was crucial to avoid setting up any authority or authoritative body, "even an elected one."[81] Nor should there be revolutionary leaders as such; "friends of the people", as he called revolution-minded intellectuals, should limit themselves to inciting people to take action, showing them the way but not taking charge. Revolution could be dramatic and violent, taking the form of an uprising, but, Bakunin asserted, revolutions could be "peaceful", taking shape through "a slow and systematic but at the same time radical transformation of...[political and] economic life."[82]

Anarchists and democracy

Neither Proudhon nor Bakunin was impressed with the mechanisms of democracy, because democracy, if anything, promised to develop an even more powerful state, in which individuals would be even more effectively supervised, regulated, controlled, and repressed than under openly despotic or autocratic systems. In his book *Idée Générale de la Révolution aux XIXé Siècle* (1851), Proudhon specifically rejected the democratic principles of separation of powers, suffrage and representation, bicameral legislature, and majority rule. The purpose of all of this, according to Proudhon, was to assure the subordination of citizens to the state, of the poor to the rich, and of the lower classes to the upper classes.[83]

In place of democracy, Proudhon hoped to see society organized on a new basis, in which, among other things, the following principles would be honored:

1. full economic equality for all;
2. emphasis on the identity of interests and an end to intergroup antagonisms;

3. the universal proliferation of comfort; and
4. "the sovereignty of reason."[84]

In the years 1936-1939, in the context of the Spanish Civil War, Spanish and Catalan anarchists established agricultural cooperatives, abolished money, established the principle "to each according to his needs," and reached decisions at the local level on the basis of communal consensus. But the anarchists were on the losing side of the struggle and, when the war ended, the experiment in anarchism died. After the Spanish anarchist project had failed, Jaime Balius, an anarchist himself, reflected on the debacle and concluded that, in order to have stood a chance of success, the Spanish anarchists striving to carry out a revolution would have required revolutionary leadership.[85] But leadership is precisely what the anarchists repudiated. So far history seems to have judged that anarchism is therefore intrinsically and crucially flawed.

Conclusion — Radicalism in the Age of Hegel

Hegel cast a long shadow over the nineteenth century. Saint-Simon, Proudhon, Bakunin, Kropotkin, and, of course, the Young Hegelians all read Hegel's writings, mining them for insights into the challenges they faced. Like Hegel, all of these nineteenth century thinkers and activists nurtured hopes that the future would bring better conditions for people, sometimes linking those hopes to the belief that people could build more harmonious societies. And like Hegel, they wrestled with questions of morality, spelling out – except for Stirner – their expectations of what it means to be a good person.

6.1

Pyotr Kropotkin

Pyotr Kropotkin (1842-1921), a professional geographer and anarchist born in Moscow, served as an army officer in Siberia from 1862 to 1867, and used the time to study animal life. He also explored the region and sketched a theory of the structural formations of mountain ranges. Although he had prospects of a distinguished scientific career ahead of him, he declined an appointment as secretary of the Russian Geographical Society in 1871 and dedicated the rest of his life to fighting for social justice. He joined a revolutionary circle which was disseminating anti-state propaganda in St. Petersburg and Moscow and was put in prison in 1874. He escaped from prison in 1876 and made his way first to Switzerland, then to France, and eventually, in 1886, to England. His best known books are *The Conquest of Bread* (1907) and *Mutual Aid: A factor of evolution* (1909). In the latter work, he argued that there was an inborn tendency in all living things to help others of their own species, and pointed to many examples in the animal world. However, he argued that, as governments grew stronger, the natural human tendency to mutual aid has weakened. He believed that, if the state were to be dismantled, this tendency would reassert itself and people could regulate their lives on the basis of consensus and mutual aid. He returned to Russia after the Bolshevik Revolution and died in the town of Dmitrov, near Moscow.

Notes

1   See, for example, Roger Pielke, Jr., "Should Scientists Rule?", in *The Breakthrough* (7 January 2013), at http://thebreakthrough.org/index.php/voices/roger-pielke-jr/should-scientists-rule/ [accessed on 4 July 2013].

2   As quoted in Elliot H. Polinger, "Saint-Simon, the Utopian Precursor of the League of Nations", in *Journal of the History of Ideas,* Vol. 4, Issue 4 (October 1943), p. 477.

3   Frank E. Manuel and Fritzie P. Manuel, *Utopian Thought in the Western World* (Cambridge, Mass.: The Belknap Press of Harvard University Press, 1979), p. 591.

4   *Ibid.,* p. 593.

5   Henri de Rouvroy de Saint Simon and Barthélemy Prosper Enfantin, *Oeuvres de Saint-Simon et d'Enfantin* (Paris, 1865-78), Vol. 18, p. 148, as quoted in Walter M. Simon, "History for Utopia: Saint-Simon and the Idea of Progress", in *Journal of the History of Ideas,* Vol. 17, Issue 3 (June 1956), p. 317.

6   *Oeuvres de Saint-Simon et d'Enfantin,* Vol. 15, p. 127, as quoted in Simon, "History for Utopia*"*, p. 324.

7   W. Stark, "Saint-Simon as a Realist", in *Journal of Economic History,* Vol. 3, Issue 1 (May 1943), p. 54.

8   W. Stark, "The Realism of Saint-Simon's Spiritual Program", in *Journal of Economic History,* Vol. 5, Issue 1 (May 1945), p. 27.

9   *Oeuvres de Saint-Simon et d'Enfantin*, Vol. 4, p. 187, as quoted in Stark, "The Realism", p. 26.

10 *Oeuvres de Saint-Simon et d'Enfantin*, Vol. 1, p. 238, as quoted in *Ibid.*, p. 25.

11 *Oeuvres de Saint-Simon et d'Enfantin*, Vol. 1, p. 57, and Vol. 3, p. 35, as quoted in *Ibid.*, pp. 26, 28—29.

12 Manuel and Manuel, *Utopian Thought*, p. 596.

13 Concerning Saint-Simon's political ideas, see Ghita Ionescu (ed.), *The political thought of Saint-Simon* (London and New York: Oxford University Press, 1976).

14 Henri Comte de Saint-Simon, *New Christianity*, trans. by Rev. J. E. Smith (London: B. D. Cousins and P. Wilson, 1834), p. 4.

15 *Ibid.*, p. 27.

16 *Ibid.*, p. 45.

17 *Ibid.*, p. 42.

18 As quoted in Manuel and Manuel, *Utopian Thought*, p. 614.

19 *Oeuvres de Saint-Simon...publiés par Olinde Rodrigues*, as quoted in Stark, "Saint-Simon as a Realist", pp. 48—49.

20 Henri de Rouvroy de Saint-Simon, *De la reorganization de la société européene*, ed. Alfred Péreire (Paris, 1925), as quoted in Simon, "History for Utopia", p. 328.

21 Stark, "Saint-Simon as a Realist", pp. 49—50.

22 *Ibid.*, p. 53.

23 *Oeuvres de Saint-Simon et d'Enfantin*, Vol. 4, p. 61, as quoted in Stark, "The Realism", p. 33.

24 As quoted in Polinger, "Saint-Simon, the Utopian Precursor", p. 479.

25 *Oeuvres de Saint-Simon et d'Enfantin*, Vol. 4, p. 45, as quoted in Stark, "The Realism", p. 28.

26 *Ibid.*, p. 32.

27 Claude-Henri Saint-Simon, "Letter from an Inhabitant of Geneva to His Contemporaries" (1803), reprinted from *The Political Thought of Saint-Simon*, edited by G. Ionescu (Oxford: Oxford University Press, 1976) and posted at www.marxists.org/reference/subject/philosophy/works/fr/st-simon.htm [accessed on 8 April 2008].

28 See Hans-.Christoph Schmidt-am-Busch, Ludwig Siep, Hans-Ulrich Thamer, and Norbert Waszek (eds.), *Hegelianismus und Saint-Simonismus* (Paderborn: Mentis, 2007).

29 Michael Allen Gillespie, *Nihilism before Nietzsche* (Chicago: University of Chicago Press, 1995), p. 141.

30 Walter Stewart, *Nietzsche – My Sister and I: A Critical Study* (Bloomington, Ind.: Xlibris Corp., 2007), p. 51.

31 William H. George, "Proudhon and Economic Federalism", in *Journal of Political Economy*, Vol. 30, No. 4 (August 1922), p. 539.

32 David McLellan, *Karl Marx: A Biography*, 4th ed. (Basingstoke: Palgrave, 2006), pp. 21, 170.

33 See Alice M. MacIver, "Saint-Simon and His Influence on Karl Marx", in *Economica,* No. 6 (October 1922), pp. 238—245.

34 Nadia Urbinati, "John Stuart Mill on Androgyny and Ideal Marriage", in *Political Theory,* Vol. 19, No. 4 (November 1991), pp. 634, 637; regarding gender equality, confirmed in Gertrude Himmelfarb, *On Liberty & Liberalism: The Case of John Stuart Mill* (San Francisco: Institute for Contemporary Studies, 1990), 201.

35 Pere Enfantin, as quoted in Bonnie S. Anderson and Judith P. Zinsser, *A History of Their Own: Women in Europe from prehistory to the present,* Vol. 2 (New York: Harper & Row, 1988), p. 377.

36 Editorial in *La femme libre,* as quoted in *Ibid.,* p. 377.

37 Manuel and Manuel, *Utopian Thought,* p. 615.

38 *Ibid.,* p. 628.

39 Regarding the Young Hegelians, see William J. Brazill, *The Young Hegelians* (New Haven, Conn.: Yale University Press, 1970); and David McLellan, *The Young Hegelians and Karl Marx* (London: Macmillan, 1969).

40 Zvi Rosen, "The Radicalism of a Young Hegelian: Bruno Bauer", in *The Review of Politics,* Vol. 33, No. 3 (July 1971), pp. 380, 396.

41 Paul Lawrence Rose, *German Question / Jewish Question: Revolutionary antisemitism in Germany from Kant to Wagner* (Princeton, N.J.: Princeton University Press, 1990), p. 268. For further discussion, see Douglas Moggach, *The philosophy and politics of Bruno Bauer* (Cambridge: Cambridge University Press, 2003).

42 Rose, *German Question / Jewish Question,* p. 270.

43 Ernst Barnikol (1972), as cited in Martin Hundt, "War Bruno Bauer Junghegelianer?", in Klaus M. Kodalle and Tilman Beitz (eds.), *Bruno Bauer (1809-1882). Ein 'Partisan des Weltgeistes'?* (Würzburg: Verlag Königshausen & Neumann GmbH, 2020), pp. 177-178.

44 See Douglas Moggach, "Bruno Bauer", in *Stanford Encyclopedia of Philosophy,* First published 7 March 2002; substantive revision 10 November 2017, at https://plato.stanford.edu/entries/bauer/ [accessed on 22 August 2020], p. 5 of 13.

45 Hundt, "War Bruno Bauer Junghegelianer?", p. 177.

46 Rose, *German Question / Jewish Question,* p. 272.

47 As quoted in *Ibid.,* p. 271.

48 James A. Massey, "The Hegelians, the Pietists, and the Nature of Religion", in *The Journal of Religion,* Vol. 58, No. 2 (April 1978), p. 108.

49 Todd Gooch, "Ludwig Andreas Feuerbach", *Stanford Encyclopedia of Philosophy,* First published 9 December 2013; substantive revision 17 November 2016, at https://plato.stanford.edu/entries/ludwig-feuerbach/ [accessed on 24 August 2020], p. 2 of 23.

50 Jacek Uglik, "Ludwig Feuerbach's conception of the religious alienation of man and Mikhail Bakunin's philosophy of religion" [hereafter, "Feuerbach's conception and Bakunin's philosophy"], in *Studies in East European Thought*, Vol. 62, No. 1 (March 2010), p. 21.

51 Ludwig Feuerbach, *The Essence of Christianity*, 2nd ed., trans. by George Eliot (New York: Harper & Bros., 1957).

52 Marilyn Chapin, Massey, "Censorship and the Language of Feuerbach's 'Essence of Christianity" (1841)", in *The Journal of Religion*, Vol. 65, No. 2 (April 1985), pp. 175, 179, 183-184.

53 James A. Massey, "Feuerbach and Religious Individualism", in *The Journal of Religion*, Vol. 56, No. 4 (October 1976), p. 372.

54 Peter C. Hodgson, "Editor's Introduction: Strauss's Theological Development from 1825 to 1845" to David Friedrich Strauss, *The Life of Jesus Critically Examined*, trans. from the 4th German ed. of 1846 by George Eliot (Philadelphia: Fortress Press, 1972), p. xxiv, as quoted in Wesley Wildman, "David Friedrich Strauss (1808-1874)", in *Boston Collaborative Encyclopedia of Western Theology*, at people.bu.edu/wwildman/bce/strauss.htm [accessed on 24 August 2020], p. 2 of 9.

55 Marilyn Chapin, Massey, "David Friedrich Strauss and His Hegelian Critics", in *The Journal of Religion*, Vol. 57, No. 4 (October 1977), pp. 347-348.

56 James C. Livingston, *Modern Christian Thought: From the Enlightenment to Vatican II* (New York: Macmillan, 1971), p. 174, as quoted in Wildman, "David Friedrich Strauss", p. 2 of 9.

57 Wildman, "David Friedrich Strauss", p. 2 of 9; and Gustav Krüger, "David Friedrich Strauss", in *The American Journal of Theology*, Vol. 4, No. 3 (July 1900), pp. 516-517.

58 Massey, "David Friedrich Strauss and His Hegelian Critics", p. 342.

59 Wildman, "David Friedrich Strauss", p. 3 of 9.

60 See Archibald B. D. Alexander, "Kuno Fischer: An estimate of his life and work", in *The Journal of Philosophy, Psychology and Scientific Methods*, Vol. 5, No. 3 (30 January 1908), pp. 57-64.

61 Martin Buber, "Moses Hess", in *Jewish Social Studies*, Vol. 7, No. 2 (April 1945), pp. 137-148; and Isaiah Berlin, "The Life and Opinions of Moses Hess", chapter in Henry Hardy (ed.), *Against the Current: Essays in the history of ideas* (Princeton, N.J.: Princeton University Press, 2013), pp. 267-316.

62 Max Stirner, *The False Principle of Our Education, or humanism and realism* (New York: Ralph Myles, 1967).

63 See also John Henry Mackay, *Max Stirner: Sein Leben und sein Werk* (Berlin: Schuster & Loeffler, 1898); and R. W. K. Paterson, *The Nihilist Egoist: Max Stirner* (Oxford & London: Oxford University Press, 1971).

64 As quoted in Lawrence S. Stepelevich, "Max Stirner and Ludwig Feuerbach", in *Journal of the History of Ideas*, Vol. 39, No. 3 (July–September 1978), p. 456.
65 Max Stirner, *The Ego and Its Own*, trans. by Steven Byington, ed. by David Leopold (Cambridge: Cambridge University Press, 1995), p. 53.
66 *Ibid.*, p. 175, emphasis as given.
67 *Ibid.*, p. 183.
68 *Ibid.*, pp. 190, 193, emphases as given.
69 Robert C. North makes this argument in *The World That Could Be* (New York: W. W. Norton, 1978).
70 Petr Alekseevich Kropotkin, *Mutual Aid: A factor of evolution* (New York: Knopf, 1909, 1916).
71 George Woodcock, *Anarchism: A History of Libertarian Ideas and Movements* (Harmondsworth: Penguin, 1962), p. 30.
72 William H. Harbold, "Justice in the Thought of Pierre-Joseph Proudhon", in *The Western Political Quarterly*, Vol. 22, No. 4 (December 1869), pp. 723–741, especially p. 723.
73 Pierre-Joseph Proudhon, *What is Property?*, ed. & trans. by Donald R. Kelley and Bonnie G. Smith (Cambridge: Cambridge University Press, 1994), pp. 196–197.
74 *Ibid.*, p. 42.
75 *Ibid.*, p. 61.
76 Frederick M. Watkins, "Proudhon and the Theory of Modern Liberalism", in *The Canadian Journal of Economics and Political Science*, Vol. 13, No. 3 (August 1947), p. 434.
77 Uglik, "Feuerbach's conception and Bakunin's philosophy", pp. 19-20.
78 As quoted in Marshall S. Shatz, "Introduction", to Michael Bakunin, *Statism and Anarchy*, trans. & ed. by Marshall S. Shatz (Cambridge: Cambridge University Press, 1990), p. xiv.
79 M. Bakunin, "Church and State", in George Woodcock (ed.), *The Anarchist Reader* (Glasgow: Fontana/Collins, 1977), p. 82.
80 Bakunin, *Statism and Anarchy*, p. 182.
81 *Ibid.*, p. 198.
82 *Ibid.*, p. 200.
83 Pierre-Joseph Proudhon, "The Old Society – and the New", in Woodcock (ed.), *The Anarchist Reader*, pp. 291–292.
84 *Ibid.*, p. 293.
85 As cited in Agustin Guillamón, *The Friends of Durruti Group: 1937–1939*, trans. from Spanish by Paul Sharkey (Edinburgh & San Francisco: AK Press, 1996), p. 92.

Karl Marx and the Class Struggle

Sabrina Ramet

Summary: Marx viewed history in terms of class struggle. In his time, although he recognized the existence of aristocrats, peasants, and beggars, among others, he believed that the central struggle was between capitalists and the proletariat (the working class). Under capitalism, workers were exploited, and there was no hope that social justice could be realized within a capitalist system. Moreover, as in any system, capitalism had developed an ideological and religious superstructure which legitimated the system of exploitation and reinforced the alienation already resulting from the capitalist system itself. For these reasons, Marx was committed to the cause of promoting revolution and, eventually, to eradicating religion, in the hope of creating a socialist society in which people would live in harmony.

Karl Marx was more than just a political thinker. He was also a trained philosopher, a self-trained economic historian and political economist, a journalist and commentator on current events, and a professional revolutionary. In this chapter, the emphasis is on his revolutionary thought and revolutionary activity, and his economic ideas will be discussed only to the extent necessary to understand his central concern, which was to hasten the overthrow of capitalism.

He abhorred capitalism for at least three reasons. First, he objected to the social, political, and economic inequality associated with the capitalist system. Second, he objected to the exploitation of industrial workers by capitalists (see discussion, below). And third, he believed that the capitalist system, together with its religio-ideological superstructure, fostered *alienation*. Marx inherited the idea of alienation from Hegel, and used the term "to refer to a situation in which our own activities and products take on an independent existence and become hostile powers against us."[1] Marx placed his greatest emphasis on what he called *alienated labor*, referring to the fact that, in a system of wage labor, the worker does not control the terms of his work or own the commodity he produces; he is, accordingly, alienated from both the process and the product. But Marx saw other forms of alienation as well; specifically, he argued that "the social relations of the market and the atomized individuality associated with it are forms of alienation which limit individuality and freedom"[2] (see the discussion of *The German Ideology*, below). And, from Ludwig Feuerbach, he took over the idea that religion too fostered alienation, by referring the potential for good to God's grace; as Christian religion taught, one cannot be a good person except through the grace of God. Marx believed that was false and that it promoted alienation. Worse yet, "[r]eligion reconciles us to an alienated life and makes it *seem* tolerable to us; it offers us illusory meaning for a mode of life which, without this illusion, would be experienced directly for what it is: unredeemed meaninglessness."[3] Accordingly, he rejected (Christian) religion as detrimental to the interests of the working class. As Amy Wendling has noted, Marx continued to be preoccupied with the problem of alienation throughout his life, arguing in his later works that the introduction of machinery and the assembly line into the production process only intensified alienation by rendering workers' daily routine "dull and repetitive".[4] Alienation figured also as a central organizing theme in his magnum opus, *Capital*, though in that context he often used the term "machine" as code for *alienation*.[5]

But, in spite of his concern about alienation, Marx was committed to a collectivist view of politics, in which the cause to be championed was not that of individual rights but, rather, that of the working class. Moreover, his embrace of the concept of the dictatorship of the proletariat and the associated concept of class warfare suggest a despair, even renunciation, of any notion of compromise with those classes he identified as oppressors. Such an approach did not lend itself to democratic politics.

Revolutionary Thought and Politics, 1837-1848

Marx was born in Trier in 1818, earned his doctorate at the University of Jena in 1841 (with a dissertation on the ancient Greek philosophers Democritus, who developed an atomic theory of the universe, and Epicurus, who resolved good and evil into pleasure and pain). He came of age, philosophically, in the course of the years 1843-1846. It was also during those years that he met Friedrich Engels (1820-1895), a young man from Wuppertal, beginning what proved to be a lifelong friendship and one of the most celebrated literary collaborations in history. Their first collaboration, entitled *The Holy Family, or Critique of Critical Critique*, published in 1845, was an unbridled attack on Marx's erstwhile friend, Bruno Bauer. Marx was an itinerant revolutionary – though his repeated moves were not always by choice. He moved from Prussia to Paris in October 1843, only to be expelled from France in January 1845, because of his revolutionary activity. Thereupon, he took refuge in Brussels, but he was, in turn, expelled from Belgium in early March 1848. In the meantime, the situation in France had changed (temporarily), and he returned to Paris, only to return to Prussia the following month. Moving back to Paris for the third time, Marx was once again expelled from France, in July 1849. By August 1849, Marx had crossed the English channel and he and his family moved into a flat in Chelsea. In April 1850, they were expelled from their Chelsea flat, and took up residence elsewhere in London.

For the last four decades of Marx's life, his thought formed a largely coherent whole, with a clear focus on the goals of liberating the working class, ending exploitation, and overcoming alienation. His central values were self-actualization, human freedom, equality, adequate living conditions for all, fair wages, and non-exploitative work conditions. During these decades, inconsistencies were, for the most part, restricted to secondary matters, such as whether or not to support the cause of Polish independence[6] (which was, in any event, conditioned by considerations of whether Polish independence would further or obstruct the cause of social and political revolution) and whether there were any prospects for revolution in Russia[7] (with Marx originally pessimistic but later coming to believe that there were such prospects in Russia's case). The preceding 25 years were, however, years of intellectual growth, in which Marx worked his way first through the writings of Kant and Fichte, then through Schelling and Hegel, and finally through Feuerbach, before defining his own position in the course of 1844-1846.[8] Kant and Fichte remained important for Marx only until he turned 19; then, during his first year at the University of Berlin (1837), he converted to Hegel, who had criticized Kant for idealism. From Hegel he assimilated the *dialectic* – defined as the theory of the union of opposites, in which in the course of conflict a new synthesis or reality emerges, which merges (or "sublates", in Hegel's terminology) aspects of the two original opposites. *Dialectical materialism*, thus, is an approach to history which is sensitive to change and which understands change as occurring through challenge and conflict between opposing forces or principles, while holding that material conditions and the mode of economic organization are the most important, but by no means the exclusive, driving force for historical change.[9] By 1843, he had embraced Feuerbach, having come to see Hegel too as an idealist, only to reject Feuerbach as well as an idealist by 1845.[10] By "idealist" he meant someone immersed in the world of ideas and not addressing issues affecting working people. Even so, he continued to admire Feuerbach's analysis of religion as fostering self-alienation, but criticized him for his exclusive focus on religion, as if breaking with religion could ever be sufficient to overcome alienation. Feuerbach had restricted himself to interpreting the world, but had offered no program for change. In response, and signalling his transcendence of Feuerbach, he wrote: "...philosophers have only *interpreted* the world, in various ways; the point, however, is to *change* it."[11]

There are two works which mark the maturation of Marx's thought: his *Economic and Philosophic Manuscripts* of 1844 (sometimes called the 'Paris Manuscripts'), and *The German Ideology*, written together with Friedrich Engels, during the years 1845-46. In the former work, Marx credited Hegel with having achieved a breakthrough, but it was only a limited breakthrough, as far as Marx was concerned: "...the entity which Hegel supersedes in philosophy is...not real religion, the real state, or real nature, but religion itself already as an object of knowledge, i.e., dogmatics."[12] Or, as David McLellan has put it, Marx had come to the conclusion that Hegel took account "only...of man's mental activities – that is, of his ideas – and that these, though important, were by themselves insufficient to explain social and cultural change."[13] As already mentioned, he continued to view alienation as a central problem, but he concluded that the economic sphere was the locus of the problem and, more specifically, that private property – including, of course, and perhaps fundamentally private ownership of the means of production – was both the source and the consequence of alienated labor.[14] If religion may be viewed as part of the superstructure legitimating capitalism (see Box 7.1), then it is not enough to combat only the vehicle of legitimation, let alone to make it the primary focus of attention (as Marx believed Feuerbach did); rather, the fight had to be carried over into the economic realm.[15]

At the time he wrote the *Economic and Philosophic Manuscripts*, Marx's orientation was normatively driven and normatively justified. Then, at the end of 1844, Max Stirner's *The Ego and His Own* was published. As woolly as Stirner's blanket nihilism was, he presented a challenge which Marx felt he could not ignore, viz., the argument that *nothing* can be normatively justified. Marx, who had met Engels for the first time in November 1842 and who forged a lasting friendship with him in the course of 10 days in August 1844, now turned to a refutation of the by-now-unemployed nihilist. Engels joined Marx in composing the lengthy manuscript which bears the title, *The German Ideology,* and the seriousness with which they viewed Stirner's challenge may be discerned in the fact that the portion of *German Ideology* devoted to Stirner – which makes up well over half of the book – is by itself quite a bit longer than Stirner's book. Curiously, rather than confronting Stirner's nihilism head-on, they attacked an inversion of his argument, presenting "Saint Max" as a holy man, as if he had been seeking to defend the very institutions which he had, in fact, been mocking. *The German Ideology*'s importance does not lie, however, in its sarcastic treatment of Stirner, let alone in the attendant dismissal of "Saint Bruno" (Bauer) and the rest of the Young Hegelians (with a marked exemption for Feuerbach), but rather in its development of a distinct political vision. For Marx and Engels,

> [t]he ideas of the ruling class are in every epoch the ruling ideas...The class which has the means of material production at its disposal, consequently also controls the means of mental production, so that the ideas of those who lack the means of mental production are on the whole subject to it. The ruling ideas are nothing more than the ideal expression of the dominant material relations.[16]

Thus, for example, the ideology of individualism serves to undercut the common interest which should unite the working class, and, thereby, to underpin the capitalist system. Or again, in their view, nationalism figured as an essential component in the armoury of the bourgeois state, deluding German workers, for example, into thinking that they shared more important interests with German junkers than with the working class in France or England.[17] Their understanding of the source of values extended also to morality. Marx and Engels had no use for Natural Law or, for that matter, for Benthamite-style utilitarianism. In their view, there was no such thing as a universal, timeless morality; rather, there were only various moralities, developed and adapted to meet the needs of the ruling class in each epoch and in each country or region. In their view, "morality has always been class morality," which is to say, the morality of the ruling class in each historical epoch.[18]

Citizenship and morality.

In the nineteenth century, the norms of the noble and aristocratic class were being challenged by the rising commercial classes, centered in the cities. Historically, the term *bourgeois* had referred to those free people living within the enclosed space of the medieval French *bourg,* who were obliged to perform certain services for the resident nobility. They were distinguished also from serfs. In the *ancien régime,* members of the noble class were entitled to bear arms, a right denied to members of the bourgeoisie, even though the latter enjoyed other rights denied to serfs.[19] The term was the closest equivalent, prior to 1789, to the term *citizen.* In revolutionary France, the term *citoyen* was introduced to designate a citizen, and the term *bourgeois* started to take on pejorative overtones.[20] Interestingly, in German, the word *Bürger* is the standard term for a citizen, while the word *Bürgerlich* is given as the translation of the adjective *bourgeois.*

For Marx and Engels, the moral ideas of any society reflect the interests of the ruling class as well as changes in the division of labor and technological advances.[21] By the 1840s, bourgeois morality, to use the Marxist term, was ascendant and the old morality of the nobility and the aristocracy was only faintly visible. Of course, in referring to bourgeois morality, Marx (and Engels) were scarcely touting it as providing a universal standard; nor did they make such a claim on behalf of proletarian (communist) morality. For them, bourgeois morality was characterized by quiescence, by seeking one's own advantage within the system, by either behaving legally or seeking to appear to be behaving in accordance with the law, and by abjuring revolution. Bourgeois morality was the morality of people who just wanted to fit in, to work within or at least appear to be working within the society's dominant normative framework. The bourgeois, thus, was a conformist.

Kant and Hegel, in reflecting on the moral challenges posed by revolutionary currents in Europe, contrasted the morality of the citizen (with duties to the functioning state) with the moral codes applicable to the individual (the categorical imperative for Kant, the duties to family and community for Hegel). By contrast, for Marx, what the state calls morality is merely the behavioral code which is useful for the ruling class. In any event, Marx and Engels did not refer to the duties of citizens qua citizens. Morality, for them, was rather relative to class and hence, as the class nature of society changes, aspects of the dominant moral code likewise change.

The Communist Manifesto.

Marx championed freedom in work (among other things) in his *Economic and Philosophic Manuscripts* and, with Engels, in *The German Ideology*. For them, freedom should be understood to involve a person's control over his or her life,[22] thus revealing an implicit normative aspect. As George Brenkert has put it, "In the full and rich sense which they [Marx and Engels] attribute to [the] 'freedom' of man fully and consciously controlling his activities and nature, it *is* a moral term." Freedom consists in living how one "ought to live and act."[23] Thus, they dismissed the bourgeois concept of freedom, which they said amounted to no more than "free trade, free selling and [free] buying."[24] Bourgeois freedom was freedom for the bourgeoisie, not for the proletariat, and accordingly, injustice and class struggle were built into the capitalist system. Defining themselves as *communists*, they declared their commitment to seek to overthrow the capitalist system, emancipate the proletariat (the working class), and abolish the class system. In the *Communist Manifesto* of 1848, they credited Henri de Saint-Simon, Charles Fourier, and Robert Owen with having offered "most valuable" insights and "practical measures…such as the abolition of the distinction between town and country, of the family, of the carrying on of industries for the account [and profit] of private individuals, and of the wage system."[25] In the accompanying 10-point program, they demanded:

1. Abolition of property in land…
2. A heavy progressive or graduated income tax.
3. Abolition of all right of inheritance.
4. Confiscation of the property of all emigrants and rebels.
5. Centralization of credit in the hands of the state…
6. Centralization of the means of communication and transport in the hands of the state.
7. Extension of factories and instruments of production owned by the state: the bringing into cultivation of wastelands, and the improvement of the soil generally in accordance with a common plan.
8. Equal liability of all to labor. Establishment of industrial armies, especially for agriculture.

9. Combination of agriculture with manufacturing industries; gradual abolition of the distinction between town and country, by a more equable distribution of the population over the country.
10. Free education for all children in public schools. Abolition of children's factory labor in its present form.[26]

At that point, a welfare state would come into being, giving way, over time, to a communist system which would operate according to the principle, "From each according to his ability, to each according to his needs!"[27]

Communist society would also, Marx and Engels claimed, overcome the division of labor, under which "...each man has a particular, exclusive sphere of activity, which is forced upon him and from which he cannot escape. He is a hunter, a fisherman, a shepherd, or a critical critic, and must remain so if he does not want to lose his means of livelihood."[28] But, they continued in a celebrated passage,

> ...in communist society, where nobody has one exclusive sphere of activity but each can become accomplished in any branch he wishes, society regulates the general production and thus makes it possible for me to do one thing today and another tomorrow, to hunt in the morning, fish in the afternoon, rear cattle in the evening, criticise after dinner, just as I have a mind, without ever becoming [a] hunter, fisherman, shepherd or critic.[29]

Shorn of the rhetorical and utopian flourishes, the point here is that communism makes possible the realization of true human freedom.

In the short run, in place of the bourgeois concept of freedom noted above, Marx contended that "Freedom consists in converting the state from an organ superimposed upon society into one completely subordinate to it."[30] But, for both Marx and Engels, the state could be understood only as an engine for the suppression of subordinate classes in the interest of the ruling class. Thus, as long as there would be remnants of the defeated bourgeoisie, the ruling working class would need a state apparatus. It seemed to follow, as Engels put it, that "As soon as there is no longer any social class to be held in subjection and as soon as class rule is removed, a state is no longer necessary" and thus simply withers away.[31] "State interference in social relations becomes, in one domain after another, superfluous," Engels explained, "and then dies out of itself; the government of persons is replaced by the administration of things, and by the conduct of processes of production. The state is not 'abolished'. It dies out."[32]

The question then was how to bring about this revolutionary transformation. From the very beginning, Marx and Engels stressed the need for organization and, against counterarguments from the Russian anarchist Bakunin, also the need for revolutionary leadership. Marx developed a theory of history (see Box 7.2), which highlighted class struggle and suggested that revolution and the eventual victory of socialism were inevitable. However, he was also convinced that revolutionary work and political organization could accelerate history, and bring about revolution, and hence socialism, sooner rather than later. The involvement of Marx and his wife Jenny, as founding members of the German Workers' Educational Association in 1839, bears witness to this belief (and came at a time when Marx still counted himself as one of Hegel's disciples!). Later, in the *Communist Manifesto*, Marx and Engels called explicitly for the revolutionary overthrow of the bourgeois state.

Revolutionary Thought and Politics, after 1848

In 1864, in his "Address to the Working Classes", Marx declared that "the lords of land and the lords of capital will always use their political privileges for the defence and perpetuation of their economical monopolies...[To] conquer political power has therefore become the great duty of the working class."[33] The Address was prepared for the International Working Men's Association – later known as the 'First International' – which was formed by a group of trade unionists in 1864 and which Marx joined that same year. Although not the formal president of the International (until 1872), Marx soon became its dominant figure. He would prepare the program for the London delegates attending the Geneva Congress in 1866 and stressed, therein, the need to exact reforms within the existing bourgeois state frameworks, and highlighted that the first stage could only involve securing the passage of "general laws, enforced by the power of the [bourgeois] state."[34] This was a dramatic retreat from his overt espousal, during the years 1847-48, of revolutionary action, but it was a tactical move, reflecting Marx's assessment of what was possible in the wake of the failure of the continent-wide revolutions of 1848. He added that, in working within the framework of the bourgeois state to exact reforms, "the working class[es] do not fortify government power. On the contrary, *they transform that power, now used against them, into their own agency.*"[35]

In 1871, Marx wrote *Civil War in France*, reflecting on the experiences of the Paris Commune and its effort to break completely with the "ready-made state machinery". In this context, Marx reversed himself and now warned that "...the working class cannot simply lay hold of the ready-made state machinery, and wield it for its own purposes."[36] On the contrary, the bourgeois state apparatus would have to be abolished, and replaced by a proletarian state apparatus. As Marx would explain in "Critique of the Gotha Program" (1875), "Between capitalist and communist society lies the period of the revolutionary transformation of the one into the other. There corresponds to this also a political transition period in which the state can be nothing but the revolutionary dictatorship of the proletariat."[37] This dictatorship of the proletariat would complete the suppression of "bourgeois remnants" and assorted reactionaries and begin the transformation of society. Eventually, as already noted (and presumably only once the state had withered away) the society would operate according to the aforementioned principle, "from each according to his ability, to each according to his need." However, in the initial phase of transformation, the operative principle would be "from each according to his ability, to each according to his contribution." Furthermore, in the early phase of building communism, unequal individual talents and productivity would therefore be rewarded, resulting in a right to unequal treatment for some.[38] This inequality would prevail, however, only in the transition phase, and the state which would "wither away" was not the *bourgeois* state, which had to be demolished as soon as practical, but the *proletarian* state, the dictatorship of the proletariat.

Marx and Engels lived in a time of rising nationalism, which mobilized hatreds and fears against entire peoples. It was also a time when writers such as Wollstonecraft and Mill had begun to underline the injustice done to women in bourgeois society. Marx and Engels took these problems seriously, but argued that a socialist revolution would not only begin the process of granting women full equality in society and political life, but also demobilize national hatreds, promoting proletarian internationalism in their stead. As for religion – yet another source of problems in their view – this would gradually wither away under socialism. Hence, it was not necessary to organize to fight specifically gender inequality; indeed, this might even be counterproductive, by diverting revolutionary resources away from the struggle for socialism.

The Civil War in France, in which Marx summarized the lessons he had learned from studying the Paris Commune and adapted to his revolutionary theory, sold 3,000 copies within two weeks. The book induced fear and consternation in various European capitals, including London, Paris, and Madrid, where the legally constituted International was now viewed as a conspiratorial threat.[39] Overnight, Marx came to be known as the "red terrorist Doctor", which immediately made the International seem more of a threat than it had seemed prior to the appearance of the book.

Meanwhile, Mikhail Bakunin, who had joined the International in 1868, had been trying to steer it in an anarchist direction and the resulting rivalry between Marx and Bakunin was undermining efforts to achieve anything like consensus within that organization. The International held Congresses in 1866 (Geneva), 1867 (Lausanne), 1868 (Brussels), 1869 (Basel), and 1872 (The Hague). But the large influx of new members during the 1860s involved mainly followers of Bakunin, who had large numbers of supporters, among other places, in Switzerland.[40] Bakunin tried his best to bring the 1872 Congress back to Geneva, but Marx managed to have it held in The Hague; in fact, Marx had skipped previous Congresses – exerting his influence through his supporters and through documents he prepared – but attended the Congress in The Hague, which Bakunin skipped. In his speech at that Congress, Marx reiterated his original and lately reaffirmed doctrine for the revolutionary abolition of the bourgeois state, urging that the workers "…must overthrow the old political system sustaining the old institutions. If they fail to do this, they will suffer the fate of the early Christians, who neglected to overthrow the old system and who, for that reason, never had a kingdom of this world."[41]

It was only now, with the International on the eve of irrelevance, that Marx was elected its president (by a vote of 32 to six, with 16 abstentions).[42] After Marx's election was announced, Engels rose to propose that the seat of the International's General Council (in effect, its executive committee) be moved to New York. Everyone in the hall knew that this would sound the death knell for the International, but Marx and Engels had decided that the International had become too dysfunctional to be useful and wanted to marginalize it, if not kill it off. They had their way and the measure passed (with 26 votes in favor, 23 opposed, and six abstentions). But before breaking up, the delegates to the Congress took one final vote, expelling Bakunin from the ranks of the organization.[43] The International was now only a limp relic of its former self and dissolved itself in 1876.

Das Kapital (1867) and Marx's Last years, 1872-1883

Marx started writing *Capital* shortly after finishing work on the *Economic and Philosophic Manuscripts* and, as early as 1845, claimed that he was nearly finished with the writing of what would come to be seen as his magnum opus.[44] He was dogged by bouts of illness during the 1850s, which were possibly also the most difficult years of his life financially. He set aside the manuscript to work on *Contribution to the Critique of Political Economy*, which he completed in January 1859. Then, instead of returning to work on *Capital*, he entered into a largely meaningless polemical exchange with Karl Vogt, a professor at the University of Bern. But by 1860, he was once more back in the reading room of the British Museum, where he had done much of his previous research. In the years 1861-1863, he took more than 1,500 pages of notes and jottings. In March 1864, having received a small inheritance from his mother, Karl Marx moved, with his family, into a spacious mansion with a large garden, with a separate room for each of his daughters; they might not have been able to afford it, but for a second windfall when, on 9 May 1864, Wilhelm 'Lupus' Wolff died, leaving Marx £820.[45] The Marxes now redecorated the house, bought an assortment of pets for their children, and took a three-week vacation in Ramsgate.

Marx's research included reading the works of classic economists Adam Smith (1723-1790) and David Ricardo (1772-1823), as well as Pierre Le Pesant, sieur de Boisguillebert (1646-1714), and François Quesnay (1694-1774). Of these, Ricardo had perhaps the greatest influence on Marx, contributing to shaping Marx's theory of political economy; in particular, Ricardo had already described class relations as adversarial and had employed a modified version of the labor theory of value.[46] Marx criticized Smith for believing that work was "*necessarily* an imposition"[47] and took Ricardo to task for having accepted certain allegedly faulty conclusions offered by Smith. In spite of his criticism, however, Marx was impressed by the works of Smith and Ricardo, but it was in the writings of the Left-Ricardian, Thomas Hodgskin, that he encountered the labor theory of value in its pure form, viz., the notion that the value attached to any commodity derives entirely and solely from the labor put into its production.[48] "Orthodox Marxism", fashioned in the early years after Marx's death and later by Vladimir Lenin, the Russian revolutionary, had Marx agreeing with Hodgskin; but this is a distortion of Marx's thought, which was more subtle.[49] In fact, in *Critique of the Gotha Program*, Marx wrote that "Labor is not the source of all wealth [or value]. Nature is just as much the source of use values."[50] More than two decades after starting work on the manuscript, Marx finished volume 1 of *Das Kapital* on 2 April 1867 and received the proofs on 5 May 1867, his 49th birthday. Wheen has described *Das Kapital* as "a vast Gothic novel whose heroes are enslaved and consumed by the monster they created."[51] In any event, the book established Marx's reputation as a major thinker.

Marx's argument in *Capital* was that the wealthy in society had become so through "conquest, enslavement, robbery, murder, [and] briefly force"[52] and that this process of "primitive accumulation" had despoiled workers of the property by which they could work and live independently, thus reducing them to slaves, even chattels, of the capitalists. Marx believed that developments associated with the Reformation, such as the suppression of the monasteries, accelerated the process of "expropriation of the people".[53] The establishment of overseas colonies in India, the East Indies, Africa, and the Americas also figured prominently in the consolidation of capitalism, with the "discovery of gold and silver in America... [and] the beginning of the conquest and looting of the East Indies" contributing to "the rosy dawn of the era of capitalist production."[54]

At first, Marx recounted, small entrepreneurs were able to operate alongside their wealthier counterparts. But the greed of the wealthier strata – and greed figures as an important explanatory variable in Marx's analysis – came to threaten the small businesses. In time, the system of small enterprises was

> ...annihilated. Its annihilation, the transformation of the individualised and scattered means of production into socially concentrated ones, of the pigmy property of the many into the huge property of the few, the expropriation of the great mass of people from the soil, from the means of subsistence, and from the means of labour, this fearful and painful expropriation of the mass of the people forms the prelude to the history of capital...The expropriation of the immediate producers was accomplished with merciless Vandalism, and under the stimulus of passions the most infamous, the most sordid, the pettiest, the most nearly odious. Self-earned private property, that is based, so to say, on the fusing together of the isolated, independent labouring-individual with the conditions of his labour, is supplanted by capitalistic private property, which rests on exploitation of the nominally free labour of others, i.e., on wage labour.[55]

It is at this point that Marx's theory of surplus value comes in. Marx held that products were sold at their real value and that the value of any product derived from "the quantity of labour necessary for its production in a given state of society, under certain social average conditions of production, with a given social average intensity, and average skill of the labour employed."[56] If then, the laborer were paid for the value of his work, there would be no profit for the capitalist. Given the assumption that products would be sold at their real value,[57] the only way for the capitalist to make a profit would be to pay the workers *less* that the value of their work; the difference between what the workers are paid and the price of the commodities they produce is what Marx called surplus value. In Marx's view, thus, exploitation was built into the capitalist system.

But there was a way out, a path already sketched in the *Communist Manifesto*. And now, in *Capital*, in a memorable passage, Marx wrote:

> Along with the constantly diminishing number of the magnates of capital, who usurp and monopolise all advantages of this process of transformation, grows the mass of misery, oppression, slavery, degradation, exploitation; but with this too grows the revolt of the working-class, a class always increasing in numbers, and disciplined, united, organised by the very mechanism of the process of capitalist production itself. The monopoly of capital becomes a fetter upon the mode of production, which has sprung up and flourished along with, and under it. Centralisation of the means of production and [the] socialisation of labour at last reach a point where they become incompatible with their capitalist integument. Thus [this] integument is burst asunder. The [death] knell of capitalist private property sounds. The expropriators are expropriated.[58]

It took four years before sales of *Das Kapital*, volume 1, crossed the 1,000 mark and many readers found the early chapters impenetrable. But, with the passage of time, both its reputation and its influence grew. The first translation into a foreign language was the Russian translation, which appeared in 1872; the Russian edition was quickly sold out.[59]

Marx did not live long enough to see volumes 2 and 3 of *Capital* published. In his last years, Marx was in declining health, as years of poor nourishment caught up with him, resulting in the spread of painful carbuncles all over his body. He ignored his physician's advice to get regular physical exercise and to cut back on his working hours, and failed to get sufficient sleep.[60] His wife too was in poor health, passing away on 2 December 1881. Marx himself died on 14 March 1883 and was buried three days later in Highgate cemetery. Marx had left his notes and manuscripts in Engels' hands; his devoted friend, who had helped him so often in the past, now prioritized the collation, editing, and organization of those manuscripts. Engels' commitment bore fruit in July 1885, with the publication in Germany of volume 2 of *Das Kapital;* volume 3 followed in November 1894.

Marx's Importance

Few political writers have had as much impact on the course of history as Karl Marx. Just seventy years after his death there were self-professed Marxist systems functioning in at least 12 states, and the number would increase subsequently until it reached a peak of 21 communist states in the early 1980s. Then came the big political crash of 1989-90, when most of these erstwhile Marxist systems committed themselves to new political directions (variously liberal-democracy, nationalist pseudo-democracy, hybrid state-capitalism/free enterprise), and after 2010 to illiberal authoritarianism.[61]

Few, if any, scholars believe that Marx's political progeny were actually consistent with Marx's thinking, although a few scholars still make exceptions for Lenin and Trotsky. But where Marx had talked of the working class taking and exercising power, even if only for a transition period through the agency of a "dictatorship", one looks in vain for any suggestion on his part that the dictatorship by a single individual or clique, such as practised, among others, by Josif Stalin, Mao Zedong, Fidel Castro, Kim il Sung, Nicolae Ceaușescu, or Enver Hoxha, might be in any way positive. It is widely understood that Marx's thought contained a number of unresolved tensions, e.g., between his *determinism* (expressed in his confidence that history was inexorably moving toward proletarian democracy automatically, as it were) and his *voluntarism* (expressed in his conviction that it was necessary to organize and fight to bring about this inevitable future). This tension between determinism and voluntarism would later be reflected in frictions between Soviet determinists (Nikolai Bukharin and Mikhail Tomsky) and voluntarists (Grigorii Zinoviev and Evgenii Kamenev); the former, inspired by their confidence that history could move only in one direction, advocated a moderate line, including the toleration of private agriculture and a certain amount of free enterprise; the latter, by contrast, insisted that the Soviet state assume responsibility for propelling history forward by suppressing free enterprise altogether and instituting forced agricultural collectivization.

But in terms of addressing the question as to the extent to which Marxist-Leninist systems of the twentieth century could be said to be true to Marx, one can begin by noting that:

1. Marx called "not [for] the abolition of property generally but [for] the abolition of bourgeois property," i.e., the appropriated economic "power to subjugate the labor of others by means of such appropriation."[62]

2. Marx specifically rejected the notion of state-run education, calling instead for the state to establish minimal requirements in education and to appoint inspectors to enforce adherence to these standards.[63]

3. While calling for a revolutionary dictatorship of the proletariat to effect the transition from "bourgeois democracy" to a "socialist" regime, which would in turn undertake the construction of communism, Marx envisaged communism as a system in which the administrative and political functions would be "completely subordinate" to society, rather than vice versa.[64]

Box 7.1

Marx on religion

Marx viewed religion as a mechanism for legitimating and supporting a particular socio-political order and, accordingly, was convinced that, when the political order changes, so too does its accompanying religious superstructure. In capitalist society, he argued, religion supports exploitation and social injustice, by – among other things – deferring believers' hopes for justice to divine judgment in the 'afterlife'. Thus, for him – as he put it in *Contribution to the Critique of Hegel's Philosophy of Right* – religion was "the sigh of the oppressed creature" and "the opium of the people." For Marx, religious doctrines were human concoctions, which not only sustained human injustice but also reinforced alienation. Hence, Marx was convinced that only an atheist could be reliably committed to the socialist cause, which is to say to realizing justice on earth. But the complete disappearance of religion can occur only after the victory of communism.

Box 7.2

Marx's theory of history

Marx developed a theory of history, outlining the evolution of societies through certain stages. As the story is usually told, he believed that societies began with primitive communism, then evolved into slave-holding societies, which in turn gave rise to feudalism. When feudalism had exhausted its possibilities, capitalism gradually developed and, once reaching an advanced stage – amid sharpening class conflict and class struggle – would be overthrown through revolution by the communists, who would establish a dictatorship of the proletariat, building socialism, which would eventually ripen into communism. But this standard account is rigid, and Marx was not prepared to lock himself into a rigid scheme. On the contrary, he allowed that Great Britain might make the passage from capitalism to socialism *without* a revolution, evolving gradually. He also came to the conclusion that Russia might be able to skip the stage of advanced capitalism and move directly from a semi-feudal/incipient capitalist stage to revolution and the building of socialism. Moreover, Marx followed the course of the American Civil War with great interest and was keenly aware that the system of slavery in the American South had been introduced after capitalism was already in place. History was, for him, the history of the class struggle, but not all societies would march in identical formation to the identical outcome.

Notes

1   Sean Sayers, *Marx and Alienation: Essays on Hegelian themes* (Basingstoke: Palgrave Macmillan, 2011), p. 5.
2   *Ibid.*, p. 58.
3   Allen W. Wood, *Karl Marx*, 2nd ed. (New York & Abingdon: Routledge, 2004), pp. 13-14 (commas added).
4   Amy Wendling, *Karl Marx on Technology and Alienation* (Basingstoke: Palgrave Macmillan, 2009; paperback ed., 2011), pp. 1, 2.

5   *Ibid.*, pp. 4, 205. See also Marx's discussion of alienation in *Grundrisse: Foundations of the Critique of Political Economy*, trans. from German by Martin Nicolau (London: Penguin Books, 1993), pp. 452-455, 470-471, 515, and passim.

6   H. Malcolm MacDonald, "Marx, Engels, and the Polish National Movement", in *Journal of Modern History*, Vol. 13, No. 3 (September 1941), pp. 324-329.

7   David McLellan, *Karl Marx: A Biography*, 4th ed. (Basingstoke: Palgrave Macmillan, 2006), p. 410.

8   *Ibid.*, p. 24.

9   See Engels' letters as extracted in Andrew G. Walder, "Marxism, Maoism, and Social Change", in *Modern China*, Vol. 3, No. 1 (January 1977), pp. 110-112, 114.

10   J. E. Seigel, "Marx's Early Development: Vocation, Rebellion, and Realism", in *Journal of Interdisciplinary History*, Vol. 3, No. 3 (Winter 1973), pp. 498, 500—501, 507.

11   Karl Marx, "Theses on Feuerbach", in Lewis S. Feuer (ed.), *Karl Marx & Friedrich Engels: Basic Writings on Politics and Philosophy* [hereafter, *Basic Writings*] (Garden City, N.Y.: Anchor Books, 1959), Thesis XI, p. 245 (emphasis in the original).

12   Marx, *Economic and Philosophic Manuscripts*, in Karl Marx and Friedrich Engels, *Collected Works, Vol. 3: 1843-1844* (New York: International Publishers, 1975), p. 341 (emphases removed).

13   McLellan, *Karl Marx*, p. 111.

14   Marx, *Economic and Philosophic Manuscripts*, p. 279.

15   See *Ibid.*, pp. 296-297, 341.

16   Karl Marx and Friedrich Engels, *The German Ideology*, 3rd rev. ed. (Moscow: Progress Publishers, 1976), p. 67.

17   See Joseph A. Petrus, "Marx and Engels on the National Question", in *Journal of Politics*, Vol. 33, No. 3 (August 1971), pp. 804-805.

18   Friedrich Engels, "On Morality" (extract from *Anti-Dühring)*, in Robert C. Tucker (ed.), *The Marx-Engels Reader* (New York: W. W. Norton, 1972), p. 667.

19   Paul E. Corcoran, "The Bourgeois and Other Villains", in *Journal of the History of Ideas*, Vol. 38, No. 3 (July-September 1977), p. 479.

20   *Ibid.*, pp. 482, 484.

21   For further discussion of the ideas of Marx and Engels as regards morality, see George G. Brenkert, "Marx, Engels, and the Relativity of Morals", in *Studies in Soviet Thought*, Vol. 17, No. 3 (October 1977), pp. 201-224, especially pp. 202, 204, 206, and 216.

22   *Ibid.*, p. 213.

23   *Ibid.*, p. 213 (Brenkert's emphasis).

24 Karl Marx and Friedrich Engels, "Manifesto of the Communist Party" (1848), in Feuer (ed.), *Basic Writings*, p. 22.

25 *Ibid.*, p. 38.

26 *Ibid.*, pp. 28-29.

27 Marx, "Critique of the Gotha Program" (written in 1875), in Feuer (ed.), *Basic Writings*, p. 119.

28 Marx and Engels, *German Ideology*, p. 53.

29 *Ibid.*

30 Marx, "Critique of the Gotha Program", p. 126.

31 Engels, as quoted in Nicholas Churchich, *Marxism and Alienation* (Rutherford, N.J. & London: Fairleigh Dickinson University Press & Associated University Press, 1990), p. 272.

32 Friedrich Engels, *Socialism: Utopian and Scientific* (1880), in Feuer (ed.), *Basic Writings*, p. 106 (emphasis removed).

33 As quoted in Paul Thomas, *Karl Marx and the Anarchists* (Abingdon & New York: Routledge, 1980; this edition, 2010; paperback, 2012), p. 262.

34 As quoted in *Ibid.*, p. 273 (emphasis removed).

35 As quoted in Ibid. (my emphasis).

36 Karl Marx, *The Civil War in France* (1871), in Karl Marx, *Later Political Writings*, ed. & trans. by Terrell Carver (Cambridge: Cambridge University Press, 1996), Section III, p. 181.

37 Marx, "Critique of the Gotha Program", p. 127 (emphasis removed).

38 *Ibid.*, pp. 118-119.

39 Francis Wheen, *Karl Marx* (London: Fourth Estate, 1999; paperback ed., 2000), pp. 331-333.

40 Thomas, *Karl Marx and the Anarchists* pp. 316, 319.

41 As quoted in *Ibid.*, pp. 343-344.

42 Wheen, *Karl Marx*, p. 343.

43 *Ibid.*, pp. 343-344, 347.

44 *Ibid.*, p. 229.

45 *Ibid.*, pp. 266-267.

46 See, inter alia, David Ricardo, *On the principles of political economy & taxation*, 2nd ed. (London: John Murray, 1819); and *The works of David Ricardo, Esq.*, collated by J. R. McCulloch (London: John Murray, 1846).

47 McLellan, *Karl Marx*, p. 281 (my emphasis).

48 Norman Levine, "*Das Kapital:* A Critique of the Labor Theory of Value"; in *Critique: Journal of Socialist Theory*, Vol. 36, No. 1 (April 2008), pp. 91-92.

49 *Ibid.*, pp. 105-106.

50 Marx, "Critique of the Gotha Program", p. 112 (emphases removed).

51 Wheen, *Karl Marx*, p. 305.
52 Karl Marx, *Capital*, A new abridgement, ed. by David McLellan (Oxford & New York: Oxford University Press, 2008), chap. 26, p. 364.
53 See *Ibid.,* chap. 27, esp. p. 367.
54 *Ibid.,* chap. 31, p. 376.
55 *Ibid.,* chap. 32, pp. 378-379.
56 Marx, *Value, Price and Profit* (1865), ed. by Eleanor Marx Aveling (New York: International Publishers, 1935), chap. 6, p. 33 (emphasis removed).
57 *Ibid.,* chap. 6, p. 36.
58 Marx, *Capital,* chap. 32, pp. 379-380.
59 Ewa Borowska, "Marx and Russia", in *Studies in East European Thought,* Vol. 54, No. 1-2 (March 2002), p. 93.
60 Jerrold Seigel, *Marx's Fate: The Shape of a Life* (University Park: The Pennsylvania State University Press, 1978; paperback ed., 1993), pp. 383-384.
61 Concerning the illiberal authoritarianism in Hungary beginning in 2010 and Poland beginning in 2015, see Sabrina P. Ramet, *Alternatives to Democracy in Twentieth-Century Europe: Collectivist visions of modernity* (Budapest and New York: Central European University Press, 2019) – chap. 6.
62 Marx and Engels, "Manifesto of the Communist Party", pp. 21, 23.
63 Karl Marx, "Critique of the Gotha Program," in Feuer (ed.), *Basic Writings,* p. 130.
64 *Ibid.,* p. 126.

8

The End of Philosophy:
Friedrich Nietzsche and the
Transvaluation of all Values

Torbjørn L. Knutsen

Summary: Friedrich Nietzsche came from a religious family and was destined for the priesthood. But in the course of his theological studies he lost his faith. Unsatisfied with a simple atheistic rejection of God's existence, Nietzsche proclaimed that "God is dead". It was a clever formulation, which implied that God once had been alive and raised a variety of questions concerning the circumstances surrounding the death of God and the consequences for human society. As Nietzsche addressed these questions, he developed an original and radical criticism not only of Christianity, but of modern society and its culture – including the established giants of German philosophy. He launched zinging attacks on Kant, Hegel and others, arguing that they had written little more than so many variations on a dishonest Christian theme. Nietzsche was, ultimately, a cultural critic. He was a philologist, not a philosopher. Yet, he developed a radical alternative philosophy of ethics and a genealogy of morality. He was a revolutionary, and demanded a "transvaluation of all values" so that an oppressive Christian culture could be replaced by true liberty, based on philosophical insight, creativity and art.

His many critics called Nietzsche a nihilist and charged him with undermining social values and destroying late-19th century moral philosophy. They were right – and Nietzsche recognized that they were right (although he protested the nihilist label). His earliest arguments rocked German culture; his later ones shattered the whole Christian, Enlightenment-based civilization. "I am dynamite", he boasted towards the end of his life.

Nietzsche fired torpedoes against modern, Western philosophy. His works were little read when he was alive, and it took some time before the torpedoes detonated. He received a wider audience just as he was collapsing into madness around 1890 – first in Germany and Scandinavia and then in France. When Nietzsche died in 1900, the power of his argument exploded. So did his fame. As Europe descended into World War I, readers hailed his diagnosis as prophetic. However, others condemned him, claiming that he abandoned the very ideas of truth and universal values. It did not help his reputation that his claims were embraced by leaders of the German Nazi party during the 1930s. For many years after World War II, Nietzsche was seen as a 'Nazi philosopher'.

During the 1950s, assessments changed. As his manuscripts were re-edited and retranslated, he was presented as a complex and multifaceted social philosopher. During the 1960s, he was rediscovered in the English-speaking world. During the 1970s he was hailed as an inspiration for critical theorists and post-structuralists. Since then, he has found admirers among 'anarchists, feminists, Nazis, religious cultists, Socialists, Marxists, vegetarians, avant-garde artists, devotees of physical culture, and archconservatives'.[1]

Obviously, many of his new fans have misunderstood his arguments – it is, for example, hard to see how Nietzsche's contempt for the popular masses could harmonize with a socialist outlook, or how his frequent misogyny could dovetail with feminist stands. Many readers have simply selected from Nietzsche's variegated texts a pliable passage and bent it to their partisan purpose.

There are many reasons why Nietzsche has been so deeply misunderstood. One is that he is different – he did for example not present a consistent philosophical system like other 19th-century German philosophers. Another is that he is undefinable and elusive. His writings are fragmentary – his books composed of a handful of essays (often poetic or polemical) or collections of epigrams and aphorisms (quite often paradoxical snippets). Finally, one book would often contradict another. Nietzsche's texts, in other words, are open to diverse interpretations.

So, how can we find "the real" Nietzsche? How can we best capture the ideas of this indefinable, elusive, and controversial thinker? This chapter suggests that the most suitable approach follows a strict biographical line.

Its first part sketches a portrait of young Nietzsche, on the assumption that the most formative periods in a person's life are the teen-age and student years. This part lingers on a few persons who exerted some special influence in his young years – on intimate friends and important authors. The second part presents Nietzsche's books chronologically, highlighting the development of a few central ideas. This part will be cast in terms of an evolution in three stages, respectively entitled "tragedy", "years of wandering", and "maturity". The third and concluding part adds a few comments that place Nietzsche in historical context. Nietzsche was a "free thinker". He must be understood as a child of his times.

A Biographical Sketch

Friedrich Wilhelm Nietzsche was born in 1844, in Röcken, a small Prussian village near Leipzig. His father was a Protestant pastor and a German patriot – who named his son to honor King Friedrich Wilhelm IV of Prussia. His mother was a pastor's daughter. It was expected that the boy would study theology and follow a family tradition.

Nietzsche's Childhood and Youth
Friedrich Nietzsche was only 6 years old when his father died (in 1849) of a degenerative brain ailment. He left a young wife and three children – Friedrich, who was five, Elisabeth, who was three and a baby boy who died only a few weeks after his father. They were evicted from their home. The young widow and her two surviving children travelled to Naumburg, where they moved in with the late Pastor's mother and her two unmarried daughters. Here Friedrich grew up, in a household of women who fussed about him.

Young Nietzsche transferred to a Naumburg school in 1854. He did well and was praised at school and at home. Two years later he received a stipend which allowed him to transfer to a Protestant school in Pforta, close by. School Pforta, located within the thick walls of a former Cistercian monastery near Naumburg, was one of the strictest and best preparatory schools in Germany. He arrived at Pforta with the intention of studying theology.

In the new environment, the young teenager expanded his interests. He learnt to play the piano and to appreciate music and became obsessed with the great romantic composer Robert Schumann as well as with Richard Wagner. Always the voracious reader, Nietzsche read Ludwig Feuerbach, Friedrich Lange, and other critics of the Christian theology. He wrote an essay on "Fate and History" in which he criticized the central teachings of Christianity.

The Budding Academic
The school in Pforta was swept up by the Greek revival that washed across 19th century Europe. It instilled in German academics a deep fascination and a particularly romanticized understanding of ancient Greece.
The Young Greek Scholar

In 1864, Nietzsche transferred to the University of Bonn to study theology. It was a big change from the strict discipline at Pforta. He enjoyed life. He drank beer with his fellow students. He took classes in horseback-riding. He became a good rider and retained a fondness for horses throughout his life. He cultivated his interests in music, developed decent skills at the piano, and excelled in improvisations. He admired Richard Wagner and embraced Wagner's Schopenhauerian argument that music represented an unmediated entry into an authentic level of spirit and will. Nietzsche, who could spellbind fellow students with long improvisations on the piano, experienced this himself.

Nietzsche studied Greek under Professor Friedrich W. Ritschl, who quickly noticed Nietzsche's academic imagination and exceptional analytic gifts. Under Ritschel's attention, Nietzsche put theology aside and took up philology. In 1865 he wrote to his sister, Elisabeth, that he had "lost his faith".

That same year, Nietzsche left Bonn for Leipzig. His mentor, Professor Ritschl was offered a teaching post in Leipzig. Nietzsche moved with him. In Leipzig he made great progress. Ritschl was impressed and published one of Nietzsche's (1867) analyses of an ancient Greek poet in the journal that he edited, the *Rheinisches Museum*.

In 1867, Nietzsche was called up for military service. He interrupted his studies and, due to his skill with horses, he was placed with a cavalry company. Here he suffered a riding accident and was discharged. He was transported to Basel for a long and painful convalescence. His health, which had never been good, now took a permanent turn for the worse. After the accident, he would suffer more frequent attacks from headaches and nausea.

But he read voraciously in Basel. When he returned to Leipzig in 1868, his skills in ancient Greek were much sharpened. He wrote thoughtful articles on ancient texts that were published in philological journals. He was 24 years old and earning a reputation in philological circles as a young and promising scholar of ancient Greek.

Nietzsche and Science
Nietzsche delved into ancient philology. But he also had other interests. He read broadly. He gleaned papers and magazines for news about music and literature. And he read about advances that took place in the sciences. He was especially interested in biology and medicine, which related directly to his own precarious health. He noted how breakthroughs in the life sciences placed theology and old-fashioned philosophy under increasing strain.

The new sciences emphasized empirical evidence. This fueled a strong materialist strain in Germany's intellectual life and accentuated a long-evolving reaction to the idealism which had long dominated German philosophy. Nietzsche joined in, expressing doubts about Kant's distinction between *noumena* and *phenoumena* because it implied that we can *never* obtain certain knowledge about anything. He grew weary of Kant's abstract, reason-based philosophy, and favored Schopenhauer's more material approach.[2] We live in a material world. The inanimate objects of this world are directly observable. Its animate objects may be difficult to understand, for their observable representation hide their true essence, not as undeterminable *noumena* (as Kant asserted) but as Will – or, more precisely, as a will to live. In Schopenhauer's view, the behavior of living beings is driven by a fundamental desire to live. Human behavior is driven neither by reason nor by ethical ideals, but by a blind, irrepressible desire for survival.

Nietzsche was convinced by Schopenhauer and by natural scientists such as the geologist James Hutton, who argued that the world was millions of years old. Also, he accepted the implication that the Bible's account of the world being created in six days could not be literally true. He was intrigued by Ludwig Feuerbach's materialist attack on Christianity, but not entirely convinced. He was more impressed by Friedrich A. Lange[3] who delivered sophisticated critiques of both religion and of the simple, materialist viewpoint. Finally, Nietzsche was awestruck by the American essayist Ralph Waldo Emerson. A professor at Pforta had noted Nietzsche's interests and given him a German translation of Emerson's first volume of essays. Nietzsche read and re-read these essays with pencil in hand. He found in Emerson a preacher's son who, like himself, struggled with questions of faith. He filled the book's margins with carefully written comments, that expressed doubt about the old arguments of theology and established principles of faith.

Philology, Philosophy and War.

In 1865, Professor Ritschl recommended Nietzsche to a vacant chair in philology at the University of Basel in Switzerland. Nietzsche was only 24 years old, and the recommendation was absurd on the face of it: such chairs were occupied by established scholars. Nietzsche did not even have a doctoral degree. Yet, the University of Basel took a chance on him and offered Nietzsche a chair in classical philology on the strength of his considerable promise and on Ritschl's glowing recommendation.

War and Trauma

Nietzsche had scarcely made his inaugural lecture before war broke out between France and Germany. He was called up for military service once more. Due to bad eyesight and poor health, he was placed in a medical unit in the Prussian army. It was his second military service and it left him permanently damaged. The young academic was traumatized by his first-hand experience of modern, industrial warfare. Visiting battle zones and carrying out maimed and wounded young men, he was emotionally shaken, and he contracted diphtheria, dysentery, and other dangerous diseases.

Severely ill, he was hospitalized in 1870, treated and eventually discharged from service. He returned to Basel to recover. He followed the war in Swiss newspapers, and was appalled to read that the German army had marched victoriously into Paris, occupied Versailles, and declared the establishment of a united German Empire. Nietzsche found the declaration preposterous. He considered the new Empire an inauthentic, entirely hollow construct.

Colleagues and Friends in Basel

Nietzsche began to teach classical philology in Basel in 1871. The reception among the university faculty was cool. His appointment to the rank of professor had raised eyebrows. He was absurdly young, inexperienced, and frail – his body was still weak from bouts with diphtheria and dysentery and his mind troubled by post-traumatic stress. And he did not have a doctoral thesis or a dissertation. However, Franz Overbeck and Jakob Burckhardt recognized his analytical gifts. They welcomed him kindly.

Overbeck arrived at the University at the same time as Nietzsche. He was nearly ten years older and appointed professor of New Testament Exegesis and Old Church History. The two new professors rented rooms in the same building and struck up a close and lasting friendship. Although Overbeck could be offended, if not shocked, by Nietzsche's rants against Christianity, he remained a caring friend throughout Nietzsche's life.

Jacob Burckhardt was the university's respected Professor of Cultural and Art History. He was a native of Basel and showed Nietzsche around town. The two of them took long, peripatetic walks and, although they were separated by a generation – Burckhardt was 50 to Nietzsche's 25 – they discovered many similarities. Both had started out as students of theology, lost their faith, and immersed themselves in Schopenhauer and the history of ancient

Greece. Both were skeptical of Kant, and they rejected Hegel's notion of History as mankind's spiritual progress. Burckhardt's sober view of life in ancient Greece and his reservations about Plato did much to modify Nietzsche's idealized assessments of antiquity, and to develop his predilection for the pre-Socratics. Both admired Schopenhauer and disliked Bismarck. They were both suspicious of mass culture and of democratic reform. Finally, Burckhardt was familiar with Charles Darwin's theories, and argued that the core of history was humankind's struggle to survive on earth.

Heinrich Köselitz would become a third important friend in Basel. He was young student of music, but took classes from Burckhardt, Overbeck, and Nietzsche. He developed a deep admiration for Nietzsche. Köselitz helped Nietzsche during his fits of illness, often acting as servant and secretary. He would read aloud to Nietzsche during his intermittent spells of near blindness. He would take dictation. He would prepare Nietzsche's manuscripts and galleys, sometimes intervening to finalize the text. Nietzsche considered this helpful visitor a blessing and affectionally called him "Peter Gast".[4]

Wagner and Schopenhauer

But the most influential friend during Nietzsche's Basel years was Richard Wagner. His ambition was to strengthen the German nation and renew its culture through his music. Nietzsche wholeheartedly supported Wagner's argument. The great composer had been his artistic hero for many years – ever since he heard *Tristan and Isolde* and recognized that Wagner's genius beautifully expressed Schopenhauer's philosophy. So, he was thrilled when Wagner invited him to his magnificent villa on Lake Lucerne. And since Wagner was an admirer of Schopenhauer, the influence of Schopenhauer on young Nietzsche became doubly strong.

They both agreed with Schopenhauer that we live in a material world, whose physical representations instill in all living things an unquenchable desire for satisfaction. Whoever obtains the object of his desires – who unites his will with its representation – soon tires of it, leaves it behind and develops desire for another object, and then another. He will never reach contentment. In this way endless desire leads to endless suffering, argued Schopenhauer. He concluded that there is only one solution: to deny material temptation by living aesthetically – to find enjoyment in non-material representations, such as art and music.

Wagner and Nietzsche accepted Schopenhauer's theory of art, according to which music was sense perception without material representation. It was communication without words. It was direct access to the Will. Nietzsche, who had read Schopenhauer's *World as Will and Representation* with tears in his eyes, agreed wholeheartedly: music provided direct access to important aspects of the human essence in ways that neither reason nor religion could.

Finally, Wagner and Nietzsche saw eye to eye on Schopenhauer's criticism of Christian theology. He had observed that men of faith simply could not understand atheism. First, they thought that atheism led into moral relativism and that anyone who doubted the spiritual universe of Christianity would lose all sense of morality and slide into a tolerance of sinful if not evil acts. This was just nonsense, argued Schopenhauer. There was no reason why the one would necessarily follow from the other. Second, men of faith automatically assumed that anyone who denied God would take the side of Satan. Schopenhauer brushed this aside as childish. Schopenhauer's refutation made a profound impression on Nietzsche: God and Satan were a conceptual pair inhabiting the same Christian universe. Those who accepted one would also accept the existence of the other. And conversely, those who doubted the existence of God would obviously also doubt the existence of Satan.

This point, that different arguments might not really be that different because they were unified by coexistence in the same logical universe, made a deep mark on Nietzsche.

The First Period: Tragedy

Nietzsche was mesmerized by Wagner's Schopenhauer-derived theory of music and awestruck by the way the great composer received him in his home. And he was charmed off his feet by Wagner's new wife Cosima, the daughter of Franz Liszt. She charmed Nietzsche – and was one of the women who played an important role in his life. In 1872, he presented her with five essays as a gift for her 35th birthday. One of them is of special interest to the political scientist: it is entitled "The Greek State", and it foreshadows some of Nietzsche's later arguments.[5]

This essay was written at a time when German interest in ancient Greece reached its zenith – around the time when German archeologist Heinrich Schliemann searched for ancient Troy and uncovered remarkable treasures. Schliemann's discoveries captured Nietzsche's imagination – as it captured that of the entire German nation. It was generally held, that ancient Greece was remarkably advanced in art, literature, and philosophy. Nietzsche observed that this advancement belonged to pre-Christian times, and that it doesn't occurr in a society which was steeply hierarchical. Civilization doesn't have to be Christian to be advanced. And great art goes hand in hand with great inequality. Indeed, social inequality may well be a precondition for great art, he argued. "In order for there to be a broad, deep fertile soil for the development of art, the overwhelming majority has to be slavishly subjected to life's necessity in the service of the minority," he wrote.[6] Greek art would never have reached the levels of the sublime if had not been for the many slaves that toiled in misery. Societies that are built on liberal notions of justice and socialist demands for equality and for "equal sharing of the pain," will never become great civilizations; they will always be condemned to cultural poverty, he opined.[7] This idea, that there is a connection between social inequality and high culture, would echo through most of his books.

Dionysus and the Spirit of Music

Cosima read Nietzsche's essays and encouraged him to write at least two of the books promised by his prefaces. This he never did. However, the exploration of the differences between ancient Greece and modern Germany was repeated in his first book, which was printed later that year: *The Birth of Tragedy from the Spirit of Music* (1872). Nietzsche had pushed aside work on his doctoral dissertation in order to complete it. It bore echoes of Burckhardt's reservations about Plato and Socrates. And it oozed with admiration for Richard Wagner.

The Birth of Tragedy is built around two important distinctions. The first is the distinction between two principles in Greek culture, the Apollonian and the Dionysian. The Apollonian principle represented reason and order. The Dionysian principle represented emotion, wine, and abandon. This distinction was not new with Nietzsche, and the originality of his book does not depend upon it. Rather, its novelty lies with Nietzsche's use of this distinction to criticize German culture. First, he disparaged traditional German philologists who advocated the primacy of Apollon, Reason and Socrates. Nietzsche, instead, affirmed the importance of the Dionysian principle.

Second, he argued that the reason why ancient Greek civilization was so superior was that these two principles were in balance and harmony, and he analyzed the dramas of Aeschylus and Sophocles to make the point. However, this harmony did not last, Nietzsche continued. The Apollonian principle gained influence as Greek philosophy evolved. As Greek culture was increasingly influenced by Reason, Greek society lost its spontaneous freedom. Nietzsche singled out Socrates as the main culprit of this cultural degeneration. He hailed the pre-Socratic period as superior because of its harmony and its musical spirit. The post-Socratic period, brought about by the rise of philosophy, pushed critical reason beyond its natural limits. Logic undermined itself and introduced an instability during which one school of thought quickly replaced another.

Toward the end of the book Nietzsche made his third original move: he applied his analysis of ancient Greece to Bismarck's Germany. He argued that the culture of the new German *Reich* bore an uncanny resemblance to Greek culture after Socrates. It could only be saved, Nietzsche continued, if it embraced a Dionysian principle – especially through the spirit of music as reflected in the Schopenhauer-inspired works of Richard Wagner.

The great composer read *The Birth of Tragedy* and praised it enthusiastically. But no one else did. The book was passed over in silence. The few reviewers who noted its publication, slaughtered it. Nietzsche was deeply disappointed. It came on top of new bouts of ill health and dissatisfaction with his university duties. His headaches got worse and more frequent. Yet, he began to write a series of critical essays on art and culture. He projected 13 essays but completed only four. The first two were ringing critiques of German culture. The other two extolled the genius of Arthur Schopenhauer and Richard Wagner, respectively.

His four essays were gathered in one volume in 1876 and published under the title *Untimely Meditations*. By the time the book was issued, Nietzsche had received a double shock. First, he had read an early version of Wagner's *Parsifal* and saw at once that Wagner had strayed from the Schopenhauerian strivings of the will and from Dionysian principles; the great composer had slid into German mythology and Christian mysticism! Nietzsche's admiration collapsed. In addition, he was shocked to hear that Wagner had corresponded with a medical doctor and proposed that Nietzsche's weak eyesight and ill health might be the result of unhealthy sexual habits.[8] Nietzsche was deeply offended and broke all contact with Wagner.

The rupture did not seem to cause the Wagners more than puzzlement. But for Nietzsche it was a big deal. It meant the loss of a mentor and a friend. In addition, it meant a blow to the argument that supported his *Birth of Tragedy* and it weakened the answer that Wagner had provided to the question of how life could remain meaningful without God: life gets meaning through artistic creation. Now, Nietzsche cast about for other answers. Soon, he would find them in the life sciences.

Evolutionary Perspectives

After the break with the Wagners, Nietzsche descended into a deep depression. His number of students and his health declined. In the fall of 1876, the university granted Nietzsche a year's leave of absence with pay. He travelled to Italy with two friends – two students of philosophy who were also depressed and in dubious health. All three travelled to Italy to rest and regain their strength. One of them was Albert Brenner, a tubercular poet. The other was Paul Rée, a veteran, like Nietzsche, from the Franco-Prussian War.

Rée knew English well (Nietzsche did not). Rée had read Darwin and drew on him for a book he had written on moral philosophy. He called himself an evolutionary ethicist. During their long walks, he presented Darwin's argument. Nietzsche was impressed. He seized upon the idea of human beings as biological organisms subject to principles and laws that governed evolution in the animal kingdom. He saw in Darwin a new scientific methodology. It did not rely on the mechanical notion of causality of the physical sciences, or on the abstract teleology of Hegelian philosophy. Darwin offered a different logic. It was a logic of functionality which hinged on mechanisms of adaptation and evolution.

Nietzsche was already familiar with the concept of evolution – he had encountered it in both his theological and his philological studies. However, whereas this old concept was tied in with notions of *telos*, Darwin's new concept was not. For him, humanity was guided by no greater purpose. Humans belonged to nature and were nothing special in the greater order of things. Darwin's theory of evolution appealed strongly to Nietzsche because it had no teleology and no God.

Darwin could explain evolution without resorting to divine principles. And it employed a functional logic that Nietzsche could use in philology, the field in which he had scholarly expertise. From this usage emerged Nietzsche's "genealogical" approach. He would use it to trace the lineage of concepts. But he would not just document its changing meaning (its etymology) over time, he would also identify the historical carriers of the concept and discuss the social basis of its changing meaning.

When Nietzsche returned to Basel, his health had improved. His mind was filled with new ideas and his notebooks with several hundred observational notes. He was more interested in these notes – some of them doubting the existence of God, others emphasizing the power of scientific reason – than in the old arguments of ancient philology, which he now taught with little enthusiasm. His students lost interest in his lectures. His paralyzing migraines returned. He took drugs to ease the recurrent pain and entered a vicious circle.

In the spring of 1879, he resigned from his post at Basel. The university gave him a small pension; just enough to sustain him for the next ten, sane years of his life. During these years he suffered bouts of illness. He sought health in the mountains of Switzerland during summer and in northern Italy in winter. He kept suffering from his illness. But he also kept on writing. Over the next ten years he produced ten remarkable books.

The Second Period: Years of Wandering

His writings changed during this period. The changes are evident in *Human, All too Human*,[9] which was printed in 1878. First, the form is new; it is composed of aphorisms – short texts, ranging from a few words to a few pages. The book is not the outcome of deskwork; it is a peripatetic product. Nietzsche worked as he walked. He wandered for hours at a time, thinking and ruminating as he did so. Sometimes he stopped to write down a thought or an insight. *Human, All-too-human: A Book for Free Spirits*, is composed of notes by a solitary wanderer, around 500-600 notes in all.[10]

Second, the content is different. There is a change of tone, which is indicated already on the first page – in a dedication to the memory of Voltaire, a representative of the Enlightenment and a spokesman of Reason. *Human All-too-Human* is marked by a fading of the Dionysian principle and Schopenhauer's (and Wagner's) theory of the saving grace of art and music. The book upgraded the Apollonian principle and the guiding light of Reason. Whereas Nietzsche had earlier decried Socrates, he now exalted him. While he had earlier emphasized culture and perceived humanity as being justified by the production of the creative genius, Nietzsche now extolled the exact methods of empirically-based life science.

Finally, Nietzsche's skepticism about Christianity became more pronounced. Indeed, the book expanded his skepticism to all established belief systems. This became more pronounced in his next two books: *The Dawn* (1881)[11] and *The Gay Science* (1882).[12]

The Dawn: Thoughts On the Prejudices of Morality (1881) is composed of nearly 600 aphorisms or maxims, several of them deeply skeptical of religion in general and Christianity in particular. There cannot be an almighty God, not in a world that is so filled with stupidity, cruelty, and human suffering, Nietzsche argued. And since God does not exist, there can be no divine principle that rewards good behavior and punishes ill. In fact, there cannot be any divine sanction associated with keeping or breaking moral norms.

Nietzsche did not present his case in the simple, materialist atheism of authors like Feuerbach – he did not claim that God did not exist, or that God was a figment of human imagination. Rather, he posited that God is dead. This was the same formulation that Fyodor Dostoevsky had used a few years earlier, and it allowed Nietzsche to ask the same questions: Was God once alive? When did He die? How did He die? What are the consequences of His death?

Dostoevsky argued that with the death of God everything became permissible[13]; that if God is dead, then everyone can claim to be God.[14] Nietzsche disagreed. He argued – with a nod to Schopenhauer – that God's death would not necessarily mean that all moral codes collapse. On the contrary, it may liberate humanity. It may replace a fictitious God with an honest, reason-based moral code fashioned by superior thinkers. Besides, God's death will have no consequences until it dawns upon humanity that God really *is* dead. And this dawn will be long in coming, Nietzsche suggested, because God's death will be too shocking to contemplate for most people. They will avoid it because it will make them feel abandoned by their mighty protector. Consequently, humans will cling to their old values, inventing secular versions of their old theologies.

From this proposition, Nietzsche made a radical attack on modern philosophy in general and German philosophy in particular. Philosophers do little more than create endless variations on the old themes of Christian theology. He argued, with echoes of Schopenhauer, that their thoughts are limited by their conceptual universe. They simply cannot imagine that God can be dead. Those few who could, tended to think that humanism is a viable alternative; however, this is nothing but a secularized version of the ancient Christian values, argued Nietzsche. As the philosophers sit "in their old caves" and repeat comments concerning the shadows on their wall, they miss out on the exhilarating possibilities of freedom that had opened up before them. Nietzsche's subsequent books elaborated on God's death, on liberation, and on unimaginative philosophers trapped in their old conceptual universe.

In *The Gay Science* (1882), another collection of short texts (nearly 400 in all), Nietzsche let a madman announce that God is dead and elaborate on the cause of death: "*We have killed him* – you and I", the madman announced. "All of us are murderers".[15] The murderer is, in fact, modern man and his scientific methods, Nietzsche explained. As the Enlightenment evolved and produced modern science, it undermined humanity's need for God.

Nietzsche followed up the madman's announcement with the proposition that God's death may liberate the human spirit. But he also issued a strong warning: Religion has an important function in society. Its God may be fictional, but is nevertheless beneficial, in the sense of helping humans cope with the challenges and problems of life. Liberation, thus, comes with a cost! In the absence of God, mankind must define its own values and norms and cope with life on its own. The big question is whether post-Christian man is up to the task. Is he able to independently define values and set his own goals? Nietzsche is not at all sure. He thinks that instead of liberating the human spirit, humanity will sink into pursuits of immediate and simple pleasures.

In earlier books, Nietzsche had portrayed Christian man as a small, cringing coward. Later he added a portrayal of post-Christian man as even more pitiful – "a smaller, almost ridiculous type, a herd animal, something eager to please, sickly, and mediocre – the contemporary European".[16] He did not elaborate much on the nature of post-Christian man – this he would do in his next book under the sobriquet "the Last Man". Instead, he expanded upon the notion of the herd. Humans are herd-animals, he averred. And consequently, moral beliefs are always group beliefs. The individual can only ascribe values to himself as a member in a herd.[17] He coined the term "herd-mentality" as a disparaging reference to ideas that are intellectually weak, but which nevertheless are politically strong because they are held by so many.

This notion now emerged as a central idea in Nietzsche's thinking. It expressed a disagreement with the Darwinian notion of the "survival of the fittest". The strong will never dominate the species, argued Nietzsche. The fittest and most highly evolved species might not lead anywhere at all; rather, chances are that it is the most common and most numerous beings that will dominate the world.

Nietzsche was deeply troubled by this thought. He was distressed by the prospect that the multitudes of simple pleasures would define and dominate the values and culture of modern society. This distress fed into a dislike for the popular masses; a disdain for organizations of mass mobilization – working men's associations, unions, and labor parties. It also ties in with an admiration for the strong individual; for the determined man who resists the communal view, who bucks the influence of the majority and breaks out of the moral consensus of the herd.

There are new ideas in the books that Nietzsche wrote in the five-year period between 1878 and 1882. But these ideas emerged into fuller maturely a few years later. They were first expressed in four slim volumes published between 1883 and 1885, in which Nietzsche presented a fable about an old Persian sage. These books, collected in one volume in 1885 and published as *Thus Spoke Zarathustra*,[18] marks a transition to the third and mature period in Nietzsche's philosophy.

The Third Period: The Mature Philosopher

Zarathustra emerged from a personal humiliation – a head-over-heels infatuation with Louise Salome, a creative and intelligent Russian woman who rejected his marriage proposal and instead eloped with his good friend Paul Rée. Descending into a new depression, Nietzsche began his fable about Zarathustra, the ancient sage. It is easy to see Zarathustra as a projection into whose character Nietzsche placed his own preoccupations. Zarathustra was a prophet and – like Nietzsche – "a friendless wanderer who moves from place to place." At the beginning of the first book (published in 1883), Zarathustra speaks to any bystander who will listen. At the end of the last book (completed in 1885), Zarathustra speaks only to himself. The most important clue to *Zarathustra*, according to Walter Kaufmann, "is that it is the work of an utterly lonely man."

Transition

Nietzsche, who had long criticized Christianity, now launched into active hostility. But more importantly, in *Zarathustra* he announced an alternative to the Christian faith. In the opening pages, Zarathustra, who had lived alone in the mountains for a decade, returned to humanity. He entered the marketplace of a village and told people there that God was dead. Then he presented himself as the prophet of the "Superman" *(Übermensch)*.

The Superman is one of Nietzsche's most famous creations. However, Nietzsche did not devote many pages to him. Also, it is a bit unclear who or what the Superman is. There is a Darwinian cast about him: Nietzsche noted how there was first the prehistorical ape which evolved into historical man, who may eventually fashion a future Superman.[19] But the Superman is more than a product of evolution. Nietzsche used him as a contrast to the Christian ideal of the meek and pliable.

As Nietzsche followed up his first volume of *Zarathustra* with a second and a third, the Superman dropped out of the story as Nietzsche moved on to other themes. One of these was the notion of the "eternal return".[20] Another theme was the idea of the "will to power". He introduced this as a characteristic property of the Superman – so that, although Nietzsche did not develop the theme of the Superman, his presence could be said to linger in this notion of "will to power".

The Superman also lingered in the elitist notion of a superior class of cultured and insightful individuals which now took pride of place in Nietzsche's books. When Nietzsche introduced the Superman in *Zarathustra*, he contrasted him with "the herd". He continued to use the idea of the herd as a contrast to his notion of a cultured elite of creative geniuses in subsequent books. The herd consists of a mass of "small and pitiable men". The elite, by contrast, consists of a few noble and superior individuals who want to be by themselves, "being able to be different, standing alone and having to live independently." The herd consists of sheep or happy pigs. The noble elite possesses "will to power".[21]

A reasonable interpretation of this "will to power" is that it represents Nietzsche's final break with Schopenhauer. Nietzsche replaced Schopenhauer's pessimistic notion of suffering caused by "endless desire" with an optimistic idea based on the ancient Greek idea of the "endless recurrence". Nietzsche argued that the Superman lives life completely. He is self-consciously present in every moment, intensely and to the full. If he were offered a chance to live his life again, he would not change a thing.

Dynamite

Zarathustra may be Nietzsche's most famous book, largely because of the striking figure of the Superman and its poetic and prophetic style – excessively prophetic, some would say, as if Nietzsche wanted to write a parody of the Bible.[22] It is not his best book. But it introduces themes and ideas which Nietzsche was to elaborate in *Beyond Good and Evil* (1886), *A Genealogy of Morals* (1887), and *Twilight of the Idols* (1888).[23] *Zarathustra* is a transitory work. It leads into a period in which Nietzsche re-read his old titles and wrote new introductions to them. He reviewed his production and developed an ambition of tying his arguments more tightly together and developing a consistent philosophical system. The three books that follow were philosophy at its most seductive.

Beyond Good and Evil was Nietzsche's final collection of aphorisms – nearly 300 of them, grouped into nine thematic parts that give the argument shape and focus. They add up to a criticism of Modernity and reintroduce questions that Nietzsche broached already in *The Birth of Tragedy*: What is wrong with German culture? Why are German philosophers so subservient to ancient Hebrew tribal myths? How can a new and better culture be constructed? Nietzsche began by attacking the most famous of the modern philosophers – Descartes, Spinoza, and, especially, Kant (whom Nietzsche calls "the Great Chinaman of Königsberg").[24] Nietzsche finds them all wanting. He thinks that they are dogmatic and lacking in imagination.

In one of the first aphorisms, he seized the Stoic precept for "living according to nature" and used it as an example of how philosophy imposes laws upon nature and thereby "creates the world in its own image". This notion of "nature" is an important term in these final books. So is the idea that "nature" is so much more than the philosophers can imagine. Nature is uncontrollable and "prodigal beyond measure". It cannot be tamed or tyrannized over. Here Nietzsche distanced himself from his old hero, Schopenhauer, criticizing him for having too benign an image of nature and for thinking that the nature of the Will is self-evident.[25]

Nietzsche first cast suspicion on the motives of Schopenhauer and the other old philosophers. They had not embraced "nature", he argued. Instead, they had imposed their own moral outlook on nature. They had read into nature what they wanted to find.[26] They had drawn excessively on Christianity, and this had blinded them and made them unable to grasp Life, which was bigger, richer and more dangerous than these traditional philosophers would ever allow. Christianity had imposed a slave mentality upon human thought and culture, Nietzsche argued.

Nietzsche's diagnosis was foreshadowed in *Zarathustra* and earlier books – i.e., the idea that past philosophers have been locked in a Christian outlook and that Christianity had imposed upon them the metaphysics of a "herd morality". Nietzsche now formulated a prognosis: future philosophers would have to think differently, he argued. In *Beyond Good and Evil* he explained why and how. Past philosophers had been shaped by Christian theologians and their idealistic precepts of universal morality, of rational science, and notions of equality and democratic participation. They had been blinded by Christian priests, so they could not see nature, life, or reality. Future philosophers would have to reject them all. They must make a clean break and embrace a new "master morality". They must acknowledge that human reason is limited, and that morality is historically and culturally contingent – that it changes with time, place, and people. A new philosophy must be developed by a new generation of "free thinkers". They will realize that the old distinction drawn between good and evil is superficial if not haphazard. That traditional categories and norms are so tightly tied in with the Christian religion that they are unsuited for capturing both nature and human life.

In *Beyond Good and Evil* (1886), Nietzsche referred to Christianity as a worthless succor for the weak and lazy who seek merely comfort, pleasure, and peace. He could see no value in their "herd morality" or "slave morality" and, frankly no value in them as human beings, except as a stock for breeding recruits for a future elite. "A people," Nietzsche noted, "is nature's detour to arrive at six or seven great men – and then to get around them."[27]

A Genealogy of Morals (1887) probes these ideas more deeply in three long essays. The first of them is the most significant as it contrasts the "slave morality" of the masses who flee nature with the "master morality" of the few, great men. Here Nietzsche located the origins of slave morality in the Judeo-Christian religion, and especially in what he termed *"ressentiment"*. He argued that Christianity evolved in the late Roman Empire among slaves who lacked will, strength, and stomach to pursue their own desires. Instead, they invented a philosophy that made a virtue of their weakness. Nietzsche saw this as an act of creative compensation on the part of the cowardly, poor, and powerless. Their desires were natural. But they fled nature and found an excuse for their lack of agency by turning inward and "compensat[ing] for it with imaginary revenge."[28] Too weak and inept to get what they wanted, they converted their envy into a hypocritical creed, denouncing their desires as sinful and evil. Out of such condemnations of natural desires emerged the Christian slave morality.

This argument flowed from Nietzsche's use of the genealogical approach. He documented the changing meaning of the concept of morality through time. In addition, he identified the historical carrier of its meaning (the Jews and early Christians) and he discussed the social circumstances – the relations of power – under which its meaning changed.

These two books – *Beyond Good and Evil* and *A Genealogy of Morals* – are critiques of the West in general and of German culture in particular. He received praise from old friends – like Jacob Burkhardt. He also received compliments from new readers – from influential men such as Hippolyte Taine in France, August Strindberg in Sweden, and George Brandes in Denmark. Brandes introduced Nietzsche to a wider audience by preparing a series of lectures on Nietzsche's philosophy at the University in Copenhagen.[29]

As his fame spread, Nietzsche felt that he needed a text that would serve as a short introduction to his work. In August 1888, he wrote – day and night – a short volume of about a hundred pages: *Twilight of the Idols*. It is a succinct summary of Nietzsche's mature philosophy. It is also his last sane work.

This short book is introduced by 44 aphorisms – some of them Nietzsche's most famous one-liners. It then launches into a discussion of Socrates and Plato, the classical entry into Western philosophy. Using the genealogical approach, Nietzsche argues that these two thinkers lived in decadent times and developed decadent arguments that put Western philosophy on a fatefully wrong track. Socrates emphasized reason to an "absurd" extent. Plato repudiated sense perception and, instead of examining nature, turned his attention to an imaginary world of eternal ideas. Later, Plato's decadent, life-denying ideals were uncritically absorbed by Christianity. Not only did the Christians imagine an eternal "Heaven", but they also argued that this fiction was ultimate reality. Their fantasy was, in turn, embraced by Western philosophers who cast the observation of their senses into doubt, removed nature from their purview, denied the real world, and rejected Life.

Nietzsche was critical of Germany and German culture. He condemned "democracy, together with hybrids such as the 'German Reich', as the form of decline of the state".[30] He blamed Immanuel Kant especially for this sorry decline because Kant vehemently denied that the world is knowable. But Nietzsche also shot some disapproving arrows at French and British writers for good measure. He added insults to their names and rejected them all.[31] He despised Christians who worked to "improve" man – who worked to *tame* man and to *breed* a particular kind of man. And he loathed the liberal reformers and the leaders of the labor movement. For when God died, these "improvers of mankind" carried on the old, Christian, life-denying fantasies.[32] "There are no worse and no more thorough injurers of freedom than liberal institutions," Nietzsche complained.[33] As for the socialists, they had simply secularized Christian morality and continued its rejection of the real world.[34]

Only for Emerson did he hold high regard, together with men of action and genius – like Caesar, Napoleon, Goethe, and Thucydides.

Coda

Examining German society of his day, Nietzsche observed a decline which he attributed to prioritizing politics over the intellect. German politics was in tension with German culture, he argued in *The Twilight of the Idols*. "One lives off the other. One thrives at the expense of the other. All great ages of culture are ages of political decline," Nietzsche wrote.[35] He noted that France had lost the Franco-Prussian war when it was culturally dominant in Europe, whereas German culture descended into vulgarity after Prussia's victory in 1871 and Bismarck's proclamation of Empire. With a nod to classical Greece, in which philosophy reached a height of sophistication as society was immersed in the Peloponnesian Wars, Nietzsche made a sweeping generalization: "what is great culturally has always been unpolitical, even *anti-political.*"[36] *Twilight of the Idols* was the last of his books that Nietzsche saw published. For just as he was receiving recognition, his lucidity failed him.

It was not the last book he wrote. In fact, he wrote furiously during 1888 and completed three more manuscripts. The most substantial of them is *The Antichrist.*[37] It was meant to be the first of four books that together would constitute his ambitious new project, "The Transvaluation of All Values". Nietzsche dashed off *The Antichrist* in a hurry. The book is uneven in style, repetitive, filled with flaws and factual errors, and it raised his attacks on Christianity to new, shrill heights. The next two books distracted him from his planned quartet on the transvaluation of all values. *The Case of Wagner* is a short and angry explanation for why Nietzsche parted ways with his one-time idol and friend. The same day he finished it – on 15 October 1888, his 44th birthday – he began *Ecce Homo*[38] and finished it in three weeks. It was a kind of autobiography and betrays the sharp decline of his mind.

This decline is also reflected in letters that he wrote during the final months of 1888. George Brandes in Copenhagen and August Strindberg in Stockholm received odd messages and noticed that something was amiss. Two of Nietzsche's friends in Basel, Jacob Burckhardt and Franz Overbeck, also received enigmatic letters and sensed that something was terribly wrong.

Overbeck travelled to Turin, where he found Nietzsche confused and catatonic in a hospital. The doctors told him that Nietzsche had suffered a mental breakdown on the street on 3 January 1889 and had slid into mental isolation. Overbeck sent for Nietzsche's mother. She first checked him into a mental institution in Jena. Then she took him home to Naumburg. He had slid into a permanent darkness, from which he would never escape.

Conclusion

Friedrich Nietzsche's books are fragmentary composites of essays that are often polemic, and aphorisms that are often paradoxical. On first encounter, his texts can be confusing. Upon closer familiarity, Nietzsche's main message is clear enough: The West is in deep trouble! The Christian, enlightened, modern West is heading for civilizational crisis. This was a powerful message at the time. It attracted increasing attention from the 1890s on.

Nietzsche was not a traditional political philosopher. He did not base his arguments on the rational assumptions of the Enlightenment, and he did not elaborate on modern rights and duties. He was as iconoclastic in his political philosophy as in his theology: He moved away from the set points of modern political thinking. His books did not really discuss the main subject of political philosophy, viz., the relationship between the state and the citizen. Nietzsche was not concerned with the state; and his view of citizenship was close to non-existent. He was interested in language and culture – he was a philologist, after all. He peered into the abyss on the brink of which modern Europeans lived their lives. When he wrote about people, he was mostly interested in great men, whom he placed in a cultural context.

Nietzsche did not discuss the state or state power. "Power *makes stupid*," he wrote.[39] He did not care for the state as an administrative organization; his view was short and dismissive – the state was for him an empty idol – as "the coldest of cold monsters. Coldly it lies; and this lie slips from its mouth: 'I, the state, am the people.'"[40] He did not care for the state as a country; he was more interested in Europe as a whole. And he was not really interested in citizens; he considered them a "herd", a great mass of self-centered people of limited potential.

Nietzsche, in short, was not a political philosopher in the conventional sense of the term. He was concerned with culture and with the supremely talented, creative individual. The men "who live dangerously".[41] His contributions made a deeper impact on the field of psychology than on political science – Sigmund Freud and Carl Gustav Jung were both influenced by Nietzsche's concepts of the unconscious, of sublimation, and of repression.[42]

Nietzsche was an extreme individualist. Georg Brandes hit the nail on the head when he coined the term "aristocratic radicalism" to characterize his philosophy. What kind of politics is associated with this kind of attitude? We may find a clue by viewing Nietzsche's writings in the context of his times.

Nietzsche in context

"His times" begin in 1860, when Nietzsche left a sheltered family life to attend the Protestant school in Pforta. It ends in 1889, when Nietzsche suffered a psychological breakdown, which left him in mental darkness. Nietzsche lived and worked during the thirty years that span these two dates: a period in which Europe's political landscape was shaken and reshaped and when major questions prompted debates on culture and political philosophy. Historians Palmer and Colton offer a pithy summary of the period: European politics, they write, was

> ...marked by hitherto unparalleled material and industrial growth, international peace, domestic stability, the advance of constitutional, representative, and democratic government, and continued faith in science, reason and progress. But in these years, in politics, economics, and basic thinking there were forces operating to undermine the liberal premises and tenets of European civilization.[43]

Nietzsche contributed to these undermining forces. Already as a young student of theology, he expressed a deep skepticism toward the "science, reason and progress" of the period. He favored the sensitive Dionysus over the rational Apollon. However, when he transferred from theology to philology (and when he broke with Wagner), he moved toward the Apollonian view, admiring the scientific method of empirical observation and logical reasoning. He developed an interest in the natural sciences – although he had no natural-science training and did not follow scientific news systematically. He was intrigued by discoveries in electricity and magnetism and fashionable arguments in vitalism and organicism.

While he paid attention to developments in the natural sciences, he neglected the rapid evolution of the social sciences. There is no indication that he paid much consideration to the breakthroughs in economics or sociology of his time. It is a curious neglect, since he raised many of the same questions concerning the "unparalleled material and industrial growth" of society – questions that Tönnies, Sorel, Simmel, Durkheim, Marx, Weber, and other social theorists would expand upon during Nietzsche's decade of darkness. In particular, Nietzsche noticed the mobilization of the popular masses, he observed the social changes that followed, and he feared the consequences.

Nietzsche emerged as a major skeptic of mass mobilization and mass politics, and an advocate of cultural elitism. When read in the context of the age, Nietzsche appears as a reactionary thinker, siding with what Palmer and Colton see as forces that "undermine the liberal premises and tenets of modern, European civilization."[44] In fact, as the century drew toward its end, Nietzsche's elitist politics harmonized with the most reactionary resisters of modernity and progress of the age.

All first-hand accounts agree: Nietzsche was physically small, near sighted and modest; he was polite and correct in all his behavior. As a writer, by contrast, he saw the great mass of people as incurably stupid and worthy only of subordination. He was unapologetically contemptuous of mass life, but admired the talents and the "great spirits" of history. He drew a sharp distinction between two kinds of morality. On the one hand was the slave morality of the unintelligent majority. On the other was the master morality of the intelligent elite.

Nietzsche despised the slave morality. He saw it as a product of the *ressentiment* of the inferior masses and associated it with two inventions of early Christianity: the rejection of the real world and the proposition that all souls were equal before God. He argued that with the death of God, these inventions were taken over by "progressive" movements – by liberal reformers and by the labor movement. He saw these as Christian cults under new names. Toward the end of his life, he expressed a particular hatred for the "socialist rabble, the chandala apostles, who undermine the instinct, the pleasure, the worker's sense of satisfaction with his small existence – who make him envious, who teach him revenge".[45]

Nietzsche admired the master morality of the intelligent, active and culturally dominant elite. This was a morality of creativity and freedom. Nietzsche sought to elaborate upon it in his ethical and political thinking. But since he found very little with which to work in a Western tradition that had been entirely dominated by Christianity, he had to create this master morality himself – out of whole cloth as it were.

It is easy to see how these elitist ideas could be picked up by groups on the political right, for example by the leaders of the German nationalists and the fascist movement. Nietzsche's sister played a crucial role in the way these ideas were appropriated by the leaders of the German far right. In 1889, Elizabeth Nietzsche-Förster returned to Germany – the widow of German nationalist, anti-Semite and Aryan agitator Bernhard Förster – from a failed colonial venture in Paraguay.[46] She assumed possession of her brother's literary estate. With some help from Paul Rée, she organized her brother's many notes, sketches and fragments – his *Nachgelassende Fragmente* or *Nachlass*. She established the *Nietzsche Archive* in Naumburg (in 1894), published an admiring biography of her brother (1895), and worked tirelessly to boost his reputation. She republished his books and put together new volumes from his unpublished fragments.[47]

Her editing was affected by her ideology, which became increasingly associated with German militarism and National Socialism. The most notorious example of this was the posthumous book *The Will to Power*,[48] which she cobbled together from Nietzsche's notes, added elements from his *Nachless*, and published in 1901. Through her efforts, Nietzsche's writings were introduced to the intellectual elite of the German nationalist movement and then the Nazi party. She became a Party member in 1930. Her *Nietzsche Archive* received financial support from the Nazi state thereafter. When she died in 1935, Adolf Hitler attended her funeral together with several high-ranking German officials.[49] In 1940, Adolf Hitler visited the Nietzsche Museum in Sils Maria and let himself be photographed besides a bust of Nietzsche.

Nietzsche, however, was hardly a National Socialist. He never advocated the superiority of the German race and culture (on the contrary, his criticism of Germany was consistent and strong throughout his works) and he never disparaged the Jewish race. (He criticized the Jewish religion, as he criticized all religions, but he also expressed admiration of Jewish art and culture.) However, his main orientation was reactionary. His elitism, his skepticism of the popular masses and his derision of socialism – "the fantastic younger brother of an almost decrepit despotism"[50] – made it easy to place him on the extreme right of Germany's political spectrum.

Nietzsche's writings inspired Continental thinkers early on – men such as Sigmund Freud and Carl Gustav Jung.[51] His arguments first found their way to the English-speaking world through refugees and immigrants – among them Hans J. Morgenthau, whose political Realism is informed by Nietzsche's anthropology, and Ayn Rand, whose novels were influenced by the Nietzschean idea of an elitist morality.[52] Thinkers such as these read Nietzsche in very different ways. A steady stream of new translations and new editions of his works have yielded an even greater variety of readings and interpretations of Nietzsche's ideas. As the 21st century evolves, it may be useful to subject his reactionary criticism of progressive ideas to careful study. It may spark new insights into identity politics and a deeper understanding into populist movements that attack institutions of progress, equality, egalitarianism, and liberal democracy.

Notes

1   See Steven Aschheim, *The Nietzsche Legacy in Germany* (Berkeley and Los Angeles: University of California Press, 1992), *passim*.
2   See "Schopenhauer as Educator", in Friedrich Nietzsche, *Untimely Meditations* (Cambridge: Cambridge University Press, 1997), pp. 125-97.
3   Friedrich A. Lange, *History of Materialism* (Boston: James Osgood & Co., 1877 [1865]).
4   Köselitz would go on to publish books and music under the name Peter Gast (meaning «guest» in German).
5   Friedrich Nietzsche, "The Greek State", in *On the Genealogy of Morals*, trans. from German by Carol Diethe (Cambridge: Cambridge University Press, 1994)., pp. 176-187.
6   *Ibid.*, p.178.
7   *Ibid.*, p. 179.
8   Sue Prideaux, *I Am Dynamite: A Life of Friedrich Nietzsche* (New York: Tim Duggan Books, 2018), pp. 167ff.
9   Friedrich Nietzsche, *Human, All too Human* (extract), trans. by Walter Kaufmann in Walter Kaufmann (ed.), *The Portable Nietzsche* (London: Penguin, 1986), pp. 51-64.
10   The numbers vary with various editions
11   Friedrich Nietzsche, *The Dawn* (extract), trans. by Walter Kaufmann in Kaufmann (ed.), *The Portable Nietzsche*, pp. 76-92. The book's original title, *Morgenröte. Gedanken über die moralischen Vorurteile*, has also been published as *The Dawn of Day* and as *Daybreak: Thoughts on the Prejudices of Morality*
12   Friedrich Nietzsche, *The Gay Science*, trans. from German by Thomas Common (New York: Macmillan, 1924).
13   Fyodor Dostoevsky, *The Brothers Karamazov*, trans. from Russian by Constance Garnett (New York: The Modern Library, 1996 [1880]), pp. 259ff.
14   Fyodor Dostoevsky, *Devils*, trans. from Russian by Constance Garnett (London: Wordsworth Classics, 2020 [1872]).
15   Nietzsche, *The Gay Science*, § 125 (p. 167f).
16   Friedrich Nietzsche, *Beyond Good and Evil: Prelude to a Philosophy of the Future*, trans. from German by Marion Faber (Oxford: Oxford University Press, 2008), p. 52.
17   Nietzsche, *The Gay Science*, § 116 (p. 160).
18   Friedrich Nietzsche, *Thus Spoke Zarathustra*, trans. by Walter Kaufmann

in Kaufmann (ed.), *The Portable Nietzsche*, pp. 103-440.

19 ibid. p. 124.

20 If Nietzsche conceives of the Superman as a product of human evolution, it is a conception that does not sit comfortably with the idea of the eternal return; on the face of it, they seem to be contradictory.

21 Nietzsche, *Beyond Good and Evil*, § 201 (p. 87).

22 Robert C. Holub, «Introduction», in *Nietzsche, Beyond Good and Evil*, pp. vii-xxv.

23 Friedrich Nietzsche *Twilight of the Idols* (extract), trans. from German by Walter Kaufmann, in Kaufmann (ed.), *The Portable Nietzsche*, pp. 463-564.

24 Nietzsche, *Beyond Good and Evil*, §210 (p. 104)

25 *Ibid.*, §9, §19 (pp. 10, 18f).

26 *Ibid.*, §23 (p. 23f).

27 *Ibid.*, § 126 (p. 66).

28 Nietzsche, *On the Genealogy of Morals*, p. 21.

29 See Georg Brandes, *Friedrich Nietzsche* (London: Heinemann, 1889).

30 Nietzsche, *Twilight of the Idols*, p. 543.

31 Nietzsche referred to Schiller as "the Moral-Trumpeter of Säckingen", Victor Hugo as "the pharos at the sea of nonsense", Michelet as "the enthusiasm which takes off its coat", Carlyle as "pessimism as a poorly digested dinner", and J.S. Mill as "insulting clarity" (in *ibid.*, pp. 513ff). *The Twilight of the Idols* shows that Nietzsche's respect for Schopenhauer had faded; his admiration for Emerson, however, remained undiminished (*Ibid.*, p. 522).

32 *Ibid.*, 501f.

33 *Ibid.*, p. 541.

34 Friedrich Nietzsche, *The Antichrist*, trans. from German by Walter Kaufmann in Kaufmann (ed.), *The Portable Nietzsche*, (1986g), §57 (p. 646f)

35 Nietzsche *The Twilight of the Idols*, p. 509

36 *Ibid.*

37 Friedrich Nietzsche, *Antichrist*, trans. from German by Walter Kaufmann, in Kaufmann (ed.), *The Portable Nietzsche*, pp. 565-657.

38 Friedrich Nietzsche, *Ecce Homo*, (extract), trans. from German by Walter Kaufmann, in Kaufmann (ed.), *The Portable Nietzsche*, pp. 657-660.

39 Nietzsche, *Twilight of the Idols*, p. 506.

40 Nietzsche, *Thus Spoke Zarathustra*, p. 160).

41 Nietzsche, *The Gay Science*, §283 (p. 97).

42 See Richard Waugaman, "The Intellectual Relationship between Nietzsche and Freud", in *Psychiatry*, Vol. 36, No. 4 (November 1973), pp. 458-68.

43 Palmer and Colton, *A History of the Modern World* (New York: Alfred A. Knopf, 1971), p. 603.

44 *Idem*

45 Nietzsche, *The Antichrist*, p. 647.

46 Ben Macintyre, *Forgotten Fatherland: The Search for Elizabeth Nietzsche*

(London: Bloomsbury Publishing, 2013).

47 Mazzino Montinari, *Reading Nietzsche* (Chicago: University of Illinois Press, 2003)

48 Friedrich Nietzsche, *The Will to Power: An Attempted Transvaluation of All Values*, trans. from German by Anthony M. Ludovici (London: T.N. Foulis 1914).

49 See Macintyre, *Forgotten Fatherland, passim.*

50 Friedrich Nietzsche, *Human All-Too-Human*, trans. From German by Helen Zimmer (London: George Allen & Unwin, 1924), § 473 (p. 343).

51 See Waugaman, "The Intellectual Relationship", pp. 458-67.

52 Shoshana Milgram, "*The Fountainhead* from Notebook to Novel" in Robert Mayhew (ed.), *Essays on Ayn Rand's "The Fountainhead"* (Lanham, MD: Lexington Books, 2007), pp. 3-41; and Lester H. Hunt, Lester H. (2016) "Ayn Rand's Evolving View of Friedrich Nietzsche," in Allan Gotthelf and Gregory Salmieri (eds.), *A Companion to Ayn Rand* (New York: John Wiley, 2016), pp. 343-350

Afterword

Jonathon W. Moses

I am trained as a political economist, with a strong interest in the subject matter covered in the preceding chapters. In other words, I am neither philosopher nor an expert on 19th century Germany. As a consequence, I read these chapters like most of you: as a wonderfully accessible introduction to a remarkably varied collection of (mostly) German thinkers.

While this anthology offers a concise introduction to "German Moral and Political Philosophy" for the period 1785 to 1908, it is difficult to corral these sundry authors and brand them with a single iron. This is a wide-ranging intellectual herd, fenced in by time, territory, and gender. I suggest that we start by examining, briefly, those fence lines.

In showcasing the 19th century, this collection is framed by revolution. At the start of the period, and to the west, Enlightenment thinking was recasting political reality in the wake of the American (1776) and French (1789) Revolutions. To the east, the same sources of inspiration had been wielded by Catherine the Great (Empress Regnant of Russia from 1762 to 1796) to catapult the Russian Empire into a great European power. The promise of Enlightenment and the shadow of Revolution hung heavily over German thought from the start of this period to the end, when Germany comes to face World War One, the October Revolution in Russia (1917), and its own November Revolution (1918).

In between these revolutionary bookends lies a country under construction. As Torbjørn Knutsen describes in the introduction (p.3), the thinkers covered in this book "did not live in a state but in a fictional empire (the Holy Roman Empire of the German People) held together by a common language." As a German Empire came into being—from an amalgamation of smaller principalities, and under threat from strong states abroad—German thought was understandably preoccupied with nation-building and the need to find a German path into the modern world.

But this very context may help to explain the third feature shared by the authors in this collection: they are all men. In other European contexts, where state boundaries had been settled and Enlightenment thinking had made stronger inroads, we begin to see the development of a nascent feminist movement. By the end of the 19th century, the voice and influence of women thinkers, authors and activists was on the rise across much of Europe. Germany, again, was the odd man out.

In short, our authors have introduced us to a wonderfully intricate dialogue, stretching across more than a century and more than a nation, but confined solely to men. While the works discussed were produced between 1785 and 1908, the lives of the German authors under consideration mostly overlapped with one another (the exception is Nietzsche). This can be seen in Figure 1, which portrays the lifespans of the German authors covered in this work, in chronological order.[1] From this figure it is possible to see two temporal waves: the first generation of thinkers was born in the 18th century (before 1780), and includes Kant, Hamann, Herder, Fichte, Schleiermacher, and Hegel. The second wave was born after 1800, the last of whom—Friedrich Nietzsche—lived most of his short life in the second half of the 19th century.

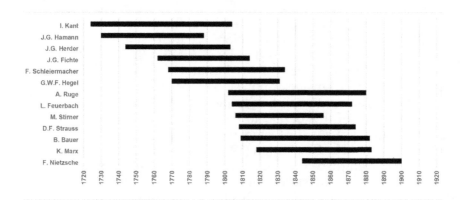

Figure 1: Author timeline

I have a hunch that many young readers will be unfamiliar with the underlying political context, from which these ideas sprout. For this reason, I will use the Afterword to elaborate upon one of two central themes that unite these sundry authors: there is more than one route to political modernity. Although I hesitate to use the term, in light of its chequered political past, this is the lesson of the *Sonderweg,* or the separate path, to which several of the chapters refer, and to which I will return later. While much of the Sonderweg's lesson has been lost to contemporary politics, I will close this chapter by reflecting briefly on its continued relevance.

It is important for me to emphasize that this theme is just one of several described above. The preceding chapters have covered much contested terrain in early modern German thought, including citizenship, morality, religion, methodology, and the role of the state. As our title suggests, these disparate themes can be fruitfully collected under two rubrics, moral and political. This Afterword is focused on the latter. In doing so, I do not mean to ignore or devalue the important moral and religious themes that reverberated throughout the chapters on Kant, Hegel, Schleiermacher, Nietzsche, and the others. I am simply covering the area I know best.

A Germany in the making

It is possible, but not easy, to speak of Germany in 1875. The first unification of Germany had begun only four years earlier, in 1871, when princes from across a number of German states gathered at the Palace of Versailles (in France!) to proclaim King Wilhelm I (of Prussia) as the Kaiser (Emperor) of Germany.

In particular, the Imperial State of Germany was a political hodgepodge that drew from twenty-six states, seven principalities, six grand duchies, five duchies, four constituent kingdoms, three free Hanseatic cities, and one imperial territory. It brought together a number of south German states (absent Austria), with what was called the North German Confederation. The North German Confederation, in turn, was itself only four years old (born in 1867) — an offspring of the Austro-Prussian War, whose peace treaty allowed Prussia to create a federal state in Northern Germany.

This disparate collection of states and polities had previously gathered under a number of confederal arrangements for over a thousand years, most recently under the umbrella of the Holy Roman Empire. Nevertheless, their political identities remained remarkably parochial — especially after the Thirty Years War — in an arrangement sometimes referred to as *Kleinstaaterei* ["small-statery"]. To give you an idea of these divided states of affairs, an *Atlas of European History* estimated that there were as many as 294 to 348 German states in existence at any given time during the 18th century.[2] When the Holy Roman Empire collapsed (in 1806), the German-speaking areas were divided into hundreds of local customs areas, each surrounded by tariff barriers that deterred commerce and exchange. To create a common political community, it was first necessary to cut down this forest of barriers.

Figure 2: Zollschranken[3] [Customs barriers].

Note: The caption "*das lichten eines hochwaldes*" might be translated as "the clearing of a tall forest".

The Zollverein

Much of the groundwork for German unification was cleared by the German Customs Union, or Zollverein,[4] where several sovereign states agreed to integrate their economies without first agreeing to an overarching political union. In particular, the Zollverein was an agreement to reduce internal barriers to trade, while maintaining a common trade policy vis-à-vis the outside world. To facilitate this, the Zollverein included a population-based revenue distribution scheme, a governance structure with a regular member state congress meeting annually, and rules that constrained member state use of public monopolies and producer taxes.[5]

It is important to point out that a customs union is *not* an economic union, and it is distinct from a free trade area. A customs union lies somewhere in between these two forms of economic integration—a goldilocks solution that allows states to balance the economic benefits of integration while maintaining a certain degree of political autonomy. A free trade agreement allows member states to exchange goods within a specified area without imposing tariffs or other types of trade barriers. But a free trade agreement does not extend to other areas of economic policy, including tariffs or trade barriers with the outside world. For example, the European Free Trade Area (EFTA) is a free trade area: its member states remain free to negotiate their own trade policies with outside (third party) states. An economic union, on the other hand, requires member states to jettison much of their economic sovereignty. For example, the European Union is an economic union that severely limits member-state fiscal, regulatory, procurement and monetary policies.[6] A customs union like the Zollverein lies somewhere in between these two integration options: it places some restrictions on member state sovereignty (in that it eliminates both internal tariffs and trade restrictions), but it also imposes a shared trade policy vis-à-vis third-party states. Members of a customs union share a common tariff policy with the outside world, but they are still free to pursue their own autonomous economic policies. This allows member states more economic sovereignty than they can expect in a full-blown economic union (or unitary state).

The seeds of the Zollverein were first planted in 1818, when Prussia began to modernize its own customs and tariff structures. Prussia then signed its first customs union agreement in 1828, which led to the 1834 Zollverein agreement that united seven German states. Over the course of the next 18 years, several other states followed suit and joined the union—the last being Oldenburg in

1852.[7] While the early years of the Zollverein allowed member states some degree of political autonomy, much of this autonomy was eroded with the arrival of the German Empire in 1871, when the Kaiser took over control of the customs union.

In building this new economic and political community, Germans were surrounded by many sources of inspiration. Although European liberal thought and the Enlightenment provided sufficient intellectual support for unification, they tended to question dynastic and absolutist approaches to political development. This did not stop the Prussian King. While the German Empire was formally organized in a way that afforded member states equal influence; in practice, Prussian interests dominated. Executive power was vested in the German Kaiser, who could appoint and dismiss the Chancellor of his choosing. The other states in the Empire retained their own governments, but other aspects of sovereignty were restricted (e.g., the printing of stamps and the issuing of coins).

The Empire was not without democratic features (although it is important not to exaggerate these) and the early years of Otto von Bismarck's rule (1871-1890) as Chancellor can be characterized in fairly liberal terms. There was universal (male) suffrage, but it was channelled through an electoral system that over-represented rural areas. Political parties were also allowed to develop, but removed from real political influence. Liberalism in the German Empire was mostly a Potemkin's village, and the Empire succumbed to a more reactionary line: it eventually embraced colonialism and entered into a number of dicey foreign alliances, which ended in World War One.

German Feminism

Given this fractured nature of German political life, and its relatively illiberal tone, it is perhaps not surprising to learn that feminism had a hard time taking root in German soil.[8] Before the Empire, Germanic law (based on Salic, or Franconian law), placed women at a disadvantage in terms of property, inheritance rights, formal representation, etc. Even in the late 19th century, German women were not free to administer their own property—this was done by their male guardians.

The reasons for this male dominance are complex, but the results are clearly evident. The German unification process was dominated by men, and they framed the struggle for independence in male-dominant terms: e.g., they were building a "fatherland", and focused on the need for military prowess. Still, toward the end of the period under consideration, during the Wilhelmine period (1888-1918), we see the start of a German feminist movement, which culminated with women's suffrage in 1919.

Whereas Enlightenment thinking was opening windows of influence for bourgeois women authors and activists in other European countries—consider, e.g. Mary Wollstonecraft in England (1759-1797)—they are less prominent in Germany. One notable exception was the life and work of Sophie Mereau, whose work deserves more attention (see Box). Sophie Mereau was a well-connected and prolific writer who targeted female audiences by producing narratives that revolved around a number of women's issues. She first rose to prominence in 1791 as the only female student in Johann Gottlieb Fichte's private seminars in philosophy.

Sophie Mereau (1770-1806)[9]

Sophie Shubart was born in 1770 in Altenburg (near Leipzig) but moved to Jena in 1793 to marry Friedrich Enrst Karl Mereau, who was Professor of Philosophy and later Professor of Law (in 1880) at the University in Jena. Their home was a gathering spot for Jena's poets and artists, and this put the couple in contact with Friedrich Schiller (who subsequently became a mentor for Sophie's literary career), Johann von Herder, Johann Wolfgang von Goethe, and other important thinkers. In 1791, Sophie became the first woman to attend philosophy lectures at Jena University with none other than Johann Gottlieb Fichte.

In 1801, Sophie divorced Mereau, winning her the distinction of being the first woman in the duchy of Saxe-Weimar to divorce and build an independent life for herself and her daughter. As she wrote most of her best-known works under the married name of Mereau, we use this name as our reference, but she had many (at the time scandalous) extramarital relationships, and she remarried two years later, in 1803, to one of them: Clemens Bernanto.

Sophie Mereau's literary work is saturated with concern for women's issues. Her first work of poetry "France's Celebration" praised the ideals of the French Revolution. In addition to authoring a number of nature and landscape poems, Mereau contributed to almanacs, and edited several of these—including an *Almanach für Frauen ins Leben* and *Deutschland*, the latter of which published works by von Herder, von Goethe and others. Her literary work targeted women audiences by focusing on issues such as free love and women's independence (e.g., "Marie" (1798); "Elise" (1800); "Some small paintings" (1801); and "Flight to the Capital" (1806)); and she was responsible for the German translation of Montesquieu's *Persian Letters*. Her two novels celebrated freedom, love and the autonomy and independence of women. The first of which, *The Blossom Age of Sensation* (1794), was written anonymously, while parts of her (1803) *Amanda and Eduard* were published in Schiller's *Die Horen*.

Sophie Mereau was not alone, and her efforts were multiplied by a growing feminist movement. Louise Otto-Peters (1819-1895) helped to establish the *Allgemeiner Deutscher Frauenverein* [the General German Women's Association] in 1865 and Helen Lange (1848-1930) was a teacher who founded a number of different women's suffrage groups. Clara Zetkin (1857-1933) was an activist fighting for stronger women's representation in trade unions (along with suffrage and abortion rights). In 1901, Lily Braun (1865-1916) published her remarkable *Die Frauenfragen*,[10] where the continued economic oppression of women was blamed on capitalism. While the works of these women, and others like them, are not well known, a useful collection of translations can be found in Herminghouse and Mueller's *German Feminist Writings*.[11]

By the end of our period, in 1894, middle-class women could join the *Bund Deutscher Frauenvereine* (BDF) [the Federation of German Women's Organizations], which came to include 137 different women's groups (and was subsequently dissolved by the Nazi regime). The BDF was a civic organization whose members campaigned for equality with men in areas such as education, financial opportunities and political life, but the BDF excluded working-class women. These women were organized by the socialists, with remarkable success and political effect, as can be seen in the life of Rosa Luxemburg (1871-1919), a Polish-born activist who became a German citizen in 1897.

The Sonderweg

In the same way that German women were struggling to secure more autonomy in male-dominated German politics, German thinkers were negotiating the dominant ideological currents of the late 19th century, with hopes of finding their own route to political development. Many 19th century German thinkers believed in the existence of a positive "German way"— that the path taken by the German-speaking lands, from aristocracy to democracy, was unlike the paths chosen elsewhere —whether it was the materialist and utilitarian path in the West (France, Great Britain), or the more absolutist paths in the East (e.g. Tsarist Russia).[12] This section focuses on that particular German route to political modernity.

The Sonderweg can be seen as a German response to Enlightenment thought, in both English and French form, which was sweeping across Europe in the wake of Napoleon's army. In the collection above, this Enlightenment thought arrives in Germany, by way of Kant, and the rest of the book can be read as a German reaction to Kant's effort. Although I will follow the lead of our authors in calling this German reaction "the Sonderweg," it is important that we proceed with caution.

The reason for this caution is the existence of a rich and controversial literature that connects the Sonderweg in post-World War Two historiography, with reference to a modernization paradigm associated with the work of Fritz Fischer[13] and Hans-Ulrich Wehler[14] in the 1960s and 1970s.

As Curi and Alemeida make clear,[15] it is possible to trace out several different and competing approaches to the Sonderweg, including what they call "a positive *Sonderweg*" (associated with prominent scholars such as Max Weber, Gustav Schmoller, Friedrich Meinecke, and Ernst Troeltsch); "a bellicose version" developed after the November Revolution, and was subsequently appropriated by the national socialist movement;[16] and a "negative *Sonderweg* line".[17] A similar point[18] is made by Kocka's reintroduction to the "Sonderweg Debates" in the pages of *Central European History*, where he distinguishes between scholars that are sympathetic and/or critical to the approach, the latter of which are willing to draw "a straight line 'from Luther to Hitler'."[19]

We have chosen to side-line the more critical or bellicose versions of the term, and use the *Sonderweg* to describe the German reaction to the Enlightenment approaches for political development. These Enlightenment approaches to development, stemming from both France and England, emphasized universal values, methodological individualism, the use of reason, and market-based solutions.

These are the intellectual goods that Kant imported into the German marketplace of ideas. As Sabrina Ramet's chapter (Chapter 2) makes clear, Kant is primarily known for his ethical works, but his political argument is mainstream Enlightenment (with a German twist): he rejects revolution (until it succeeds) but embraces many of the underlying norms that the (French) revolution was spreading across Europe. This liberal emphasis is most clearly evident in the work that gains the most attention by my fellow political scientists, his (1795) *Perpetual Peace*, which lays out the promise of international organizations and laws—rooted in reason, universal rights, and market-based principles—that could limit sovereign authority and set the groundwork for perpetual peace.

After Kant is introduced in Chapter 2, the remaining chapters can be read as a collection of disparate reactions to Kant and this liberal approach to political development. Their collective responses sketch out a unique, German, path to political development. This *Sonderweg* is based on particular (not universal) principles; is rooted in the community and its language/culture (not the individual), and prioritizes the political over the economic. Along the *Sonderweg*, economic exchange is not an end in itself, but is a means to secure political objectives.

In one way it is curious that German thinkers were so skeptical of Enlightenment thinking and the political goods it produced. After all, Enlightenment thought provided the kind of intellectual supports that were useful in creating a new political community, as evidenced by the American Revolution and its subsequent constitution. One might speculate that this sort of thinking is exactly what was needed by a political entity like the German Empire, trying to create a state where none had previously existed. In this light, the American Revolution offered itself as a premier example of the self-created state, built on reason, from scratch. And yet it is remarkable how little attention was paid to the American revolution or American thought by the works considered in this anthology: their focus is clearly trained on the political lessons of the French and English Enlightenments. But French and British thinkers were products of settled, established states—while German thinkers were not. At any rate, not yet.

The reaction to Kant was a reaction to these Enlightenment political norms. When our focus is trained more on the political, as opposed to the moral, then it may seem odd to use Kant as the keystone to this collection. A viable alternative can be found in Kant's contemporary, Friedrich List (see Box), who had travelled to the United States, and used his American experience to sketch out an alternative route to (economic) development. List's vision of economic nationalism offers a perfect complement to the *Sonderweg* described in the post-Kantian chapters of the anthology.

Friedrich List (1789-1846)[20]

Born in Southern Germany, List was appointed Professor of Administration at the University at Tübingen in 1817. List was politically active in support of reducing internal barriers to trade in Germany (work which eventually resulted in the formation of the Zollverein in 1834), and he was elected as a deputy to the lower chamber of the Württemberg Diet. His political activities landed him in trouble: he was accused of treason, expelled from the Diet and dismissed from the University. He was eventually released from prison after promising to emigrate to America, which he did in 1825 (where he stayed until 1830).

List is often heralded as a forefather of the German historical school of economics, and he is best known today for his *National System of Political Economy* (1841).[21] This work can be seen as a product of his earlier campaign to secure a German customs union from a nationalist perspective, combined with his study of early American economic policy, especially that associated with Alexander Hamilton.[22] List advocated the use of tariffs on imported goods, while supporting free trade in domestic goods, to provide young (infant) industries with the protection they needed to mature, before being exposed to greater (international) competition.

List also recognized the need to distinguish between the rhetoric of liberalism, and its practice. The sort of free trade advocated by classical (British) economists was the economic policy of the strong, not the result of some inherent "law of comparative advantage". The law of comparative advantage was little more than a rationalization of the existing international division of labour, and it was used to prioritize (more established) British interests over those in less developed economies. List saw how Britain and the US grew out of protected markets, with strong political support. He then argued that developing countries should do as these countries practiced, not as they preached.

For List, a nation's trade policy should be used to nurture the development of its domestic industry, for the benefit of its people. When a country embraces free trade, it undermines its autonomy and its capacity to control the national economy by exposing it to the vicissitudes and instabilities of the world market and by exploitation from other, more powerful states. Worse, the logic of comparative advantage—which advocates specialization (especially in commodity exports)—reduces flexibility, increases the vulnerability of the economy, subordinates the domestic to the international economy, and threatens domestic industries.

In List, we find another important German thinker from the early 19th century. His work in the field of political economy dovetails nicely with the Sonderweg approach to modernization outlined in several of the post-Kantian chapters of this collection.

Many of the thinkers in this collection could be linked up to List's vision of the Sonderweg, where Germany needed to build a state that could protect its unique characteristics and not succumb to the rhetoric of free markets, methodological individualism, powerful international institutions, and the hegemony of reason. This

Afterword does not afford the room necessary to address each and every one of these possible connections, so I will focus now on a few of the most significant (but perhaps least known) of them.

All of the authors described in Chapter 3 were interested in linguistic diversity and cultural pluralism, and that language provided keys to interpreting reality in unique ways. It is in the work of these authors that we find a cultural justification for the Sonderweg. These thinkers questioned the centrality of reason (e.g., Hamann), and universality (both Herder and Fichte) in Enlightenment approaches. For them, political development was rooted in language, culture, and identity—it developed along evolutionary lines and was place-specific, not universal. As Fichte learned from the French occupation, the German people would need a strong and independent state if they were to preserve their distinct culture and enjoy freedom and identity. Some of this strength came from the need to secure greater economic autonomy, as Knutsen mentions in his chapter, when pointing to Fichte's remarkable book on *The Closed Commercial State*.[23] This book is so important, and yet so little read: it deserves more attention (see Box).

Fichte's *The Closed Commercial State*[24]

Fichte's book *The Closed Commercial State* (1800) can be read as a direct response to Kant's proposal for *Perpetual Peace*; it "redefined the political economy of the Kantian ideal and extended it into a strategic analysis of the prospect for pacifying modern Europe."[25]

In particular, Fichte hoped to reconcile J.J. Rousseau's ideal of free citizenship in small autonomous communities with the realities of modern commercial societies (marked, in Fichte's time, by a decline in agriculture in favor of industry and a rapidly increasing division of labour). *The Closed Commercial State* was an outline for an economic policy suited for the Sonderweg. Whereas List justified the utility of harnessing trade as an instrument of national economic development, Fichte emphasized the need to use state power to secure a more just political order at home. To secure legitimacy, the modern state had to be able to minimize the insecurities and inequities produced by an expanding capitalist economy, as these inhibited the capacity for fellow citizens to flourish. To do this, Europe needed to integrate its economies in a way that would allow its member states sufficient control over local economic conditions. Fichte wanted us to prioritize justice over efficiency, political sovereignty over economic integration.

For Fichte, Europe could not secure a perpetual peace unless the economic life of its member states could be disentangled from the competitive dynamics of the new economy. What was needed was greater sovereign authority over local economic conditions — greater opportunities for planning and tools that could create self-sufficient national economies. By controlling its own monetary policy, the modern state could bring about a moral transformation of economic relations — as this monetary autonomy could secure a more equal division of labour and wealth, without the need for massive expropriations, or the need to deter international trade. The outlines of this proposal are not all that different than those that were agreed to at the Bretton Woods conference in 1944 — and provided the international context that generated the Golden Era of post-World War Two capitalism.[26]

In Fichte's recipe for German economic development at the turn of the 19th century, the state was given a pivotal role in reorganizing society so that all of its members would enjoy the opportunity to cultivate their respective individualities, to the richest and fullest extent possible. To secure this opportunity, the state needed to guarantee its citizens a right to work.

We can see similar reactions to Enlightenment themes in Hegel's focus on a more organic form of state, where national customs and ethics were allowed greater freedom to roam (see Chapter 4). Rather than strong individuals and weak states, Hegel sees a powerful state as a precondition for freedom and dignity:

In considering freedom, the starting-point must not be individuality, the single self-consciousness, but only the essence of self-consciousness; for whether man knows it or not, this essence is externally realized as self-subsistent power in which single individuals are only moments. The march of God in the world, that is what the state is. The basis of the state is the power of reason actualizing itself as will.[27]

Each of the chapters in this collection could be used to link up to a vision of Germany pursuing its *Sonderweg*, but along different fronts. If Hegel can be said to have turned Enlightenment thinking on its head, then the authors that follow him in our collection continue the head rolling. Marx, most famously, is said to have turned Hegelian thinking on its head by prioritizing the real over the ideal, and offering a new form of Enlightenment critique, rooted in class, rather than the individual or the state (Chapter 7). Then Nietzsche, in turn, throws this all in a spin with his transvaluation of all values (Chapter 8). I do not have the space to elaborate here, but I expect that readers are already familiar with Marx's and Nietzsche's critique of mainstream economic and political development.

What we can find in all these authors is an unwillingness to surrender to the invisible laws of commerce, or to a political sphere that is drained of its autonomy. The authors of the *Sonderweg* recognize the need to prioritize the political and the moral over the narrow logic of market exchange.

Conclusion

In most respects, the *Sonderweg* resulted in a dead end. While Kant, Marx, Hegel, and Nietzsche are still able to muster large audiences in the English-reading world, most of the other authors in this collection receive much less attention, and are of interest mostly to a specialized group of readers.

After World War Two, German thought was marginalized, and the *Sonderweg* was marginalized along with it. Although Kant remains very popular (because he reaffirmed the utility of Enlightenment thinking), many of the other thinkers included in this collection have been placed in intellectual mothballs, as a new Germany and a new Europe rose from the ashes of the Second World War.

When I conducted a Google Book N-gram search in the English-language for all the German authors in this collection, Kant and Marx were clearly the most referenced, with Kant's popularity growing strongly after 1980. Hegel and Nietzsche were less popular (scoring about half of Kant's and Marx's references), with all the other authors in this collection trailing far behind.[28] To give you an idea of the spread in popularity, Figure 3 provides a snapshot from the year 2019, the last year for the N-gram data.

Figure 3: English-Language Google Books Ngram, 2019.

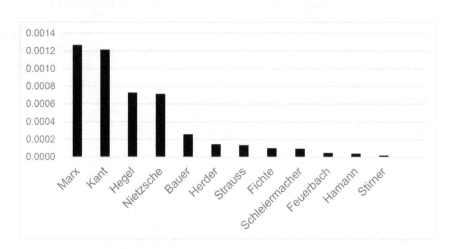

Source: Google Books Ngram Viewer, https://books.google.com/ngrams. Accessed 12 January 2023.

Note: There is much controversy over the actual scoring techniques used by the Ngram viewer, so this figure should be taken with a grain of salt. The vertical axis reports the use of these author names, relative to all the words published in 2019 in English language books.

But the new Europe is remarkably similar to the old. Like Germany in the late 19th century, Europe has spent the last part of the 20th century trying to create a new political constellation, by uniting a number of autonomous states into a common market and a new type of state: a European Union. In so doing, Europe has drawn heavily from a liberal tradition that descends directly from Kant and the enlightenment tradition, with a focus on international institutions promising perpetual peace.

Like German integration, European political integration was fuelled by a drive to integrate markets. The post-war European Community also started as a customs union but slowly evolved into an economic union that has placed greater and greater restraints on the political powers of its member states. This increased integration (both in scope and depth), was heavily informed by market principles, and the desire to establish a common market. This European Union was built on the sort of universal principles embraced by Enlightenment thinkers and resulted in four new freedoms: the freedom of mobility for goods, services, capital, and labor. But these are market-affirming freedoms, not life-affirming freedoms. The resulting EU is similar to the German Empire, in that member states have sacrificed a great deal of political autonomy to secure some of the benefits of economic integration.

Contemporary followers of the thinkers reviewed in this anthology will find much in modern European politics to criticize. The European Union has introduced the sort of Enlightenment state, at the continental level, against which these authors argued so vehemently. In doing so, the European Union has made it impossible to secure the sort of authentic, sovereign, German state to which the Sonderweg led. Seen from this perspective, the Sonderweg still offers a different path to political modernity, and a critique of mainstream approaches to political development that continues to resonate.

Notes

1   This timeline does not include many of the non-German authors covered in Chapter 6 (e.g., Proudhon, Bakunin, Kropotkin, Saint Simon…). This is done mostly to make the graphic easier to read.

2   The Times, *Atlas of European History* (London: Harper Collins, 1994), p. 127.

3   Machahn, "Zollschranken." Scanned 24 July 2007. Part of the public domain. Online at: https://upload.wikimedia.org/wikipedia/commons/8/88/Zollschranken.jpg. Accessed 8 February 2022. Originally published as "das Lichten eines Hochwaldes," in The Münich-based satirical magazine *Fliegende Blätter*, Vol. 6, No. 140 (1847), p. 157.

4   This is not to suggest that the customs union created the political union, although this argument is common enough. Smaller member states benefited economically from the customs union, and they often used this new source of revenue to strengthen their resistance to Prussia and Berlin and to secure greater political independence. See Hans-Hoachim Voth, "Prussian Zollverein and the bid for economic superiority", in P. Dwyer (ed) *Modern Prussian History, 1830-1947* (London: Routledge, 2001), pp. 109-125.

5   Florian Ploeckl, "The Zollverein and the sequence of a customs union." *Australian Economic History Review* Vol. 55, No.3 (2015): 277-301, p.278; Florian Ploeckl, "A novel institution: the Zollverein and the origins of

the custom union", in *Journal of International Economics* Vol. 17 (2021): 305-319, p. 306. For more background on the Zollvereien, see Arnold Price, *The Evolution of the Zollverein* (Ann Arbor: University of Michigan Press, 1949) and Richard Bazillion, "Economic integration and political sovereignty: Saxony and the *Zollvereien, 1834-1877*", in *Canadian Journal of History* Vol 25 (1990), pp. 189-213.

6   Jonathon W. Moses, *Workaway: The Human Costs of Europe's Common Labour Market* (Bristol: Bristol University Press, 2021); and Jonathon W. Moses, *Eurobondage: The Political Costs of Monetary Union in Europe* (Basingstoke: ECPR Press, 2017).

7   See Ploeckl, "A novel institution", p. 284, Table 1, for a list of states included, the dates of their inclusion and relevant descriptive statistics.

8   Eda Sagarra, *A Social History of Germany: 1648-1914* (London & New York: Routledge, 2017 [1977]), p. 406.

9   There is little written in English on Sophie Mereau, but some additional background can be found in chapter 3 of Todd Kontje, *Women, the Novel, and the German Nation 1771-1871* (Cambridge: Cambridge University Press, 1998) and "Sophie Mereau" in *Who's Who: The Peoples Lexicon.* https://whoswho.de/bio/sophie-mereau.html. Accessed 30 January 2022.

10   Lily Braun, *Die Frauenfrage* (Leipzig: Verlag von S. Hirzel, 2004 [1901]).

11   Patricia A. Herminghouse and Magda Mueller (eds.), *German Feminist Writings* (London: Continuum, 2001).

12   See, e.g., Barrington Moore Jr., *Social Origins of Dictatorship and Democracy* (Boston: Beacon Press, 1966); and Perry Anderson, *Lineages of the Absolutist State* (London: Verso Books, 1974).

13   E.g. Fritz Fischer, *Germany's Aims in the First World War*) [*Griff nach der Weltmacht*, 1961] (New York: W. W. Norton, 1967 [1931]).

14   E.g., Hans-Ulrich Wehler, *Bismark und der Imperialismus* (Kiepenheur & Witsch verlag, 2017 [1966]); Hans-Ulrich Wehler, "Bismark's Imperialism, 1862-1890", in *Past and Present* Vol. 48 (1970), pp. 119-155; and Hans-Ulrich Wehler, *The German Empire, 1871-1918*, translated by Kim Traynor (Hamburg: Berg Publishers, 1985).

15   Luiz Felipe Bruzzi Curi and Ian Coelho de Souza Almeida, "Beyond the *Sonderweg*: defining political economy in 19th Century Germany", in *The European Journal of the History of Economic Thought*, 2021, pp.3-4.

16   E.g. Hans-Ulrich Wehler, *Deutsche Gesellschaftsgeschichte.* Vol 3: 1849-1914 (München: C. H. Beck, 2008), p. 464.

17   As associated with Georg G. Iggers, "The Decline of the Classic National Tradition of German Historiography", in *History and Theory* Vol. 6, No. 3 (1967), pp. 382-412 and Avraham Barkai. *Nazi Economics: Ideology, Theory, and Policy*, Translated by Ruth Hadass-Vashitz (Oxford: Berg, [1977] 1990).

18   See also Helmut Walser Smith, "When the *Sonderweg* Debate Left Us", in *German Studies Review*, Vol. 31, No. 2 (2008), pp. 225-40; and Jürgen Kocka, "Asymmetrical Historical Comparison: The Case of the German *Sonderweg*", in *History and Time* Vol. 38, No. 1 (1999), pp. 40-51.

19 Jürgen Kocka, "Looking Back on the Sonderweg", in *Central European History*, Vol. 51 (2018), pp. 137-142, p. 138.

20 To learn more about List, and his approach to political economy, see William Otto Henderson, *Friedrich List: Economist and Visionary* (London: Frank Cass, 1983); David Levi-Faur, "Friedrich List and the political economy of the nation-state", in *Review of International Political Economy*, Vol. 4, No. 1 (1997), pp. 154-178; and Ha-Joon Chang, *Kicking away the Ladder: Development strategy in Historical Perspective* (London: Anthem Press, 2002).

21 Friedrich List, *The National System of Political Economy* [*Das Nationale System der Politischen Ökonomie*], translated by Sampson S. Lloyd (London: Longmans, Green and Co, 1901 [1841]). Online version at https://archive.org/details/nationalsystemp01nichgoog/page/n12/mode/2up.

22 Chang, *Kicking away the Ladder*.

23 Johann Gottlieb Fichte, *The Closed Commercial State* [*Der geschlossene Handelsstaat*], Translated and with an interpretive essay by Anthony Curtis Alder (Albany: State University of New York Press, 2012 [1800]).

24 For a contemporary introduction to Fichte's *Closed Commercial State*, see Isaac Nakhimovsky, *The Closed Commercial State: Perpetual Peace and Commercial Society from Rousseau to Fichte* (Princeton, N.J.: Princeton University Press, 2011).

25 Nakhimovsky, *Closed Commercial State*, p. 2.

26 John Gerard Ruggie, "International regimes, transactions, and change: embedded liberalism in the post-war economic order", in *International Organization*, Vol. 36, No. 2 (1982), pp. 379-415.

27 Georg Wilhelm Friedrich Hegel, *Philosophy of Right*, translated by T.M. Knox (Oxford: Oxford University Press, 1967 [1821]), § 258.

28 A similar picture can be found in mapping the French literature on these authors, while it should not be surprising to learn that a German-language N-gram provides more long-standing interest for many of the other authors.

Further reading

In addition to works by the philosophers themselves, the following secondary sources may also prove useful:

Chapter 1: Introduction

Ameriks, Karl (ed.). *The Cambridge Companion to German Idealism* (Cambridge: Cambridge University Press, 2017)

Bubner, Rudiger (ed.). *German Idealist Philosophy* (New York: Penguin Classics, 1997)

Bowie, Andrew. *German Philosophy: A Very Short Introduction* (Oxford & New York: Oxford University Press, 2010)

Haddock, Bruce. *A History of Political Thought, 1789 to the Present* (Malden, Mass.: Polity Press, 2005)

Thornhill, Chris. *German Political Philosophy: The Metaphysics of Law* (London & New York: Routledge, 2007)

Watson, Peter. *German Genius: Europe's third renaissance, the second scientific revolution, and the twentieth century* (New York: Simon & Schuster, 2019)

Chapter 2: Immanuel Kant

Beck, Lewis W. "Kant and the Right of Revolution", in *Journal of the History of Ideas*, Vol. 32, no. 3 (July—September 1971)

Beiner, Ronald and William James Booth (eds.). *Kant & Political Philosophy: The Contemporary Legacy* (New Haven, Conn.: Yale University Press, 1993)

Kuehn, Manfred. *Kant: A Biography* (Cambridge: Cambridge University Press, 2001)

Scruton, Roger. *Kant: A very short introduction* (Oxford: Oxford University Press, 2001)

Williams, Howard. *Kant's critique of Hobbes: Sovereignty and cosmopolitanism* (Cardiff: University of Wales Press, 2003)

Wood, Allen W. *Kant's Ethical Thought* (Cambridge: Cambridge University Press, 1999)

Chapter 3: The German Anti-Enlightenment

Ameriks, Karl (ed.). *The Cambridge Companion to German Idealism* (Cambridge: Cambridge University Press, 2000).

Fichte, Johann G. *Addresses to the German Nation* (Cambridge: Cambridge University Press, 2008)

Gardner, Patrick. *Fichte and German Idealism* (Cambridge: Cambridge University Press, 2010)

Nakhimovsky, Isaac. *The Closed Commercial State: Perpetual Peace and Commercial Society from Rousseau to Fichte* (Princeton, N.J.: Princeton University Press, 2011)

O'Hear, Anthony. *German political Philosophy Since Kant* (Cambridge: Cambridge University Press, 2009)

Sternhell, Zeev. The Anti-Enlightenment Tradition (New Haven, Conn.: Yale University Press, 2009)

Chapter 4: Georg Wilhelm Friedrich Hegel

Buck-Morss, Susan. *Hegel, Haiti, and Universal History* (Pittsburgh, Pa.: University of Pittsburgh Press, 2009)

Cristi, F. R. "Hegel's Conservative Liberalism", in *Canadian Journal of Political Science / Revue canadienne de science politique,* Vol. 22, No. 4 (December 1989)

Cristi, Renato. *Hegel on freedom and authority* (Cardiff: University of Wales Press, 2005)

Smith, Steven B. "Hegel's Critique of Liberalism", in *American Political Science Review,* Vol. 80, No. 1 (March 1986)

Smith, Steven B. *Hegel's Critique of Liberalism: Rights in Context* (Chicago: University of Chicago Press, 1989)

Taylor, Charles. *Hegel and Modern Society* (Cambridge: Cambridge University Press, 2015)

Chapter 5: Friedrich Schleiermacher

Brandt, Richard B. *The Philosophy of Schleiermacher: The development of his theory of scientific and religious knowledge* (Westport, Conn.: Greenwood Press, 1968, 1971; reprinted from New York: Harper & Row, 1941)

Lamm, Julia A. "The Early Philosophic Roots of Schleiermacher's Notion of Gefühl, 1788-1794", in *The Harvard Theological Review,* Vol. 87, No. 1 (January 1994)

Lamm, Julia A. *The Living God: Schleiermacher's theological appropriation of Spinoza* (University Park, Pa.: Pennsylvania State University Press, 1996)

Raack, R. C. "Schleiermacher's Political Thought and Activity, 1806-1813", in *Church History*, Vol. 28, No. 4 (December 1959)

Sockness, Brent W. "The Forgotten Moralist: Friedrich Schleiermacher and the Science of Spirit", in *The Harvard Theological Review*, Vol. 96, No. 3 (July 2003)

Sockness, Brent W. "Schleiermacher and the Ethics of Authenticity: The 'Monologen' of 1800", in *The Journal of Religious Ethics*, Vol. 32, No. 3 (Winter 2004),

Chapter 6: The Young Hegelians

Brazill, William J. *The Young Hegelians* (New Haven, Conn.: Yale University Press, 1970)

McLellan, David. *The Young Hegelians and Karl Marx* (London: Macmillan, 1969)

Massey, Marilyn Chapin. "Censorship and the Language of Feuerbach's 'Essence of Christianity'' (1841)", in *The Journal of Religion*, Vol. 65, No. 2 (April 1985)

Massey, Marilyn Chapin. "David Friedrich Strauss and His Hegelian Critics", in *The Journal of Religion*, Vol. 57, No. 4 (October 1977)

Paterson, R. W. K. *The Nihilist Egoist: Max Stirner* (Oxford & London: Oxford University Press, 1971).

Uglik, Jacek. "Ludwig Feuerbach's conception of the religious alienation of man and Mikhail Bakunin's philosophy of religion", in *Studies in East European Thought*, Vol. 62, No. 1 (March 2010)

Chapter 7: Karl Marx

Carew Hunt, R. N. *The Theory and Practice of Communism* (Harmondsworth: Penguins Books, 1963)

Carver, Terrell (ed.). *The Cambridge Companion to Marx* (Cambridge: Cambridge University Press, 1991)

Claeys, Gregory. *Marx and Marxism* (Bold Type Books, 2018)

McLellan, David. *Karl Marx: A biography*, 4th ed. (Basingstoke: Palgrave Macmillan, 2008)

Singer, Peter. *Marx: A very short introduction*, 2nd ed. (Oxford: Oxford University Press, 2018)

Wood, Allen W. *Karl Marx*, 2nd ed. (New York and Abingdon: Routledge, 2004)

Chapter 8: Friedrich Nietzsche

Detwiler, Bruce. *Nietzsche and the Politics of Aristocratic Radicalism.* (University of Chicago Press, 1990)
Gemes, Ken and John Richardson. *The Oxford Handbook of Nietzsche* (Oxford University Press, 2016)
Hollingdale, Reginald J. *Nietzsche: The Man and his Philosophy*, 2nd ed. (Cambridge & New York: Cambridge University Press, 1999)
Prideaux, Sue. *I Am Dynamite: A Life of Friedrich Nietzsche* (New York: Tim Duggan Books, 2018)
Solomon, Robert C. *Living with Nietzsche: What the Great "Immoralist" Has to Teach Us.* (Oxford & New York: Oxford University Press, 2006)
Tanner, Michael. *Nietzsche: A Very Short Introduction.* (Oxford & New York: Oxford University Press, 1996)

Afterword

Chang, Ha-Joon. *Kicking away the Ladder: Development strategy in Historical Perspective* (London: Anthem Press, 2002).
Fichte, Johann Gottlieb, *The Closed Commercial State [Der geschlossene Handelsstaat]*, translated and with an interpretive essay by Anthony Curtis Alder (Albany: State University of New York Press, 2012 [1800]).
Herminghouse, Patricia A. and Magda Mueller (eds.). *German Feminist Writings* (London: Continuum, 2001).
List, Friedrich. *The National System of Political Economy*, translated by Sampson S. Lloyd (London: Longmans, Green and Co. 1901 [1841])."
Nakhimovsky, Isaac, *The Closed Commercial State: Perpetual Peace and Commercial Society from Rousseau to Fichte* (Princeton, N.J.: Princeton University Press, 2011).
Reiss, Hans Siegbert (ed), *The Political Thought of German Romantics, 1793-1815* (Oxford: Blackwell, 1955).

CPSIA information can be obtained
at www.ICGtesting.com
Printed in the USA
BVHW052040220523
664679BV00007B/15

9 798985 221466